C000234224

How to Live in the Here and Now

A guide to Accelerated Enlightenment, Unlocking the Power of Mindful Awareness

First published by O Books, 2009
O Books is an imprint of John Hunt Publishing Ltd., The Bothy, Deershot Lodge, Park Lane, Ropley,
Hants, SO24 0BE, UK
office1@o-books.net
www.o-books.net

Distribution in:

UK and Europe
Orca Book Services
orders@orcabookservices.co.uk
Tel: 01202 665432 Fax: 01202 666219   Int.
code (44)

USA and Canada
NBN
custserv@nbnbooks.com
Tel: 1 800 462 6420 Fax: 1 800 338 4550

Australia and New Zealand
Brumby Books
sales@brumbybooks.com.au
Tel: 61 3 9761 5535 Fax: 61 3 9761 7095

Far East (offices in Singapore, Thailand,
Hong Kong, Taiwan)
Pansing Distribution Pte Ltd
kemal@pansing.com
Tel: 65 6319 9939 Fax: 65 6462 5761

South Africa
Alternative Books
altbook@peterhyde.co.za
Tel: 021 555 4027 Fax: 021 447 1430

Text copyright Paul Jones 2008

Design: Stuart Davies

ISBN: 978 1 84694 173 3

All rights reserved. Except for brief quotations
in critical articles or reviews, no part of this
book may be reproduced in any manner without
prior written permission from the publishers.

The rights of Paul Jones as author have been
asserted in accordance with the Copyright,
Designs and Patents Act 1988.

A CIP catalogue record for this book is available
from the British Library.

Printed by Digital Book Print

O Books operates a distinctive and ethical publishing philosophy in
all areas of its business, from its global network of authors to
production and worldwide distribution.
This book is produced on FSC certified stock, within ISO14001
standards. The printer plants sufficient trees each year through
the Woodland Trust to absorb the level of emitted carbon in
its production.

How to Live in the Here and Now

A guide to Accelerated Enlightenment, Unlocking the Power of Mindful Awareness

Paul Jones

BOOKS

Winchester, UK
Washington, USA

Contents

Acknowledgements

Rebecca Southworth
Professor W. Wiggins
Stephen Jones
Steve Taylor
John Jones
Janet Jones
Craig Harrison

Chapter 1

Introduction

Let him who would enjoy a good future waste none of his present.
Roger Babson

Do you suffer intrusive thoughts?
Do you plan to make changes, yet they do not happen?
Do you find it difficult to make decisions?
Do you find it hard to follow through on your decisions?
Do you sometimes find it hard to control your own thoughts?
Are you plagued by worries about the future?
Do you find yourself constantly going over past events in your mind?
Have you ever experienced paranoia or jealousy?
Are you a victim to boredom or frustration?
Do you feel a general sense of discontent?
Are you prone to low-level depression or anxiety?
Do your thoughts go around in circles?
Do you suffer internal conflict?

All these maladies and many more, stem from a disjointed relationship with time and space. When, for instance, was the last you found your mind truly focused only on where you were, and on what you were doing?

If you have answered **yes** to any of the above questions, then this book will help you, because quite simply:

This book gives you some of the quickest and simplest techniques and exercises ever developed to achieve Enlightenment, by learning to Live in the Here and Now.

Many sources would have you believe that to obtain the state
of enlightenment is to embark upon a long and hard journey. Old-
school thinking may tell you that "anything worthwhile is hard
work and will take a lot of time and effort."
Is everything that's difficult worthwhile?
Is everything that takes a short time not important?

If you have already grasped the fact that this process can be
relatively easy, quick and simple, you have already overcome the
biggest hurdle on your way to:

'Accelerated Practical Enlightenment'

- **Accelerated:** through the integration of the latest psychological
techniques, becoming enlightened has never been so quick.

- **Practical Enlightenment:** a brand of enlightenment designed
for practical, realistic living, where major changes to your lifestyle
and preferences are unnecessary. No withdrawal from
mainstream society is necessary either so throw away that loin
cloth and forget about having to live on top of a lonely mountain.

The purpose of this book is twofold;

1. To explain what enlightenment is.
2. To become enlightened.

For some readers, just the contemplation of the concepts
contained in this book will be enough for a very real shift in their
perception, but the exercises are more important. The exercises
guide your awareness in ways that are only controlled by the
unconscious mind – if you could just consciously choose to
change your mind state you would have already.

There are ways and means of manipulating your senses of the perception of time, space and values, and we will explore these in the rest of the book.

Don't worry because your current perceptions will always be there for you to fall back to if you wish. And society will, all too frequently, try to pull you back to those old ways. With Accelerated Practical Enlightenment, you will have more choice and more flexibility in your thinking, feelings and behavior.

If we were all simple robots, it would be an easy task to just make a computer program called 'keep the conscious attention focused upon the direct experience of the Here and Now.' The problem is that we humans are very complicated 'robots', running many conflicting, yet important programs, so we need to work with and around our values, emotions, beliefs, habits and self concept in order to allow that simple program that directs us towards present-moment awareness to operate effectively.

Exercises and practices to actively encourage the mind into the Here and Now are included to begin with, but there are various factors that want to constantly pull the conscious attention away from the Here and Now and so we must also consider techniques that will address the tendency of the mind to constantly want to pull its attention inwards. I developed many of the techniques and ideas you will see here in order to deal with specific problems, such as the one's you see at the beginning of this chapter. I soon began to see, though, that these problems were just various symptoms of a deeper but very simple cause, namely that we hardly ever relate to our world directly. Our minds are hardly ever fully on where and when we are.

As I began to teach people to focus not on eliminating their specific problems but instead to move towards living in the Here and Now, many clients presenting with complex interactions of problems would find spontaneous solution to a lot of those

3

problems, simply by shifting their attention towards the present moment. And so Accelerated Practical Enlightenment was born. You are looking at the synthesis of the fastest and most powerful techniques at the disposal of any therapist today all aimed at producing a rapid, permanent and very real 'enlightenment' in its truest sense.

So when would you like to get started and find out exactly why anyone would want to Live in the Here and Now? There's no time like the present!

Chapter 2

Why do you want to Live in the Here and Now?

O thoughts of men accurst! Past and to-come seems best; things present, worst.
Shakespeare, King Henry the Fourth, Part II

A man is walking on the top of a cliff side and, as he enjoys the sights and sounds, smells and feelings, he begins to hear a barking, woofing noise coming closer. Soon he begins to see a pack of wild dogs chasing him, so naturally he runs away from danger and toward safety. It is no wonder he wants to increase his comfort and decrease his discomfort. The discomfort of running very fast is outweighed by the expected discomfort of getting ripped to death by the rabid pack, so his decision is easy. As his primary mission is to escape the dogs, he runs in any direction away from the dogs, but soon he finds himself surrounded at the cliff edge by the pack. Still following his pleasure principle, he now decides to climb over the cliff to escape the dogs, so he clambers over the edge and holds onto some wild grasses atop the cliff edge. A quick look downward assures him that he cannot climb down the cliff but must remain holding onto his grass until perhaps the dogs go away. At the bottom of this very high cliff are some treacherous rocks and rough seas, his plight seems desperate, even more so he realizes, as his attention turns to the grasses that are holding him. The grasses, one by one, are beginning to break, yet as he looks up at them he spies a wild raspberry growing there. As the final grass breaks; he grabs the raspberry and shoves it in his mouth. During the fall to certain doom, a final thought flashes through his mind – a thought without words, yet I can only describe it to you here and now with words:

"This raspberry tastes delicious!"

If you are HERE reading this book, which I know you must be doing RIGHT NOW, then I guess you have at least a little bit of interest in Living in the Here and Now. Many traditional teachings rightly equate mindfulness, (*living in the here and now*) with enlightenment. The idea of mindfulness will be central to the working definition of enlightenment that we will be using. Enlightenment, as a state, is deconstructed and evaluated at length throughout the book because very often, a simple description of what you want is not sufficient to take you where you want to be. Riddles, analogies and metaphors are great but sometimes a little lacking in any practical application at the right level; a little like being told by your sports coach to score more points than the opposition without being taught how to. I've still included many examples, stories and metaphors, yet I have rendered their meaning explicit, they are there to make things clearer, not more clouded. It is my intention here to go beyond the traditional riddles and sophistry and to describe not only, specifically *what* we want, but also specifically *how* we can achieve it. With modern advances in psychological techniques, anybody can easily learn to live more in the Here and Now. There are still no shortcuts; we still have to travel the same path, yet now we can travel much, much faster.

Why would we want to Live in the Here and Now?

It's really just common sense to want to live when and where you find yourself. Sometimes, the desire to Live in the Here and Now is motivated by a desire to feel alive. This works out quite conveniently because the Here and Now is really a great place to find yourself alive. Sometimes, the desire to be Living in the Here and Now is motivated by a *moving away* as opposed to a *moving towards*, because a great deal of psychological discomfort is associated and caused by finding yourself living not in the time and place that you actually are. This is not to say that having your awareness in the future or past is undesirable per se, but there is now so much more we can do when we find ourselves in areas of our experience that are undesirable.

Now take the time to imagine for just a moment, if you will, how the ability to Live in the Here and Now will work usefully, happily and comfortably for you in the future. Where will you be? What will you be doing? When exactly will you find that this is something you are looking forward to? That's right. You have just enjoyed a pleasant, not-in-the here-and-now, experience. The ability to dissociate from our immediate experience is an essential tool for planning, learning, and living in a shared world; it is part of what makes us different from the animals. It's a gift and a curse. We don't want to Live in the Here and Now all the time, but neither do we want to be tuned out of the world all the time. You will learn how to control these two options and you will also learn how to make your own decisions as to where you want your attention to be at any moment.

A wise and enlightened individual was once asked what he did before enlightenment. He answered, "Before enlightenment, I carried water and chopped wood." When asked what he does after enlightenment, he answers, "I carry water and chop wood." I have come across many different versions of this story, one of which appears in a later chapter. Before reading any further, right now, just ask yourself what you think the lesson of this little parable is.

I have given it some thought and I think, the wise man is telling us that enlightenment is not a highly rare and extreme experience; there are no burning bushes or roads to Damascus; no angels, visitations, thunderbolts or crises are necessary. Having said this, as soon as you turn over an old perception for a new possibility, this happens instantaneously, so if you have the odd epiphany ('Ah ha' or 'Eureka' moment) from time to time, certainly don't write it off. The epiphytical experience is certainly instructive and may be sufficient to affect enlightenment, but it is not necessary. Moreover, the epiphany is short lived, like certain other things; you can't keep it up for long. Just imagine what St. Paul did after his walk on the road to Damascus, sooner or later he was back to the same old routine, at least biologically; eating, drinking, sleeping, using the toilet. Enlightenment is not the learning experience itself, but the practice in everyday life of that learning. So after enlightenment what did I do? I washed the dishes and did the ironing.

Chapter 3

What exactly does it mean to Live in the Here and Now?

Imagine you walk into a room and your friend is sitting there looking glassy-eyed and staring into space. Suddenly, as you startle him, he turns to you and says, "Sorry I was miles away then." What does this mean? He certainly wasn't miles away; he was in the room with you. Quite obviously he was speaking metaphorically; he found his attention was directed elsewhere, possibly to another time and place. Perhaps he was daydreaming. Perhaps he was imagining a past event where that witty comment eluded him, or he may have thought up a wittisicm and was rehearsing it within an imagined future. We are not really concerned here with the content of your friend's attention so much as the direction of his attention. When he was 'miles away', your friend's attention was on something other than the immediate world around him. In that moment of time, he was *living in his head*. It is no coincidence that in the English language we have many terms that refer to this dissociation of attention. As well as 'being miles away,' you may also know people who 'live in the past,' or 'live for the future.'

Let's look at the nature of consciousness to find out what it actually means to Live in the Here and Now. To Live in the Here and Now is to find your attention in the outside world. If your attention is not in the outside world, you are inside your head. You may not be fully aware of it, but you move your attention from *outside* to *inside* your head, and back again, all the time. Most of the time, a mixture of habit and reactions to external events guides whether our attention is inside or outside our head. Most of the time you can just trust your unconscious processes to govern where, and when, your attention is directed, according to

9

these factors. Sometimes though, your mind will make unuseful and/or uncomfortable choices as to where and when your attention becomes directed. We are going to learn how to take control of those times by making active choices as to where, and when, our attention will be directed.

Let's begin by modelling your consciousness; Thanks to Freud and his colleagues 'the conscious' and 'the unconscious' are common ideas in popular thought. However, to speak of 'the unconscious' is to treat the unconscious as if it were an object or structure and this will not serve our purposes here. We will treat the conscious/unconscious distinction as functional, not structural. We want to think of the term 'unconscious' as an adjective that describes things you are not immediately aware of. The term 'unconscious' is not to be taken as a noun that describes a thing. The way the 'unconscious' operates will begin to become clear as we visit Planet X. The Planet X is just a model to illustrate the tendencies and relationships of our short-term memory, which is the seat of consciousness. In order to Live in the Here and Now, we need a cognitive model of what it means to do that, so bear with me. As soon as we have looked at the model, we will be relating it back to a much better understanding of Living in the Here and Now.

The Planet X Model

Imagine a small planet called 'Planet X'. The planet is actually a disc world, like a coin, not a sphere. There is only one building on Planet X, this building is a simple castle-like arrangement. The castle consists of only a tower with one small windowless room at the top. Around the tower is the courtyard. A perimeter wall made of glass surrounds the courtyard. The rest of the planet, outside the wall, is made up of pleasant scenery.

Seven small sprites (smalls creatures) live on the planet. Each sprite carries with it a video camera. On each of the seven cameras the lenses can be made to focus very narrowly for a close-up view

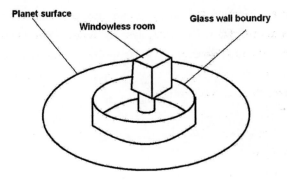

Planet surface

Windowless room

Glass wall boundry

Planet X

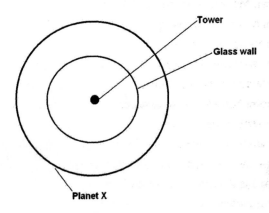

Tower

Glass wall

Planet X

or very widely for a more panoramic view. The sprites can move very, very quickly around the space only within the courtyard inside the glass wall. There are many things to see on the surface of the planet, outside and inside the courtyard, yet with only seven sprites, with only one camera each, the maximum number of things that can be seen at any one time is seven.

So, on Planet X you have your seven sprites moving around all the time, pointing their cameras at various different objects on the planet. There is an unseen watching force looking down on the planet from above in the sky, it can see everything on the planet from its vantage point. Imagine the 'Unseen Watcher' to be a cloud floating high above the planet. The 'Unseen Watcher' directs the sprites as to where to point, and how to focus, their cameras (but every now and then a sprite can influence the movement of the others - we will come to this later).

Unseen Watcher

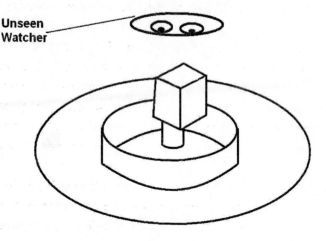

Planet X

It is possible for a camera to be pointed at, and so view, another camera. And as things of interest on the Planet X unfold, the Unseen Watcher can direct sprites to any areas of novelty. Each sprite may direct their camera towards objects within the courtyard, or they can go up to the glass wall and point their camera outside and view what is outside the courtyard. The cameras cannot be directed upwards to see the 'Unseen Watcher'; this is what makes it 'Unseen'. All the cameras relay their pictures into the windowless room at the top of the tower in the centre of the courtyard. Inside the windowless room is a 'brain' that experiences all the information relayed from the cameras.

Now, remember Planet X is really a model of your cognitive experience*, wherever the cameras are pointed represents where your attention is. The seven views, captured by all the cameras, represent the full contents of your conscious experience at any time. The planet surface, inside and outside the courtyard, represents the total amount of experience available to be viewed at any time. The environment outside the courtyard represents the outside world; the inside of the courtyard represents the inside of your mind. For every part of the planet where a camera is not pointing, to all extents and purposes it doesn't exist inside your awareness, yet it can be brought back into conscious existence very quickly again by pointing a camera on it, at the expense, however, of leaving something else unviewed (in conscious 'darkness' so to speak - unconsciousness). The glass-wall boundary that separates the outside world from the courtyard represents the boundary between our inner experience and our outer experience.

To Live in the Here and Now (to live in the world) is simply to have all your cameras pointed through the glass wall at the outside environment. In the diagram below, the squares are objects of attention, and the sprites are triangles.

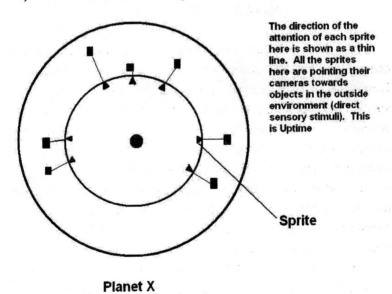

The direction of the attention of each sprite here is shown as a thin line. All the sprites here are pointing their cameras towards objects in the outside environment (direct sensory stimuli). This is Uptime

Sprite

Planet X

To live in your head is to have all your cameras pointed within the courtyard:

13

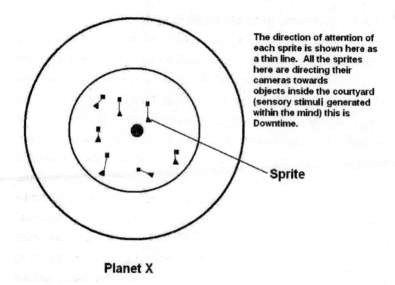

The direction of attention of each sprite is shown here as a thin line. All the sprites here are directing their cameras towards objects inside the courtyard (sensory stimuli generated within the mind) this is Downtime.

Sprite

Planet X

Whether your attention is 'in your head' or 'in the world' is really a matter of degrees, as some cameras can be pointed outside whilst some are pointed inside at the same time, but the 'Unseen Watcher' has a tendency to direct the sprites to either point all the cameras outside or inside the boundary at any one time. So, for now, we will deal with the two extremes of having all of your attention outside or all of it inside.

Imagine there are many similar planets in this imaginary universe. Some Unseen Watchers, hovering over some of the planets, will have the tendency to keep most of the cameras pointing inside until something of novelty happens outside. On other planets perhaps the Unseen Watcher will keep most of the cameras pointing outside until, for some reason, they need to be directed inside. Which kind of tendency is your Unseen Watcher displaying?

To Live in the Here and Now is to have the majority of your attention in the outside world. If all the cameras are pointing outside, you can 'lose yourself' in what you are doing (being 'in the zone' for example), if they are all inside, you could be hypnotized, daydreaming, or catatonic, for example.

When a sprite briefly controls the direction of some of the other sprites; it represents the mechanism of mind, by which we will make it the Unseen Watcher's habit to keep the sprites directing their cameras outside as the default. It's a question of either living in the world or living in your head.

You may be wondering why there are seven sprites with seven cameras. These seven sprites represent the seven 'bits' that are the limit of your short term memory. Your short term memory is the seat of the contents of consciousness. With regard to what constitutes a 'bit' of information, this is the 'object of awareness' discussed above, it may be large or small. There is much too much of the outside planet for the seven cameras to view it all at once. That is to say, there is much too much information bombarding the senses for you to be conscious of it all at any one moment. The unseen watching force, looking down, can view practically everything that happens on the planet's surface though.

It is possible for a camera to view another camera, when this happens we become aware of the direction of our own conscious awareness. When we do this the *direction* of some of our awareness actually becomes the *content* of our conscious experience. Notice that there are no mirrors on the planet; it takes one camera to view another. It is also possible to give greater attention to an object by directing more than one camera upon it. Directing all cameras towards an object of attention can represent a state of complete mental focus.

As mentioned before, the width and focus of each camera lens can be made to view a whole landscape or a single small object or any point in between. This governs exactly what constitutes a single object of awareness to us; we are constantly moving the outlines we put around objects. As a camera lens becomes more panoramic, so the field of vision is widened and it can view more, but it does this at the price of image definition.

For example, as I write these words right now, if I look up I can see a roof on the other side of my road through my window. I can either concentrate my attention on the whole roof, or a single tile. If I concentrate on the roof as a singular object, then the trees and hills behind become the background. If I concentrate on a single tile, the rest of the roof drops into my perceptual background, as only that tile is in the foreground.

So your foot, as you read this, is probably outside of your conscious awareness yet I have just directed your attention towards it – now, so to speak you have sent a sprite or two to the glass wall boundary to view the sensations of that area of the outside world. As you read the few paragraphs above, a lot of your conscious awareness is directed inwards to make pictures, sounds or feelings about the sprites, cameras, planet and so on. Just imagine now, that if a wasp suddenly stung you on the neck, your Unseen Watcher would suddenly direct most of those cameras towards viewing this area of novelty (because the otherwise constant sensation from that part of your body has suddenly changed).

Setting the Here and Now as a Default

What do you see in the above picture? You can have one interpretation of the image where a white vase is seen against a black background and then again, you can have another interpretation of the image where two silhouetted faces are seen against a white background. It is actually impossible to see both at the same time. You may think you can see both interpretations at the same time but you cannot. Your mind can flick very quickly between the two interpretations of the image but it can't perceive both at the same time. This is because your mind cannot accept one thing as both a foreground and a background at the same time. So when the vase is seen, the faces must drop into the background and when the faces are seen, the vase becomes the background.

This picture is quite neutral so you'd expect to spend a roughly equal amount of time perceiving the vase or the faces, as you flick from one to the other. You can keep one interpretation for a time, but sooner or later, the other way of seeing the image will pop back out at you. The more effort you expend, the longer you can keep one interpretation. If you completely relax your attention though, you'll notice your mind flicking backward and forward between the two perceptions almost at random.

There is a way to make one perception more obvious than the other one is. If we do this, we can set the default perception of the image; that is to say, the one interpretation that automatically springs into awareness first because we've made it easier to see.

Now as you look at the image below, you'll notice that the faces are the most obvious interpretation. You can still quite easily concentrate and see the vase again, but your perception naturally wants to make the faces the default way of perceiving this image now.

Now look at this image below, I've set the default interpretation to the vase. Once again, notice that you can still easily perceive the faces by a concentrated act of will, but whilst your mind is relaxed it will naturally tend towards perceiving the vase.

So, despite being able to consciously shift your attention between two different interpretations, your brain tends towards the interpretation that is easiest – the path of least resistance, so to speak. This is true of our perception when shifting between Living in the Here and Now and living in your head just as much as it is with the illusions above.

Just as the vase can be made the default perception in the images, so Living in the Here and Now can be set as your default direction of attention. When this happens, your attention will want to stay Living in the Here and Now automatically, with the option of deferring to the past, future, elsewhere and other minds only when necessary. Once you have set the default direction of your attention to the Here and Now you can still purposely move your attention away from the Here and Now for some practical purposes, but your mind will automatically snap back to Living in the Here and Now as soon as you relax your concentration. In this model, to Live in the Here and Now, setting your mind's default direction of attention to immediate sensory perception, is the very definition of enlightenment.

A lot of people today have their default direction of attention set as living in the past, future, elsewhere and other minds, and they only find themselves in the Here and Now as a result of some suitable novelty in the outside world that demands their attention. You can imagine that some people go around in a dream until they are either stung by a wasp, or the car in front of them brakes suddenly, or they may even get a bucket of cold water thrown over them. When these things happen, the dreamer is suddenly forced into the world to deal with whatever problem needs their attention. After the emergency is over they can slide back into the daydream. It's like they live in Downtime and only take the odd 'holiday' to Uptime, whereas to become enlightened we want to reverse that situation. (Remember, 'Downtime' describes a situation where the sprites only view the inside of the courtyard, or where you only bring your conscious attention to the contents of the inside of your head. 'Uptime' is where all the sprites view the environment outside the glass boundary, or where you direct your conscious awareness into your immediate senses and so begin to attend to the outside world.)

Many of us would like to live longer, but few of us ever consider that a more profitable exercise would be to learn how to be in the moment so we can make the most of the meagre span of our lives – a kind of damage limitation exercise on our three score years and ten. Perhaps a joke will help to illustrate:

Doctor: You only have six months to live.
Patient: Oh dear, what shall I do?
Doctor: I suggest you move in with your mother-in-law.
Patient: Why, will that help me to live longer?
Doctor: No but it will make six months *seem* like ten years.

Of course we don't have to be miserable for our perceived time to slow down or even stop it. Living in the Here and Now feels like a more 'childlike' perception of the world where time seems to be an ever-present Now, yet it is not necessary to compromise any of our other more adult functions to have this. I believe the 'fact' that time perception speeds up as we become adults is not driven by biological factors but by the way we direct our attention, and we can change this easily.

The Building Blocks of Conscious Awareness

So to recap; when you are in Uptime your awareness is directed outwards.

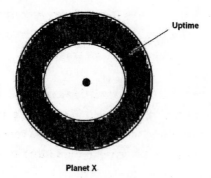

Planet X

And in Downtime your attention is directed inwards.

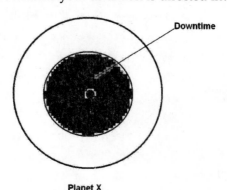

Planet X

All conscious awareness is made up out of the senses; literally everything we experience, whether real or imagined, direct or interpreted, is made up of the sensory information. Our whole world of experience is just:

1. Sight (Visual)
2. Sound (Auditory)
3. Feelings (Kinaesthetic) - There are many different feelings in the body; balance, hunger, heat etc. but they are all represented here as simply one sense.
4. Taste and smells (Gustatory) – these two senses are (for our purposes here) combined because there is so much cross-over in 'flavour' – a combination of taste and smell.

When you find yourself in Uptime, for example, you can be spread across the senses or just focused in one sense, and likewise in Downtime. So we can denote Uptime like this (below), adding in a representation of the four senses. The letters **V**, **A**, **K** and **G** denote the four senses as detailed above:

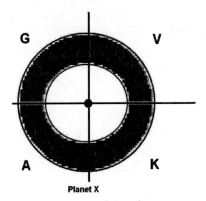

Planet X

And likewise, Downtime is denoted like this:

One of the things the Planet X model demonstrates is that your whole world, your life; literally the only things that exist for you at any time *are* the contents of your consciousness and this, in turn, is governed directly by the direction of your attention. Your attention is made up of 'sensory matter'. So whether you are outside your head or inside, you are experiencing vision, kinaesthetic (physical feelings), smells, tastes or sounds (including words). Our awareness is made up only of these things; they are the very building blocks of our experience

When you are Living in the Here and Now (Uptime), you are directly tuned into the input of your senses right now. Your conscious awareness has much less 'bandwidth' (seven bits, and I use the term 'bits' here as it is used in computer terminology to denote a discrete piece of information) than the signals your senses are constantly receiving (thousands, if not millions, of bits). Your conscious awareness is only seven bits so, for example, you literally cannot experience all your fingers as separate objects all at the same time. You can be aware of them all as clumps, but not ten individuals. Have a go right now, try to perceive all your fingers as separate objects all at the same time!

Have you done it? Well done! You have just had an experience of Living in the Here and Now (Uptime), in this particular case by having all of your conscious attention in your sense of physical feeling (**K**). See the diagram below.

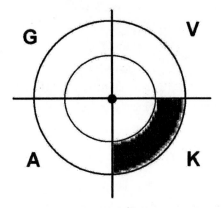

Whilst you were there trying to divide your conscious attention between your fingers, I bet you weren't thinking about that tax bill, the embarrassing moment last week or the buyer's remorse over that money-pit of a car. You might have noticed how it was easier to move *towards* Uptime than you would find it to move *away* from Downtime, even though they are really movements in the same direction. This is because nature abhors a vacuum; you cannot get rid of something without replacing it with something else. You might even have been unaware of sounds around you, the sensations in the rest of your body or any tastes or smells as you were trying.

So now you have had a little taste of Living in the Here and Now (Uptime), let's contrast that with the experience of Living not-in-the Here and Now; having your awareness directed inside your head (Downtime). The sensory perceptions you experience when your awareness is directed inside your head are always dislocated from the Here and Now. These sensations are always located elsewhere or else-when. There is no inherent goodness or badness, comfort or discomfort, rightness or wrongness about either being in Uptime or being in Downtime. It just seems to be a common malady that people find themselves stuck in unuseful loops in their heads.

Deciding Where You Want to Direct Your Attention

With regards to the direction of our awareness, we have made the distinction between Uptime and Downtime. Neither Uptime nor Downtime is desirable or undesirable per se, so another distinction must be introduced to the model to help us in our decisions regarding where we would like to direct our attention. This new dimension will be that of usefulness vs. un-usefulness. We want to be in a useful state as much as possible.

I've decided to use the distinction useful vs. unuseful in the matrix, as opposed to good/bad or pleasant/unpleasant because it is also our aim to live in existential authenticity – to be aware of the relevant facts without fear or a tendency to bury our head in the sand. Good/bad is a bad distinction in this case, and even though it would be pleasant to use the pleasant/unpleasant distinction, it seems that useful vs. unuseful is the most useful. Be aware that the usefulness of a direction of awareness in this model is not fixed, the concept of 'usefulness' in itself is only relevant to our arbitrary goals. The pain in my injured leg may be useful to stop me walking on it and making it worse, but not useful from the point of view of having a nice time. Most commonly, though, for us as humans, 'unuseful' can be equated with a certain level of discomfort.

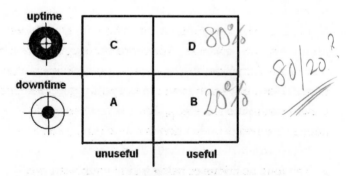

As you look at the diagram above, you'll see that the direction of your conscious awareness can be outside (Uptime) or inside (Downtime) your head and operating either usefully or unusefully.

(Inclusive question)?

There are 4 positions:

Unuseful	Downtime	A
Useful	Downtime	B (20)
Unuseful	Uptime	C
Useful	Uptime	D (LIVING IN THE HERE AND NOW) (80)

Obviously, given a choice, you will choose to find yourself in the useful two for most of the time, but with *useful Uptime* **D** being the default and *useful Downtime* **B** being the option. *Unuseful Downtime* **A** is so prevalent as a human tendency that it requires the whole of the next chapter. Examples of *unuseful Uptime* **C** could include a painfully stubbed toe – where the pain is now offering no useful information to you, or perhaps some distracting noises stopping you going into useful Downtime to concentrate on some academic work or reading.

It is the tendency to find oneself in *unuseful Downtime* **A** much more than is necessary. In fact, it is doubtable that it is ever necessary. We will begin to shift the balance by replacing it with the tendency to be in *useful Uptime* **D** (Living in the Here and Now).

Look at the diagram below, when in Downtime (whether usefully so or not), you experience sensations, either from the past or the future or from elsewhere or even from other people's minds. Now, obviously, you are not really mind reading, remote viewing and time travelling, this just represents the direction our minds go when our attention is inside (in Downtime).

The four positions of being inside your head are:
Past

Future

Elsewhere

Another mind(s)

They are all psychological dissociations from the Here and Now.

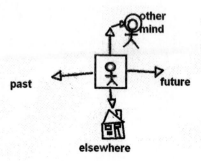

For convenience, we can represent the four dissociations of Downtime as below:

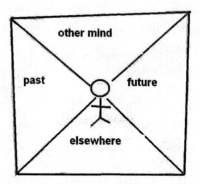

Each of the four dissociations carries with it uses and abuses, in the next chapter we will explore these.

* This is not intended to be a comprehensive model, just a metaphor that makes it easy to conceive and explain the areas of our particular interest in our quest of understanding and controlling the direction of our awareness.

Chapter 4

The Four Dissociations of the Mind that will try to pull you away from the Here and Now

Where does discontent start? You are warm enough, but you shiver. You are fed, yet hunger gnaws you. You have been loved, but your yearning wanders in new fields. And to prod all these there's time, the Bastard Time.
John Steinbeck

Past
You can never plan the future by the past.
Edmund Burke

Those who do not [learn] from the past are condemned to repeat it.
George Santayana

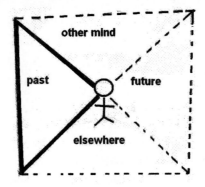

When you are in Downtime-Past, your awareness has retreated from the outside world into past events, whether 'good' or 'bad'. Now, as you drift back in your mind, it is not the content of your experience that is so important, we should be more concerned here with how useful that content is. You can relive or review a disastrous or unpleasant event usefully as well as unusefully; the same is also the case with pleasant events. Our ability to remember, replay and review the past is extremely useful for learning, or for recalling information that we need in the present. As long as you are sure of your reasons and purpose for visiting the past inside your head you are likely to be there usefully.

As I mentioned before though, it is a gift and a curse. The curse of unuseful and compulsive visits to both pleasant and unpleasant experiences of the past is Depression; I write here not only of the full blown 'clinical' (what does that actually mean?) depression. I mean, also, any event in which this mechanism operates, perhaps something as little as buyer's remorse over a pair of shoes, or the regret of last nights drunken display of Karaoke.

Depression is characterized by helplessness and hopelessness; this really makes sense because the depressed person is living in the past and, as we know, the past cannot be changed, so it's logical to have a low efficacy. Even the very seriously depressed individual still visits the outside world at times of emergency or maintenance – to avoid a wasp, or to eat, for example. It is likely that at least some of their attention will remain in the past though giving them, even at the best of times, the impression that they are not all there and displaying a distracted or vacant look.

This is not noticed so much, though, by the depressed person because, for them, the default position is that the past is in the foreground of their perception. (The Unseen Watcher has the tendency to keep most of the sprites pointing their cameras inside the courtyard). If this unfortunate individual was to remain inside for any length of time, they would habituate and not feel too bad about how bad they were feeling. It is the small visits to the outside (Uptime) that make the return to the past (Downtime) overwhelming again and again. If you want feel really cold for example, it makes sense to get really hot first, and you will feel coldest as you first leave the warmth and stand in some snow. After a bit, you'll get used to the cold, so you have to go back in the warm and come out again to get the effect of feeling cold again. The depressed individual does not choose overtly to return elastically to the past; it's the Unseen Watcher that has set the tendency to run this unuseful pattern. It seems that depression will often extinguish in time, simply because the person has had enough trial events to accidentally discover, and get into the habit of using, new patterns of awareness direction. What a pity no system existed that could have actively directed and sped up this process!

Certain beliefs can also predispose us getting pulled back to the past and these beliefs are not likely to be in our conscious awareness as they can become unquestioned truths we are not even aware of. They will show up in the way they guide our behavior, though.

Among these beliefs could be, "*if I review the past constantly, I might find a solution to my problems or some indication of how to act in the future.*" This belief has a positive intent but it causes you to focus on the past and not the actual solution of any situation that may be operating problematically for you. This belief rests on other beliefs such as, "*there is one true interpretation of events*" or "*insight equals cure.*"

Imagine you get a puncture on a wheel of your car and you take the wheel to the shop. The man in shop says, "Could have been a can, maybe a piece of glass, perhaps a rock." As he looks at the tyre, he calls out; "Ah ha! Here it is; a nail - that was your problem!" then he hands you the tyre back. You think "I don't give a s**t what caused it, what difference does that make? I want it fixed!" If you are making the decision to go into the past at all, try to be solution-focused.

Popular interpretations of Freud and his colleagues lead the common individual into the almost unquestioned belief that: "Insight will automatically lead to cure." This can drive an obsession with uncovering memories or with finding the 'one true interpretation' of a past event. Do you believe that insight always leads to a solution? Does every solution require full insight into the causes of a problem?

It is true that reviews of the past can help us learn (a review of the cause of the puncture could yield useful results if the cause is likely to happen again – a crack on the rim of your wheel causing continuously poor seals with any tubeless tyre you use, for example), but only if we know how to do it properly in useful Downtime. If you find you are having difficulty in staying in Uptime as events from the past are constantly pulling you back, it may be that the mind believes there is something you need to learn from the experience(s). After you have learned from the experience(s), your mind will no longer get pulled back to the past as the need to do so is no longer there.

The past can also pose a threat to our flexibility through our dependence on it for our sense of identification. Our sense of identity can lie in the past and threaten the present by making our thoughts and behaviors inflexible or unresponsive to the situation we actually find our selves in at any time.

This unresponsive, inflexible behavior-tendency is compounded if part of our conscious awareness is diverted away from the Here and Now (Uptime) by being in Downtime. This is similar to a computer running too many applications and so seeming to slow down or freeze. In fact, in these cases, the computer is running just as fast, but running too many applications – it's actually working *perfectly*, it's just not running *usefully* for you in the one application you are looking at. Also, when your computer runs a virus, it is running that virus perfectly, the computer is working fine, it's just that it is running unuseful software; 'unuseful' with respect to your needs and goals.

Future
The coward dies a thousand deaths.
Shakespeare [shown here as it's common paraphrase]

A man who suffers before it is necessary, suffers more than is necessary.

Expecting is the greatest impediment to living. In anticipation of tomorrow, it loses today.

The mind that is anxious about the future is miserable.
Lucius Annaeus Seneca

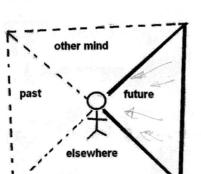

The future - brave new world, land of plenty, of opportunity, where around the next corner life may become simpler, happier, more peaceful and prosperous. It is not uncommon to see people in life chasing the next horizon. The useful side of visiting the future inside your head is obviously in anticipating and planning things; as humans we'd be lost without this ability, but it's a gift and a curse.

The unuseful side of visiting the future in your mind is Anxiety; Anxiety caused by living through fears that haven't happened and won't happen.

The very modern complaint of 'Stress' often comes from trying to balance too many variables against each other for the optimum outcome.

Many, who would reject the diagnosis of anxiety, suffer it in spades. The 'hard man' and the 'chilled out dude', among others, place such a sense of identification on their stress-proof personality that it's potential loss, or revelation as a facade, is itself a

31

subject of anxiety.

The future is not set, yet the only time we can meet it is in the present. From the perspective of your past, you are in the future right now. Today is yesterday's tomorrow. You understand it, but when will you act on it? Manyana?

One belief that can drive the attention into an imagined future is, "*I can consciously calculate all the variables and find the 'best' path if I keep running over possible future scenarios.*" Of course, all the best intentions belie this belief but the belief is based upon some faulty presuppositions such as, "*There is one 'best' path available,*" and

"*I am affected by future events per se, not my interpretation of events.*"

Stress

It is interesting that the word 'stress' (in the modern sense that it manifests itself during this current and very serious epidemic of self-diagnosis) was first used metaphorically by an engineer whose first language was not English and he has left us with a grave linguistic legacy. In engineering terminology, the stimulus is the *stress* and the result is the *strain*. A weight placed on a beam is the *stressor* and so supplies the *stress* load, and the beam's reaction to that load is the *strain*. Some beams will bend, some break.

In that most disastrous body of knowledge, known as contemporary popular psychology, 'stress' is the word used for both the stimulus and the attendant response, this bends people's thinking towards the deterministic and powerless beliefs of the victim, whose feelings and thoughts are at the mercy of external events in the world. There is no behavioral/cognitive/emotional response that is inextricably linked to any stimulus. When you can't affect how the world treats you, you certainly can still control how you treat yourself in the face of disappointment.

Speaking of disappointment, you must plan ahead adequately to get it right! If you don't have an outcome in your mind that is

Life is change. Acceptance of the now !!!

so specific and so set, that it won't ever happen, then you just haven't planned adequately to generate, within yourself, a sense of disappointment. If so, then you are doing it all wrong, you are bad at disappointing yourself. Watch out because when you discover you are bad at something you are likely to feel a bit disappointed.

set a goal then LET GO !!

Elsewhere

I'd rather be golfing.
Bumper sticker

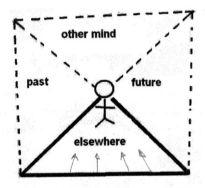

Imagine you have to work late, but all of your friends are out tonight having a good time. You wish you were there. A dread feeling that you are missing out on some of the fun that is being had in the world at this very moment comes over you. Your mind is elsewhere, not on where you are, not on what you are doing. When we are spatially dislocated in such a way, we are not just dislocated from our actual position in space, but also from the activities that are related to that place. So when we find ourselves elsewhere in our mind, we are really mentally locating ourselves not just in another place but also in another activity. Yet to recover the Now you must tune back into where you are and be mindful of the activity you are experiencing right now. In civilisation, the extreme side of the elsewhere dissociation is discontentment.

Some time ago, before I had learnt anything about hypnosis, I thought it would be great to be able to 'turn myself off' whilst doing mundane tasks. I reasoned that if I could hypnotise myself, I'd like to be able to do the washing up, and any other dreary household chores, in a zombie-like trance or off in my head, solving weighty problems, as my body went senselessly through the motions. If I had succeeded in really mentally 'turning myself off' at those times, I would have cut my perceived life span considerably. I'd also have been acting somewhat in-authentically if I'd tried to pick and choose the most pleasurable bits of my life. Even if I could cut out the unpleasant half of my experience, then what was previously mundane would automatically become the new worst parts of my life and I'd have to cut out half my experience again. If I carried on like that I'd wish away my whole life. Instead, it dawned on me that I should be mindful of the task; paying attention to every aspect of that present moment, just like our wood-chopping, water carrying friend from chapter 2. If Archimedes, during his famous Eureka! moment, was inside his head, thinking about the crown problem, he may never have become aware of the displacement of the water as he entered the tub. He has demonstrated, perhaps, that we can often trust our unconsciousness to make the lateral leaps of logic and learning if only we provide the mind/brain with some stimulus.

When engaging in a new activity (learning to drive perhaps) we are very much in our present awareness, but when we have learned that activity the mind wants again to drift inwards or to other secondary tasks. Many people prize their ability to 'multitask', oh what a wonderful computer their brain is! There is no dual chip in your brain. As you 'multitask', the care and enjoyment slips from all the tasks, this is not a good way to be. When was the last time you drove a car and enjoyed the sights, sounds, and other sensations of the activity just for what it was, instead of planning that meeting or making that shopping list in your mind?

The beliefs that belie this dissociation include, *"I can effectively* model events outside my immediate awareness," "I don't want to miss out," and "I don't want to be here, because I don't want to be doing what I am doing."

In addition to refuting the faulty beliefs, how can we avoid this jaded mind-drift after learning an activity? Well, by increasing our sensory acuity we may begin to realise that there is no ordinary moment. We shall learn more about how the 'ordinary moment' comes into existence in our minds later on, we shall also revisit our enlightened wood-chopping, water carrying friend again.

The consciousness is designed for sensation, so stay present and let the rest of the mind make what it will of what you find, trust it. So when you are enlightened what will you do? Wash the dishes and vacuum the carpet!

Other Mind(s)

During the earliest stages the child perceives things like a solipsist who is unaware of himself as subject and is familiar only with his own actions.
Jean Piaget

Prison continues, on those who are entrusted to it, a work begun elsewhere, which the whole of society pursues on each individual through innumerable mechanisms of discipline.
Michael Foucault

Hell is other people.
Sartre

In the Other Mind(s) dissociation, a person runs a simulation of another mind or minds inside their own. Like all four dissociations, this simulation may be based on outside events, but will always be contained within the mind of that individual. The Other Mind(s) dissociation, is critical to social life and any form

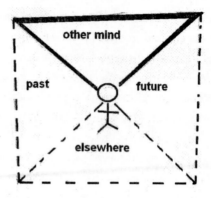

of civilisation, we could not imagine being without it, yet it can exert a high price on us from time to time. The faculty of the Other Mind(s) dissociation is developed in early childhood as differentiation between self and world develops. The internalisation of Other Mind(s) is required as control of the child begins to move from external to internal. This is not necessarily the way things must progress, as it was common in olden times to consider that the crime was in getting caught, not in the act itself (a behavioral belief that persists, yet is not confined to, the animal world). Of course pushing the idea of a 'higher sentinel', who judges us all according to fixed universal values, is of great importance for anyone who wishes to dictate how a population will experience the relationship between themselves and the universe, and by doing so, dictate their actions. The illusion will become even more compelling if you can persuade that population to experience this sentinel as outside of the mechanism of their own brain/mind.

How many times have you found yourself having an internal conversation when you are actually alone; perhaps justifying decisions you've made against the predicted criticisms of others. Who are you really having this conversation with? Well necessarily, it must be a part of yourself, there is nobody else there. Quite often the 'other' in this conversation will be someone who, in real life, is dead. Are you on the attack? Are you on the defensive? If there really are two parts of your mind conversing,

36

how do you know which one to identify with? You may be rehearsing an anticipated conversation or running over an old conversation as Past and Future will often also play a part. You might find yourself playing with ideas of what others are saying about you, whether good or bad. Do these other minds have a monopoly on the truth? Do they create or discover the 'real truth'?

The Other Mind(s) direction of Downtime can be the sneakiest. It can make itself the hardest to spot when it masquerades as a part of us; in fact, it is a necessary part of the *Myth of the Self*. For this reason, it is difficult, yet important, to become aware of how it operates. The Other Mind(s) dissociation plays a large part in defining the reality of one's social world, yet this reality (and it is real) is only relative, never absolute. The dialogue with the other represents a constant struggle to assert the truth. The nature of the Myth of the Self is such that a disproportionate amount of time you spend in the Other Mind(s) dissociation will consist of conversations regarding how you have stepped outside of somebody else's idea of 'who you are'. This happens even though that other is likely to be an internalised other (i.e. a part of your own mind). At the extreme, the Other Mind(s) dissociation could be called Paranoia where allegiance between the warring factions of the mind becomes loose or non-existent. This mechanism operates within every one of us, thought mostly at lower 'normal' levels.

Social phobia, multiple personality, split personality, guilt, shame, experience of a separate anthropomorphic God, the conscience, 'super ego?', anthropomorphism (the hallucination of humanistic feelings onto non-human objects – including animals), empathy, sympathy – all these things and many more require the Other Mind(s) dissociation at some level.

One interesting phenomena connected to this position is what I call, 'the search for external validation'. This can be seen in an over-reliance on other's opinions or simply as the need for an audience in which we may perhaps see our own reflected glory; a legitimization of our position. During pre-enlightenment, we would not be quite so happy about our happiness unless we could let other's know about it. That is why postcards, whose function is to pretend not to say "I'm having a better time than you," were invented.

Self concept and self esteem both require that we step outside of ourselves in order to interpret or judge that self. The higher self – the single point of consciousness we all are at the core - does not judge, cannot be seen by itself. So then who is the judger? Who is the interpreter of the self? Answer: it is actually a part of the mind simulating another critical mind, a third person perspective. The Myth of the Self, seeks objective clarification of the reality of what it is, yet this can never happen; it can only ever generate a reflection of what it believes itself to be. Every time we step outside ourselves to have a look, part of that self must come with us outside. We can project upon a screen, our idea of our selves (wherever that idea came from), if we like we can start to judge it too. The true centre of consciousness is the 'I' who views that idea and this self can never be directly conceived as it will always require another truer 'I' to conceive it. We will know this true 'I', this very centre of lived experience itself only as a shady reflection; only as raw experience of being in-itself.

Some of the positive intention implicit in the attention drifting off to other mind(s) are based upon faulty assumptions such as; "*I can accurately model other minds,*" "*Other minds may contain a definitive interpretation of events that I should recognize,*" and, "*Other minds hold a constant position*" (i.e. other minds hold consistent and singular thoughts.)

Beliefs

We've seen that certain beliefs and assumptions drive our attention towards the four dissociations, now let's look in more detail at the mechanism behind how they act upon our direction of attention. On the surface, it seems the mind is not serving our best interests as it pulls our attention to the *past, future, elsewhere* and *other minds*. Surprisingly, our minds are, in fact, acting in our best interests even in these cases, but the mind is acting according to a set of beliefs. Sometimes these beliefs are faulty and sometimes they are simply not consistent with our best interests overall.

There are two types of belief and we should make ourselves aware of the distinction between the two. You will, no doubt, be aware of many beliefs you hold such as:

'I believe the world is round.'

or

'I believe the government has not done enough to control the country's drug problem.'

or even

'I believe God's love is infinite.'

Now those very *explicit beliefs* are fine, we hold them as conscious and overt thoughts, but there are other types of belief we can hold. These other types of belief only really make themselves known through our behavior; they do not exist in our conscious awareness. We can call these *behavioral beliefs*. If I slip in the shower my arms will grasp for something to steady myself and, in doing so, my behavior expresses the belief, "It's better not to fall." This is so obvious, so in-built within us all that we wouldn't really include it if we were asked to list our beliefs because we take it for granted and so never really think about it.

These behavioral beliefs are very useful in so many ways as they make things happen for us automatically, but sometimes the behaviors they drive are no longer useful for us. Some of these beliefs are so endemic in our culture and society that, much like the figurative goldfish that is unaware of the water that surrounds him, we are not aware of them. Each behavioral belief may also rest upon yet further beliefs. Reflexes not withstanding, each time we exhibit any behavior we are buying into some beliefs at some level. Sometimes, if a behavioral belief is uncovered, it may seem absurd and our mind steps in to automatically protect our sense of self (Myth of the Self) by backtracking and finding an explicit belief that, by some logic, explains our actions.

Thinker/ Prover

So, if I'm bored and I eat, I'm holding the behavioral beliefs that:

'I cannot (or should not have to) tolerate boredom.'

and

'Eating will distract me from boredom.'

and further

'A short-term satisfaction is better than long term satisfaction.'

But I cannot admit this to myself, either because I do not know about the behavioral beliefs, or because they are incongruent to my sense of self. I need to find an explanation for my action and therefore come to the conclusion that I must have been hungry.

This mechanism is called 'cognitive dissonance' and can operate in hypnosis in the so called 'trance logic'. In trance logic, an individual, who is hypnotised to behave in a particular way, will, if questioned as to their motives, create an explanation that makes some sort of sense. Often, if the hypnotic subject is told they have been directed under hypnosis to act how they have acted, anxiety will be displayed along with a renewed urgency to establish their own interpretation of their motives. This is not restricted to hypnosis; we are all doing it, all the time.

This mechanism of mind means that you probably are not aware of some of your behavioral beliefs because cognitive dissonance is operating within you. By making our behavioral beliefs explicit, we can begin to question some of our assumptions. As we do so, we will find some behavioral beliefs that no longer serve us and as we find the strength to refute them we can begin to take on new, more useful, beliefs. Put simply:

1. We have some beliefs we are unaware of.

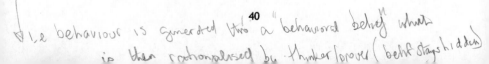

I.e behaviour is generated thro a 'behavioral belief' which is then rationalised by thinker/prover (belief stays hidden)

2. Any belief we are unaware of is, necessarily, unquestioned.

3. When we become aware of those beliefs we were previously unaware of, we can begin to question their logic and usefulness.

4. When we uncover beliefs that do not serve us, we can begin to swap them for something that does.

5. We can uncover and refute beliefs by:

    a) Making them very clear (write them down in a sentence if you like).

    b) Asking ourselves if there is consistent, rational, realistic evidence for them. Is there another way of seeing things that still fits the facts?

    c) Finally, ask yourself if your beliefs are actually helping or hindering you. A belief may seem rational yet, it if it is not serving you, there are a plethora of self-fulfilling beliefs to choose from.

You'll notice here that never have I suggested that a belief should reflect some underlying grand truth (because I don't believe it has to).

Do not confuse the way in which beliefs can be changed. With two different types of belief come two different mechanisms of change. Changing overt cognitive beliefs (explicit beliefs) takes evidence or intention and changing behavioral beliefs requires action.

Pleasantness of States

Whilst in any of the four positions of dissociation, it makes no difference to our bodies and our minds that this is all imagined. The physical and emotional results are very real for us. How pleasant the positions are is of no consequence, I could be depressing myself because things were bad in the past, or because they were so good in the past ("better than they are now, better than they will ever be again"). I can anguish myself by thinking that things will be awful in the future or by thinking things will be great in the future and feel grieved later when they aren't that great. Don't be fooled or seduced into pleasant Downtime if it is unuseful. Avoid it much in the same way you would like to avoid a drug addiction that dissociates you from any discomforts associated with reality.

Compound Dissociation

Described above are the four basic dissociations of *past, future, other minds* and *elsewhere*. There are times, probably the majority of times, when you may discover yourself having multiple dissociations of awareness; where your sense of dissociation is not confined to just one of the four basic positions. For instance, if you find your awareness in the past, you will often not be in the same location in your thoughts so you are both elsewhere and in the past. To think forward to how someone will feel in reaction to his or her surprise birthday party is to dislocate in both another mind and to the future. Don't let this confuse issues for us because it really doesn't matter. The remedy for unwanted movements of your attention to Downtime, in any of the directions, is one and the same – to direct your attention to the Here and Now.

Back to the Diagrams

The two diagrams introduced so far fit together like this: In

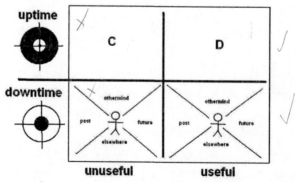

Good diagram

42

Downtime, whether useful or not, we experience a range of indirect sensations and can find our consciousness directed in a range of directions.

Chapter 5

How to direct your attention into the Here and Now and get it to stay there

But what minutes! Count them by sensation, and not by calendars, and each moment is a day.
Benjamin Disraeli

When we live in Downtime, we find our attention is dislocated in space and time. It is logical then to find that Living in the Here and Now (Uptime) is to have our attention located in space and time. This simply equates to having our awareness in our senses; hearing, sight, taste, smell and feeling. When this happens, our seven points of conscious awareness are spread across the direct senses or even all in one sense. In the Planet X model, we would see this as the sprites pointing their cameras through the glass wall looking outwards.

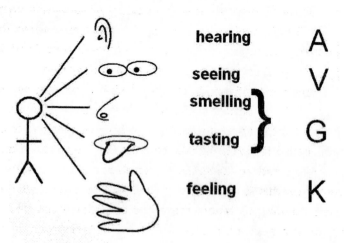

hearing	A
seeing	V
smelling	
tasting	G
feeling	K

Let's just review; to be in Uptime is to be in your immediate sensory awareness; that is to say, directly in your hearing, seeing, smelling, tasting and feeling. And to live in Uptime as your mind's default choice is Practical Enlightenment. In this chapter you will learn powerful techniques that will enable you to control whether you are in Uptime or in Downtime. Then you will be happy to find that you can use this control to override the old habits and start to set the new habits of making Uptime your default perceptual preference. Just as we were able to manipulate the default preference of perception with the vase/face illusion, so it is we can use these techniques to set the default position of our conscious attention within the senses. These three exercises are THE most important of all the exercises in the book.

Setting Your Uptime Anchor

When people feel upset, depressed, angry, anxious or any other unpleasant emotion this is always a result of the attention of consciousness drifting into Downtime (inside the head). Being in Downtime means you are mentally attaching meaning to sensation, being in the future, the past, somewhere else or inside someone else's head. There is nothing wrong with being in Downtime (to plan for the future for example), but often people find that they are not really present in the world when they would like to be, especially if that journey 'inside your head' is a painful, unuseful one - such as in depression or anxiety.

In human interaction, it is also desirable to increase our sensory acuity to reduce social hallucination and promote the tendency of the conscious awareness to become sensitive to any raw unlabelled feedback signals from the outside world. A move into Uptime and so away from simulating other mind(s) is necessary for this to take place in Uptime. You might even find yourself listening to others more and planning what you are going to say next a little less. A move into Uptime is also consistent with increasing mindfulness and contentment within the activity in which you are currently engaged.

This exercise implants a switch ('anchor'/'trigger') on your body that will take the attention of your consciousness into your bodily senses. You may find that once your attention is in Uptime you get more of a sense of being at the center of your lived world so that instead of moving through the world spatially, you feel more that it is moving around you. So, for example, on a walk to the shops, you will find less that you are perceiving yourself walking along a stationary sidewalk, and more that the sidewalk is moving underneath a stationary you. So, in a way, you are not going to the shop, you are walking with your legs and this is an act that brings the shop to you*.

After you have mastered the exercise, at any time during everyday life, if you feel your concentration drifting into unuseful Downtime, you can simply squeeze the anchor in order to bring yourself back into Uptime – that is, into your senses and into the world, into the present, into the Here and Now.

1, Relax and close your eyes. Send your attention into your body (your sense of feeling – the kinesthetic sense), try not to visualize or verbalize the sensations in your mind; just become more aware of any raw sensations. *Note that each of your senses operates through more channels than your conscious attention so whilst your entire attention can be in a single one of your senses, you can't hold in your conscious attention the entirety of any single sense (so, for example, you can concentrate your attention entirely in your body, but cannot become aware of every sensation your body is sending at any one time) - this is as it should be.*

2. Once as much of your conscious attention is focused on your body as possible, (your sense of feeling - **Kinesthetic**)

Squeeze the index finger and thumb of your right hand together to make a loop. This is your 'anchor', hold the anchor for a few moments or until you start to feel your concentration on your body wane, or your mind drift in any other way, then let your fingers relax. (You'll preferably relax your fingers before your attention starts to drift off.)

3. Repeat this simple anchoring of your other 4 senses (in no particular order.)
   Smell and taste (Gustatory)**

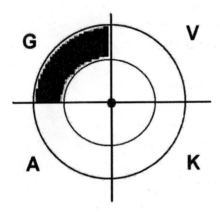

Hearing (Auditory)

Sight (Visual)

You anchor the experience of each pure sense by squeezing the same two fingers together as you find yourself fully in each sense at that time. You'll have to open your eyes for the sense of sight, of course, but be careful not to verbalize what you see, and when doing your sense of hearing, be careful not to verbally label the sounds or make pictures in your mind of what you hear. Just tune into the purest and most uninterrupted experience of each sense that you can. I have seen people almost catatonically stuck because they 'cannot let go of the labels'. Ironically, at these times, I can always see them drift massively into Downtime as they judge exactly how well or how badly they are not-judging the incoming perception. If you can't avoid the labeling, at first just go with the exercise as well as you can, and go fast too. Labeling your incoming perceptions is a lot nearer to Uptime than drifting back down inside yourself.

Repeat steps 1 to 3 until the anchor becomes a powerful trigger, repetition and persistence are vital to reinforce the trigger, allowing it to become powerful enough to serve you in any times of need.

Within the three exercises in this chapter, it is only in this first one (setting your Uptime anchor) that we deconstruct Uptime into its four sensory ingredients (V, K, A and G), this is simply to allow us to have the most powerful and focused state to anchor each time. In the next two exercises, when you use your anchor to bring your attention into Uptime, allow your unconsciousness (the unseen watcher in our Planet X model) to dictate exactly which of your senses you find yourself in. This is important; let your unconsciousness guide your awareness, just as you would allow and trust the director of a film you are watching to point the camera where he will. You concentrate on simply being aware of, and enjoying, whatever is been shown to you. <u>When in Uptime, in everyday life, the 'unconscious part' of your mind can be trusted to direct your awareness between the senses</u>.

Uptime Anchor - Roadblock Variation

In this next exercise you will learn to attach the anchor from the previous exercise to the very first signs of drifting in unuseful Downtime. This will bring your mind back into the present instead of being sucked into an unpleasant, unuseful experience. This is particularly useful if you find yourself, among other things, in habitual patterns of worry or depression, (these being signs of being pulled into the future or the past respectively). If you need to, you can repeat the exercise for different emotions as and when the need arises. Having made your Uptime anchor nice and strong (as above), we can program this to fire at the first physiological sign of drifting into unuseful Downtime.

1. First, find your physiological sign of drifting into unuseful Downtime. Close your eyes and just go inside your head and play an internal movie or thought (real or imagined, past or future, it doesn't matter) that you know will make you anxious, depressed, discontented or paranoid. The memory or thought is not as important as the feelings it creates. Just note those physical feelings, particularly the first feeling you can become aware of. For some people this may be a sinking feeling in the stomach perhaps, or racing heart, or hot hands, or a tight chest etc. (don't let these examples sway you, it could be something else. Make sure you discover your own). It can often be a subtle signal or one you have been unconscious of until now.

2. Just note the very first feeling you get that tells you this is an unuseful Downtime experience (film/soundtrack) you are playing to yourself.

3. Now, once more, let your mind wander to the same, or similar, internal representations (film/soundtrack) just so you can, again, experience the very first feeling you get that tell you that this is an unpleasant internal experience. As soon as you get the very first inkling of this sensation, squeeze your fingers together (your Uptime Anchor) and allow your conscious awareness to quickly jump from inside your head to your current senses of taste, smell, vision, sound and feeling. Do not worry if the jump is a conscious and chosen one; it will be at first, but you did it all the same.

4. Repeat. This is very important; you need to associate the very first feelings of unuseful Downtime to the jumping of your consciousness from the inside to the outside of your head and soon this will become automatic.

What you are doing here is creating an automatic association that will act as a roadblock to your awareness drifting into unuseful Downtime by catapulting your awareness into Uptime.

Setting up the Default Position of Your Attention as Uptime

Having already set your Uptime anchor and 'road blocked' the unuseful (or 'distressing') Downtime, you may find that Downtime is still largely operating as a default perception for you. Your brain/mind still, maybe, has the inclination to drop into Downtime as matter of course because it's a well known and well trodden path. The Downtime is still the path of least resistance for your system perhaps? This final variant of the exercise, below, will allow you to install a newer deeper path of least resistance with Uptime becoming the default position of your attention.

This exercise below is most important as it helps us to circumvent a paradox that can hold us back in our quest for enlightenment.

The paradox is this: 'are you in Uptime or Downtime when you make the decision about whether to be in Uptime or Downtime?' The decision seems to be taking place unconsciously and this is what is so problematic, this is the mechanism that allows or encourages the long periods of introspection where, once in Downtime, you can get trapped there for minutes, hours, days; even years.

Imagine that you are a robot and you have an on/off switch. If you switch yourself off, how can you ever make the decision to switch yourself back on again?

Yet using this technique below you are able to change that decision. We are essentially pulling ourselves up by our bootstraps; taking conscious control of our unconscious process through the back door.

This technique is incredibly easy; all you need is the determination to carry it out. The values that help you to keep up your motivation for this exercise will be ones of direct authenticity – of being alive in the real world. Most people would not sacrifice a real existence for a superficially, more comfortable virtual existence.

Many people will find the technique annoying, but if this is the case with you then you have got to ask yourself why. Perhaps you are more comfortable being removed from the world? And remember that 'useful' is not the same as 'comfortable', also keep in mind that it's possible to be comfortable about your discomfort.

All we need to do in this exercise is to attach our Uptime anchor to something that will be activated outside ourselves:

1. Buy a digital countdown timer, smaller is better, just for convenience. They are available in cooking shops and, sometimes, digital watches and mobile phones will contain them.

2. Set the timer to buzz you every fifteen minutes. When the timer goes off, fire your Uptime anchor whilst the alarm is still buzzing. You may still need to consciously review the senses one by one, and this is fine to begin with. When you are nicely in Uptime then turn off the alarm and reset it to go off in another fifteen minutes.

3. You will eventually automatically transfer your anchor from a physical touch to the audible sound too, and will no longer need to physically squeeze the anchor.

   You can play with the time interval as you wish (I once did a whole day on four minute intervals). Just continue with the exercise until you find yourself naturally and automatically in Uptime as a default. Once you have set this, it will become automatic, but you may still benefit from top-ups periodically; almost everything in our shared world seems to exert an intention of pulling our consciousness inside our heads. Perhaps do it once a week for a couple of hours at five minute intervals as a maintenance procedure.

In *The Matrix*, the hero is given a choice between taking a red pill and having his perception changed, or taking a blue pill and staying where he is, perceptually speaking. There is no third halfway option. There is no purple pill! <u>Your countdown timer and this exercise is your red pill! If you choose not to make a choice and don't do this exercise then you have, by default, chosen the blue pill.</u>

Notes on the Exercises

In the *Setting up the default position of your attention as Uptime* exercise, remember that the countdown timer is needed to manage the off-switch paradox. The temptation to implement the exercise without it is likely to lead to self-monitoring in Downtime or clockwatching in Uptime and these are both unuseful directions of the attention. It is exactly these trance-like states that the exercise is designed to avoid; making the exercise done improperly, at best, useless and most likely counter-productive. The exercise is for resetting decisions made in uncon-sciousness, so you cannot seek to consciously manipulate this. If you feel that you *simply haven't got time* to make these changes, then they are all the more indicated for the way you are choosing to live. No red pill = blue pill and you've chosen to give all your choices away. The blue pill is the staple diet of the Ostrich.

If you are still finding your brain/mind pulling your attention to Downtime, then perhaps it is because you have yet to address the meaning of that 'habit'. Habits will persist as long there is a meaning behind them and, in this case, that meaning will likely be that the Downtime, to which your conscious awareness is being pulled back, still contains positive learnings that you have not integrated yet. Try the timeline exercises in chapter 11 then return to these Uptime anchor exercises.

Incidentally, each time you ever experience a pleasant or

useful state you may wish to anchor it. It does not matter how this state came about, whether through the practice of the exercises in this book or simply spontaneously. You may wish to set different anchors for different states; so for example, if you suddenly find yourself getting an awareness of the interconnectedness of all things, you could create an interconnectedness anchor. If you find yourself suddenly very clearly perceiving the outside world devoid of any projected mind-made labels or categories then you may wish to anchor this on the same anchor point as Uptime, to strengthen the feelings of direct, uninterrupted perception.

* Do not worry that the perception that you are at the center of happenings is a form of 'egocentricity'; think of it as a more genuine (authentic) contact with your sense perceptions. As long as you realize that other people are not having the same experiences as you then this is not egocentricity, it is only 'sense-centricity'.

** I have put smell and taste together as 'Gustatory' yet you can anchor smell (olfactory) and taste (gustatory) separately here or together as a single gustatory sense – it will likely make little difference. When I have been refining this technique in my practice, I have often given the client a stimulus such as a strong mint in order to make it easier for them to focus in on the gustatory senses. In these cases it makes sense to anchor them together. Likewise, when anchoring the kines-thetic sense, some tactile stimulus may help.

Chapter 6

The Fifth Position, what it is, and how it controls the reality of your world

We have nothing to fear but fear itself.
Franklin D. Roosevelt

Whilst we can find ourselves in the past, future, elsewhere and other minds (or a combination of these) in Downtime, we can also find ourselves in the 'Fifth position', see diagram below. This 'Fifth position' is a special case of thinking, where we think *about* our thinking. A lot of thoughts will slip through our mind in a shady form, outside of our awareness. (The bubble meditation exercise later will help you to become more aware of this level of thinking.)

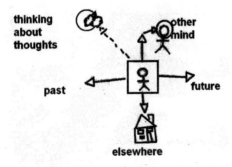

The Fifth position really operates outside all the other levels. The diagram below, returning to our more formal notation, expresses the Fifth position as being outside and above the other four directions of Downtime dissociation.

PAC + beliefs

Resistance to Now

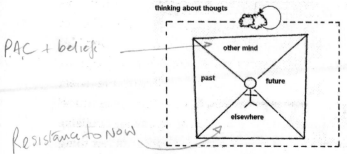

Imagine we are both in a plane about to go skydiving; we are both anxious. This seems perfectly rational, perhaps the deeper circuits of our mind are reacting to the very real perception of height and danger, yet to recognise it as rational in the moment is another thing. Imagine, as the plane climbs, we both consciously feel the anxiety symptoms (increased heart rate, sweating, butter-flies in stomach etc) yet we also begin, on an almost unconscious level, to be having feelings about our anxiety. I am fearful of the anxiety, yet you are more acceptant about your anxiety. Yes, we are both in future Downtime and at first it seems we are in Unuseful Future Downtime as we are experiencing anxiety at the base level as a range of physical symptoms.

At this point, I should mention that there is a third sky diver; he is a pig that we have taken along; we are going to chuck him out on a parachute too. Now ideally, whilst the plane is climbing, all three of us would be in a state of Useful Uptime; Living in the Here and Now, but only one of us is - the pig. This is because he has no real concept of what is going on, but we do and there is not much we can do about that. For us, this is a gift and a curse.

The demand for certainty is one which is natural to man, but is nevertheless an intellectual vice.
Bertrand Russell

Ideally, you and I would also find ourselves in the Here and Now and literally be unaware of what is to come, like the pig is. Yet for us humans to turn the mind off in this way is difficult. One idea would be for us to tune into our senses by using our Uptime Anchors, yet our minds may override this with the sheer magnitude of what we are about to do (although that 'magnitude' itself is a judgment based on our subjective values and beliefs). Our thoughts are operating as a curse at this point. Another thing for us to try would be to consciously tune into each of our senses at that very moment (and this strategy can operate very well). So I try it: I sit down and simply say to myself, 'is the temperature comfortable right now?' 'Is it too noisy for me?' 'Is the movement of the plane too violent?' 'Am I in any immediate pain?' 'Does it smell bad in here?' And so on. It is likely that all of the sensations are not too uncomfortable and if I can recognise this, I am OK. Yet the tendency of my thinking in this mode makes it likely I'll label even moderate sensations as unuseful or uncomfortable.

The way I'm thinking about my experience is operating unusefully for me. I am experiencing physical symptoms of anxiety; for me this is not OK. So I experience anxiety *about* my anxiety. Perhaps then I experience anger about my anxiety about my anxiety, then perhaps frustration about my anger, and hopelessness about my frustration. See diagram below (the chain of compound experiences, feeling or thinking one thing about another can be either long or short it doesn't matter).

hopelessness   Judgements
/   \
frustration
/   \
anger
/   \
anxiety
/   \
anxiety
(physical symptoms)

try "Drop Through"?

But let's have a look at how the pig is handling things; he is happily sat in the corner of the fuselage eating turnips. Well the pig is fearless, and fearlessness about a dangerous situation comes only with ignorance of the facts, through either a lack of the facts or an inability to comprehend them. See diagram below.

The pig is a special case; he is unable to assess the situation, but he is also unable to assess his feeling about any situation anyway, and he feels those feelings but he can't label them or feel or think

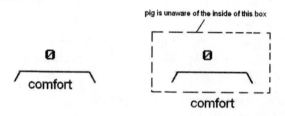

pig is unaware of the inside of this box

comfort

comfort

a certain way about them*, "*Ignorance is bliss.*" The pig is not anxious because it is not the literal raw sensations of the plane that is the problem. The problem is the unuseful thoughts in Downtime (in this case, the future – when we jump!)

But let's have a look at how you are handling the situation. You are not *fearless,* instead you are *courageous,* you have almost found a way of 'feeling the fear and doing it anyway'. Although experiencing similar physical anxiety symptoms, you have labelled them as OK. You know something very, very powerful and that is how you can be comfortable about your discomfort. You have experienced the physical symptoms, you expect them, you accept them, and you are comfortable with them. You are 'comfortable about your discomfort' – see diagram below.

comfort

dis-comfort

The tendency to be uncomfortable about your anxiety symptoms may creep into your mind a few times – see diagram

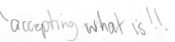

accepting what is !!.

below, yet you understand that you can still be comfortable about your discomfort about your discomfort about your discomfort about your uncomfortable symptoms. At the higher level you are still comfortable.

So you can realise that no matter how many levels of discomfort you may experience you can always go one higher to affect all the lower levels; this ultimately really leaves you with

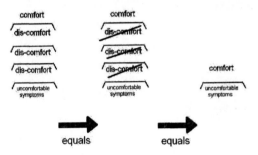

only two positions when dealing with discomfort – see diagram below.

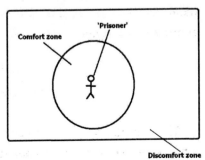

The Comfort Zone

The comfort about your discomfort allows you to get things done; it increases your comfort zone. Quite simply, it frees up your available repertoire of actions. Go where you want. Do what you want.

Accept this as a fact; it hurts (it is uncomfortable) to ride a bicycle over the Alps. So now ask yourself: how many Tour de France riders hold each of the two mental positions in the diagram above? Only by continually finding higher, or more robust, levels of comfort through which to perceive the discomfort can they keep going, the way they do, through increasing levels of discomfort**. Let's have a look at the idea of the comfort zone: in the diagram **right**, the situation is that discomfort cannot be tolerated on any level.

Once it is understood that one can feel comfortable about one's discomfort, the situation is that shown below.

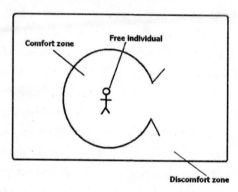

The individual is now free, and the more time that is spent outside the comfort zone, the more the discomfort zone will actually become comfortable on every level. This can happen many times as each discomfort zone effectively collapses into the newer larger comfort zone. Many people have requested more confidence, yet upon questioning they either did not really have a strong idea of the concept this unquestioningly prized trait represented, or they had a representation focused on some form of 'feeling comfortable all the time and at all levels'. This conception of confidence has an implicit intolerance of any discomfort and so this 'magical thinking' is part of the unconfident trap itself. Confidence is, more usefully, <u>the ability to comfortably tolerate discomfort when necessary</u>. And so, we don't demand comfort on every level but are free to be comfortable at the top level at least.

OK

Many of us spend much of our lives trying to control or prevent the

unexpected. Individuals who take on challenges inherently accept the possibility of failure and their feeling of doubt and inadequacy. However, many of us have been taught that we need to build a totally organised and predictable world in order for us to be OK.
Christopher S. Hyatt

Of course the mind does not want to seek out discomfort for its own sake; the trick is in knowing (deciding) just where your priorities lie; knowing at what level to set your goals and motivations. We shall learn more about this in chapter 9. In the examples above, we have been dealing with 'discomfort' to make the manipulation of those ideas more accessible but that's just one manifestation of the concept. If we take this idea out to its most general state, discomfort is only one example of the many ways in which we can be 'not OK'. Likewise, comfort is only one example of OK-ness. The really desirable (useful) frame for you to understand is that; it is OK to be not-OK. The less useful frame, again, is that it is it is not-OK to be not-OK.

$$\checkmark \quad \frac{OK}{not\text{-}OK} \qquad \frac{not\text{-}OK}{not\text{-}OK} \quad \times$$

This frame can then be expanded to all sorts of real world circumstances.

You can forgive yourself for not being able to forgive yourself.
You can feel peaceful about not being able to find any peace.
You may find that the only constant is change.
Mistakes are a chance to learn.
You could choose to force yourself to do something.
You could force yourself to choose.
Become relaxed about your tension.
Accept your sadness about your sadness.

List how many things you can do today to lessen your helplessness – oops, the depression has gone! How will you know who to be? Quickly, run to a darkened room and say to you self, "It's not OK to feel sad, there is nothing I can do about my helplessness" a hundred times or you may never get it back. I've forgotten to remember all the other examples now, or did I remember to forget?

In the past I was obsessed with the future but I know NOW, that in the future I'll put the past behind me.

Get rid of the judgement, get rid of the 'I am hurt'; you are rid of the hurt itself.
Marcus Aurelius

Some of these ideas are complex and, as you begin to continue applying them in your life, you may feel confused or frustrated. That's fantastic, what a wonderful opportunity for you to accept how your are thinking and feeling and watch the way your mind is working properly. Let me just reiterate that you know that IT IS OK TO BE NOT-OK!

There is a good reason why this is the royal road to enlightened living. Allow your mind to accept another example, again we'll use anxiety for the model but it can apply to lots of 'problems'. Just imagine that you are a school child and your enemy is the local bully, Crusher. Every time Crusher steals your lunch money this is not-OK, that's understandable. Now, as you have an immature mind your 'wish' is the complete removal from your world of this unpleasant scallywag and his naughty ways. This is understandable, but if you get your wish (Crusher is hit by a bus whilst insulting the local old people), is your situation any better? Well, on the surface, yes it is, but you are always anxious about another bully coming along. Your anxiety about the potential re-emergence of your anxiety is still operating. Another bully could come along at any moment, after all there is a vacancy - perhaps you should start interviewing applicants immediately. Warning signals should be flashing right now - VICTIM MENTALITY!

Perhaps your wish was faulty. Remember you asked for a complete removal of the problem. What if... (Ah, that old chestnut!) What if... you had wished for some way of dealing with your problem? Well you are half way there. What if... you had decided to find or create a way of dealing with this problem? Great! This sounds more like it.

So let's say you decided to learn karate, after which you effectively repelled Crusher and had the confidence that comes with the ability to apply your new solution to any other bullies that come along. Then what happens? Less potential bullies will pick you as a victim and those who do, get a bashing. Sooner or later you are no longer victim material. Fantastic, if you give a man a fish you feed him for a day; teach him how to fish and you've fed him for a lifetime. When it's raining, do you implore the sky to stop, or do you start looking for an umbrella?

It seems in life that those who can defend themselves rarely have to and the rich get richer and the poor get poorer. It's good to know the universe is working how it should be!

This brings me to another point, the so-called 'just world hypothesis'. A lot of people are discomforting themselves about injustice in the world, in the universe. Imagine you and I are out hiking, we decide to walk to the castle that is shown on the map. When we get to the correct location, there is no castle. I say, "Where is the castle? It's on the map. What is wrong with the world?" You say, "Where is the correction fluid? I'm going to correct the map."

Wake up! Take a look around yourself right now. If your map

is out of date, or indeed never was accurate, don't expect the world to change. The universe is working correctly. Justice is only ever crudely and arbitrarily created, it is never encountered. In fact, some cynics may say that the universe seems to be geared up for creating injustice. This is not surprising in light of the fact that the concept of 'justice' is, itself, a reaction to the natural tendencies of the universe, the world and nature. If justice or fairness was supposed to be an inbuilt quality of the universe it would already be here and we would not have to set up so many ways of trying to impose it.

Dealing with Problems

The annihilation or removal of our problems (obstacles to our goals) is an obvious and habitual response, and if you have the power to annihilate your problems then go ahead. This is not often very realistic in the psychological sphere, so instead the 'it's OK to be not-OK' frame sets us up for the three stages for solving a problem.

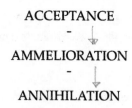

ACCEPTANCE

AMMELIORATION

ANNIHILATION

Quite often it seems we will not be able to complete the path all the way to the ultimate annihilation of our problem, yet your goal is only to walk the path as far as possible.

ACCEPTANCE - Understand that you are creating the conditions within which the situation is operating as a problem.

If you think the problem is outside of you, that thought is the problem.
Stephen Covey

64

Imagine yourself in a situation: you can't get to sleep.

You can:

a) Say to yourself; "This is terrible. If I don't sleep tonight I'll be tired at work tomorrow, I can't handle that." The anxiety may keep you awake.

b) Say to yourself; "I would prefer to be asleep but if I find it uncomfortable tomorrow at work because I don't sleep tonight, then I'll handle it." The anxiety is resolved; it is much more likely you'll fall asleep.

AMMELIORATION - The symptoms have less or no effect, even if they are still there. E.g. you may not be asleep, yet now this is no longer operating as a problem.

ANNIHILATION - The symptoms might go away now. Even though this is your ultimate preference, you do not demand it be so anymore. E.g. now that the situation of being awake is no longer causing you distress, you are more likely to fall asleep – which would represent an Annihilation of the symptoms. This is not always a possible step; sometimes the symptoms will not go away.

In my professional experience as a hypnotherapist, if a client drops out of therapy voluntarily it is most often due to a lack of comprehension or application of the understanding of the 'Acceptance - Amelioration - Annihilation' path. Such a situation would show itself up in the continuing demand for immediate Annihilation of the problem without effort and, therefore, a denial of any personal responsibility for their making a given situation into a 'problem'. This often derives, in my experience, from the faulty belief that the Acceptance phase is a surrender to infinite suffering under the weight of the problem and not a positive step towards its management and eventual reduction

(Amelioration) and even removal (Annihilation). Acceptance does not mean 'put up and shut up'; it is not a retreat but a forward movement toward the regaining of control over one's *lived* world and possibly over *the* world (at large).

Goals

There are no problems – only situations that operate as problems within certain arbitrary psychological perspectives. Now this involves that most unfashionable of concepts – 'responsibility', but on the other side of that coin is control because response-ability is your *ability* to choose how you, emotionally, cognitively and behaviorally *respond* to any situations you find yourself in. As you take control of this ability to respond, you take control of the meaning of any situation. Notice how, in situation 'a' (above), the situation is operating as a problem because of your beliefs, whereas in situation 'b' the same situation is not operating as a problem. In 'b', you have not solved the problem so much as actually avoiding creating it initially.

You also take *ownership* of your goals. You recognise it's realistic to change the things you can change and manage the things you can't change. Let's look at two imaginary goals with a common objective:

The *end* goal: "I want more people to like me more." If someone was to come into the clinic asking me this, I'd say, "OK, take a seat outside, could you show the rest of the world in." Why? - Because the ownership, the areas of the world that need manipulating, lie outside that person's control.

But look at the new goal:

The *means* goal: "I want to learn to exhibit the behaviors that will make it more likely that more people will like me more of the time, regardless of the outcome." Now, providing we can identify the right behaviors, perhaps by experimentation, then that person will find that they have the control of the variables that will make this happen. Notice that if this person still finds that no one likes them more than before, success has still been achieved; the behaviors have still been exhibited. Ownership of the goal is not lost.

We can also separate these two goals into *ends* and *means* goals. So when you ask yourself, "do the ends justify the means?" You are really asking yourself, "can I pay the price the world is asking of me to complete this goal?"

VALUES
AIMS

The *ends* goal is a wish; it encapsulates your higher motivations for wanting something but not really how to get it.

The *means* goal is an action plan; a decision. Sometimes, it may ignore or even negate the wish, but it's also more likely to achieve it.

OBJECT
IVES

Problems often arise when different criteria are applied to the *ends* and the *means*. *Ends* goals are often assessed upon the *possible vs. impossible* spectrum. If you are overweight, you know it is possible to lose weight and it may be your wish; your *ends* goal. It is possible, so you wish it and you must have it. Yet, when it comes to the decision to take action, the criteria of *possible vs. impossible* often gets replaced with *easy vs. hard* thinking. Your wish list is full of what is *possible* but the 'purse of your motivation' only has enough 'money' to buy what is *easy*. I have seen many cases where wants and expectations are based on the fact that something is possible, whereas the follow-through is based on the ease of delivery. Ultimately, all this talk of setting goals is aimed at your higher values. It will work for any level or type of goal, but just be sure about *what* you actually want and *why you want it* before wading in.

Sometimes happiness is wanting what you have, not having what you want. Like some sort of psychological crash-test dummies, everyone wants to destroy their 'wants' once they have created them. Some ways of doing this are easier and more authentic than others – we'll discuss these later. Crushing the endless stream of 'wants' may bring only illusions of happiness. Fear not, because our goal here is not happiness. It is one beyond good and evil, it is the quest for *enlightenment*.

Now goal attainment is really beyond the scope of our enquiry here, but good, solid goal-setting is important for to us as it allows the doing (in Uptime) and avoids the reviewing and previewing (in Downtime). A badly formed goal, or one resting upon shaky values, can promote the mind to drift into Downtime.

* I intend no bias or debate at all regarding the level of animal intelligences. I have included the mention of animal consciousness here just as a short hand for a non-linguistic, non-labeling, less self-aware state of mind. No doubt animals do project object/subject boundaries and have different reactions to the mind-objects they create.

** These higher values of comfort are likely to be attached to more abstract values such as pride, competition, sense of self, obligations, financial reward and all of its attendant values. Furthermore, the change in bodily state and chemistry are sure to play a factor in reducing the Lower Element (ground level) physical discomfort and may play a beneficial part in buying into the higher level values by making them more vivid, or more compelling perhaps? – Notwithstanding, a complete escape into some sort of Downtime.

Chapter 7

The Identification of Objects: What is Really 'Out There'?

Existence precedes essence.
Sartre

A common debate in perceptual theory goes something like this: "Do we see the world as it is, or do we impose meaning onto what is 'out there'?" Perhaps another look at the neutral two faces/vase illusion will help you to decide which view is correct; remember there is no secret TV in the pages of this book; the images are all completely still. You might see the two faces at exactly the same time as someone else viewing the page is seeing the vase. So decide for yourself now: Do we impose meaning, or is it 'out there'?

Well, in reality it's a bit of each, you can skip back and forth between the faces and the vase quite easily so it's true that you are creating some of the meaning yourself. On the other hand, it certainly is easier to see the two faces or a vase in the image than it is to see a dog in a hot air balloon, so you must be picking up on some hint of meaning in the World at Large (i.e. what is 'out there' in the world). So certain things are presented to us by the world and it is up to us to make meaning of them. There are many ways to make a map that still accurately reflects the territory, yet emphasises the particular aspects of the territory that we are interested in and so they are more useful for us with respect to our particular goals at that time.

In the way I've asked you the question there is no one *correct* answer, but there may be a *best* answer.

It will help to ask the question in another way. Remember that our beliefs (our maps of the world) need not reflect what is 'right', but what is *useful*.

So here goes:

Is it more useful for *you* to continue with the belief that:

a) ...meaning is out there in the world?
or
b) ...you generate meaning yourself?

Usefulness, itself, is relative to your goal though, is it not? Part of our goal in becoming enlightened by Living in the Here and Now is to control our experience and make the (perceived) world a better place to live for ourselves. We also want authenticity. So which belief will give you more power and control? I think now that it might be best here to just assume that it is indeed correct that we do impose meaning on the World at Large. In my opinion at least, I am certain that the true reality of the situation is that that's the way I'd like to see it. Choose not on the basis of 'truth', but for power (perhaps even the power to define the truth).

History is written by the victors.
Anon

70

Governments, Foucault, historians and media of all kind, have long since known that power really comes, not from the ability to change what is actually physically happening in the world but, from the ability to dictate the meaning and the interpretation of those events. We, as individuals, all have this power on a personal level to create our own meaning from what is presented to us in the world. This is not some fairytale of complete freedom *over* our conditions, but a freedom *within* conditions.

Even objects 'out there in the world' are dependant on us for their boundaries. I could go into a garden and see that it is actually made up of all smaller bits. Then I could choose to direct my attention towards one of those bits - the lawn. The lawn itself is made of smaller components - blades of grass. Each blade of grass (I might be using a microscope now) has it's own structures, cells, sub-cell structures, DNA, then molecules, then atoms and so on... So every object can be a component of a larger object whilst at the same time it is made up of smaller objects itself.

The point is that whatever is designated as 'a single object' is completely arbitrary and controlled by the observer. In the Planet X model we see that each sprite can focus narrowly or widely and this represents the ability of our perceptual systems to project boundaries around things to create objects.

The categories we transpose onto the world are not real in any external sense, but can have very real consequences for our lived world. Let's look at a few fictional examples that show how we may think erroneously about the world.

I'm watching a TV program and a boy has a gun, which makes everything invisible. He points it at a wall, it turns invisible, he points it at the school that turns invisible, he points it at his friend and she turns invisible. Do you see the error in the logic here? Physical laws are no respecters of our categories, or the legal, visual or linguistic boundaries we place round 'objects'. You'll see this error a lot in science fiction and fantasy. A gun makes a whole man disappear, including his clothes, his possessions, the gun he is holding, and the bag over his shoulder, but how does the gun know where one object finishes and another begins? Why, when Alice shrinks after eating mushrooms, do her clothes shrink, yet at the very same time, the tears which have left her eyes have not shrunk and she experiences them as a flood? How long after the invisible man eats does his food become invisible? Why can a man see a naked woman with his X-ray specs, instead of seeing a skeleton? <u>All these boundaries are in the observer, not the world.</u>

The acceptance of these boundaries as somehow real can lead to inaccurate perceptions. A man buys a motorbike, after not long, it gets a puncture, a week later his chain snaps. He not only concludes that his motorbike is unreliable, but that all of them are. In fact only two components failed; a tyre and a chain. Even within the chain, it is likely that only one smaller component, such as a single link, has failed. Yet this man generalises his misfortune out to a massive degree and never dabbles with motorbikes again. In fact, what is a motorbike? Does a trike count? Then why not a three wheeled car? How about a trike with a steering wheel, two seats next to each other, but no roof. Is that a motorbike? It's all completely subjective. Two failures in a week is a lot though, but what is a week?

Have you ever had a bad week? Was it made up of bad days that, in their turn, were made up of bad hours? How do you decide exactly when to start or stop throwing out the baby with the bath water? How many blades of grass make a lawn? When do a set of physical symptoms become a syndrome? How many short periods of sadness make a depression?

When we superimpose our identifications onto objects this is what gives them their boundaries, from our perspective at least. We can do this visually but what really gives a sense of concreteness to these boundaries is the linguistic labels that we project 'out there' to actually make these objects distinct from each other. These outlines can be set, not just around physical matter, but also more abstract concepts and even ourselves. All these boundaries are true hallucinations, but because they are largely shared, these norms are so taken for granted that amazement and awe are common when these boundaries are transgressed.

This location of the source of meaning within ourselves plays an important part in defining our response to things because it controls whether a stimulus has even been presented to the consciousness, simply through the mind's ability to define the boundaries of objects themselves. If an individual chooses a particular response to a given stimulus; let's say a phobia of snakes, then this phobia is initiated firstly by the identification of the object, 'snake'. The misidentification of a garden hose could spark it off. Likewise, the identification of snakes could generalize (wide angle) out to any reptile, or discriminate (narrow focus) down to a particular breed of snake. There are no external and set boundaries in the absolute sense, and so when an individual responds to an event in the outside world they are already a participant in as much as they created the reality of that event for themselves, even before they respond to it. Would a vegetable phobic be afraid of tomatoes? Would a bear phobic be afraid of a koala bear? Knowledge of categories and the ability to recognise them are prerequisites to creating a stimulus, a 'mind object' and these categories are always subjective. It would be very difficult for me to respond in any way to Ash trees in particular, because I don't know one tree from the next. I can respond to 'trees' or 'a tree', but not one particular breed of tree against another except the ones I know, like the Christmas or the Monkey – puzzle. If the acuity of one's ability to identify one stimulus from the next is low then responses will be become confused or generalized.

As we separate one mind-object from another, or when we classify them together, we can use different categories. If we take some objects, let's say cars on the street for example, we can slice up the 'pie' in many different ways: colour, brand, fuel type, or general design (saloon/sports/jeep /convertible etc.) Some of the cars will even span categories; a jeep can be a convertible as well, for example.

Now the choice of categories we would use will be entirely dependant on our goals, but with so many categories available with which to dissect our experience, we have a situation where things can be similar and different at the same time. An appreciation and use of these ideas can help to avoid the perception of 'ordinary moments'. Ordinary moments are times when you project nothing but similarity onto the world, and because you've seen it all before, it seems as though there is no novelty at all to attend to.

Every separate mind-object is both similar and different to every other mind-object in at least some way. From the perspectives we normally operate from, which are driven largely by survival and society; a chair and a table have more differences than two chairs. Some perspectives exist though that would perceive as much difference between the two chairs as there is between a chair and a table. The very designation of an object as table is often *structural* in that it has obviously been designed as a table. Yet, if I sit on the table and have my plate of food on the chair then from a *functional* perspective, the chair is being used as (operates as) a table and vice versa. Although the structural perspective seems more valid it is not, it is simply more consistent with regard to the aspects of reality we attend to. Everything, all meaning is up for grabs. Remember this when 'ordinary moments' seem to creep into your lived world. By all means the common distinctions, and so 'ordinary moments', will need to be used *to live* in the shared world, but they are not needed in the moments in between when one only has to *be alive*.

For an individual, conceiving a *mind-object* can drive a whole host of associated mind objects and values. Everything seems to have some connection to something else. The alarm clock, for example, is never just a clock. We don't see it just for itself anymore, now it has begun to *mean* something. It is attached to so many values that now we relate to it indirectly; to us it has become something which it is not. This is OK as long as we are aware that we are doing this and why we are choosing to do this.

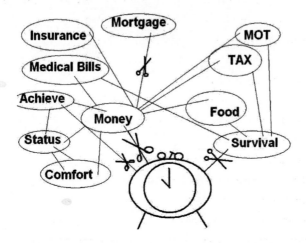

The early phenomenologists had a name for the technique of freeing up one's raw perception from the contaminating ideas and values – they called it *Bracketing*. We can never bracket-off all the values that insist on attaching themselves to our mind-objects but we can strive for as raw an experience as possible. So if you look at the face/vase illusion again, try to perceive it in a third way, as a flat image with no foreground or background. Turning the picture upside down or sideways might help a bit. This interpretation may give just a glimpse of what it is like to bracket-off the meanings from the raw sensory information, as you see the image without any of the attached meaning. The Uptime state is one approaching a bracketed experience, but the *Bubble mediation* is the exercise that really will improve your bracketing ability fast. So when we perceive things with all the extra values attached and as a means to an end, we call this seeing it *for-us*. And to perceive things without the attendant values and as an end in itself, we call this seeing it *in-and-of itself*.

Absolute vs. Practical Concepts

Each concept, each idea is, in itself, a mind-object. Justice, consistency, truth, reality, hot, cold, tall, comfort are all mind-objects themselves. Yet these concepts can never exist in and of themselves; that is to say that even though we know what they mean, the concepts can never exist in the World at Large in their purest form. One concept can never be expressed without relating to other concepts, just take a look in the dictionary to confirm this. Each word can only be described using other words which, in their turn, require other words to explain them. At the simplest level we have *binary-opposite* concepts; hot cannot exist without cold, nor tall without short, happiness without misery, and comfort without discomfort.

Even higher concepts cannot exist without something to compare themselves to. Let's look at an example from my school days to illustrate. During some sort of arbitrary assessment of my performance I was labelled 'inconsistent', I had no idea what the word meant, but was enlightened (only on this matter I might add) by the teacher. After a short while, as I took all this in, I enquired, "Am I always inconsistent?" It was my reasoning that I must be consistently-inconsistent and so could only be held to be inconsistent on a certain level; an arbitrary and subjective level. The only other alternative was that I was inconsistently-incon-sistent and this is a double negative, meaning that I was actually consistent.

This did not go down too well with the teacher at hand, and it occurred to me much later that this was due to my stepping

DUALITY!

outside of the 'socially agreed' level that everything was to be interpreted within. It further occurred to me that, actually, the concept of *consistency* itself only exists as a concept by virtue of its relationship with *inconsistency* as an opposite. Therefore, if the purity of *inconsistency* was in doubt, then the idea of *consistency* itself must be on shaky ground. How can we have *consistency* when *inconsistency* only exists at certain levels? To add to this, *inconsistency* only existed by virtue of the purity of the concept of *consistency*, which I had already thrown doubt upon.

Then it came to me: Paradoxes, the logical inconsistencies that exist in thought, are only confined to our minds. There was no consistency or inconsistency in the World at Large; no right or wrong, no good or bad, at least in their most absolute senses. Paradoxes only highlight the errors, the contradictions, in our thought processes. Yet we still use these concepts which is fine as long as we stick to the same level when discussing them, that is to say, so long as we define our frame of reference. So the purity of any concept can exist as a thought, yet it cannot be applied to the outside world as an absolute. If we attempt to apply any concept to the World at Large, it will not 'stick' across the board, but will only hold within a small frame of reference. It seems pragmatic then not to chase any concept too absolutely, because their only constant is change. No absolutes are available to us that can be applied to the World at Large. Absolute concepts will dissolve into paradox if we try to apply them at every level.

Just as my teacher was fixed at a certain level of definition, with respect to the application of the concept of consistency, so we too must remain at a single level at any one time in order to have any understanding of anything. The trick is in knowing that we don't have to be *consistent* in our choice of level from one moment to the next, and that, furthermore, we can choose as and when it suits us. If we know why it suits us, at any particular time, then so much the better - relatively speaking of course.

level of
abstraction

The Practical Concept

This brings us to the idea of the *practical concept*. The term denotes a concept that is applied pragmatically, with a respect to achievability, feasibility, and a good fit with one's everyday life. The *absolute concept* is a term that denotes the purest, rawest form of any idea and it always remains a purely metaphysical matter (only in our minds – our ideas). If we try, in vain, to apply absolute concepts to the World at Large then we will find that we have a situation upon which paradox will play a merry tune and, in so doing, will distract us from our goal of *Practical* enlightenment.

I'm sure you will agree, sooner rather than later now, that the division of our concepts into *practical* and *absolute* is an absolutely practical idea and that there are absolutely no practical reasons for not doing so. So, as we now see that the integrity of the boundaries we normally take for granted is somewhat more shaky than we previously thought, we will explore, in the upcoming chapters, how this can relate to an escape from some of the mechanisms of our minds and of our society that otherwise constantly try to entice us away from the Here and Now.

Own the World Strategy

Despite the ideal of eliminating all of the labels and values that we impose on the world, it's unlikely to be practical, even if it is possible (which I doubt). Then we are left with at least some control over which way we can perceive things, even if the number of ways we choose between is finite (this is freedom within conditions, not of conditions). Going back to Planet X, we could imagine that each sprite (managed by the Unseen Watcher) can make a few directorial decisions as to how each camera is pointed at an object of awareness.

Within our visual perception, there are differences that make the difference to us, normally these will not be operating inside our conscious awareness; they are at the *fifth position*, so it's easy to miss them. If you can tune into them then you will be able to

— Awareness!!

dictate your lived world (within limits). ←

Have a look at your phone, get it out of your pocket and have a look now. Imagine an identical phone next to this phone, but one that does not belong to you. What is the difference? How do you know yours is yours? Perhaps it has a certain personalized picture on it, or a particular scratch on it? Well just transfer all those qualities over to the imagined phone and ask yourself again. What tells you that your phone is yours? What gives you a different feeling about your phone?

On top of the pure visual sensations you are getting, what are you layering on top that gives each phone a slightly different meaning? Search for these qualities, they are your ownership strategy. This means it is the strategy your brain uses to let your mind know what you think you own and what you don't.

Let's look at another example. Imagine that you have just got off the train; as you walk over the bridge from one platform to another, you can see your car in the car park in the distance. How does it seem different to all the other cars?

Is it more 3D? Does it seem more solid? Do you model the interior of the car in your mind? After all, you know this car better than the others. Is it brighter, more real than the other cars? Is your car more detailed, at a higher resolution, than the other cars? Do you imagine yourself in it? Is it easier to imagine actually being in it? You might have a better idea of what is going on under the bonnet of the car, and the contents of the boot.

Perhaps you just have a sense that is difficult to put into words, but you can feel it.

The qualities can become obvious as you approach your car only to find it was another car of the same model and color, you were fooled. All the qualities you had used to inform yourself that this was your property now drop away from the car as you search the car park for your car - the right object to throw your sense of ownership at - making sure this time with the right car, they will stick. You were fooled for a moment but as you were on the

79

bridge, that other car *was* your car in your lived experience. You can extend that sense to anything. Now look at the public property around you, the whole environment, even ideas and institutions, what meaning do you overlay on them? Is it the one you would like, the one that's best, most useful? Why not? It can be hard to find these extra qualities because they are at the *fifth position.*

Experiment with new purchases; buy a lager at the bar and begin to notice when and how it suddenly becomes yours, and how and when it ceases to be yours anymore. Notice, if it's over on a table with other identical drinks far away, how it seems different. This is not just how you identify your drink from the others, e.g. it's the one half-full (half-empty?) on a mat touching the ashtray. No, this is about how you signify to yourself, within your own internal experience, the sense of ownership of that drink. What qualities do you overlay on top of the simple visual image that gives it meaning?

I know the previous owner of my previous car was upset to see it drive away with me in it on the day I bought it. Whilst taking it home, I fuelled it up at the local gas station, and looked at it through the window of the station whilst waiting to pay, it did not seem or feel like it was mine; it was just a car. When I got it home I had a good look, I can't remember but I might have looked out the window at it on the drive from time to time or walked around it, until I eventually, and unconsciously at this point, was able to project my ownership strategies over the simple conception of the car, now it was *my* car! The previous owner was still overlaying his ownership strategies over the visual sensation of the car as it drove off. This, coupled with the knowledge that I wasn't bringing it back, led him to experience feeling a little sad. Did the previous owner hurry inside to look at his pile of cash in the kitchen? Did the double overlaying of meaning of ownership and power that he was projecting onto that collection of pieces of paper, soothe the sadness at the loss of the large and noisy piece of steel?

Now I'm not going to dictate, or even suggest, how you should consciously choose to use these strategies to shape and give your chosen meaning to your lived experience. I have come to the personal conclusion that it is unwieldy, in a psychological sense, and so, therefore, unuseful for me, to extend my sense of self (my 'ego boundary' as some might say) to any of the following:

Objects	"Oi! Mate. Are looking at my beer?"
Places	"What are you doing on my bar stool!"
Ideas	"Who the **** is this bloke, he thinks he know more about existentialism/enlightenment/cars/chilies/whatever than me!"
Times	"Eleven o'clock! Nonsense, it's *my* birthday, give me another!"
People	"Oi! Mate. Are looking at my girlfriend?"

It can be liberating and entertaining to impose a sense of ownership, for a moment; to extend your 'ego boundary' around a cloud, or the sea, or even someone else's pint, maybe everything in sight. You can quickly and easily release the extension of ownership, the extension of self, again. A better definition, instead of the term *ownership*, might be a sense of 'connection'; a sense of primacy, a sense of having something-to-do-with. Are these values of connection ultimate in that they reflect the highest (or 'deepest') values in themselves or are they only stepping stones to some other value to be chased? Comfort? Status? Adventure? ....? Who knows!

Naturally, once you have learnt to impose and then depose ownership onto trivial objects, you might want to experiment by seeing how far you can dissolve every projection of ownership that is your current habit.

Labelling Exercise
From my personal memories of the playground, as a child, I

remember a certain game or technique which, at the time, was probably just used as a bit of a wind up. You would find a 'victim' and follow them around repeating their name constantly until it began to feel absurd and the sound of that name began to disconnect itself from the meaning it had previously. We could say that this forced a split between the *signifier* and the *signified*. This gave the pursued (the 'victim'), and often the pursuer as well, a strange sense of a 'vertigo of meaning'; a vertigo of identity even. This vertigo can lead to a twinge of anxiety which sometimes led the pursued to try to run away and so the game was often played 'on the hoof'. Incidentally, a good defence if you were the victim was to put your hands over your ears and sing loudly "La la la…! I can't hear you…! La la la…!" You will, no doubt, have experienced something like this yourself. In the labelling technique you do exactly the same thing. You might wish to continuously repeat (silently or out loud) your own name, or the name of a body part, or the name of an object in the world, or the name of an emotion, or anything you can label. The purpose of the exercise is to disrupt the boundaries we project onto our mind-objects. You too will feel the vertigo of meaning and maybe anxiety; nevertheless, try to continue. As you begin to force a more direct and un-interpreted perception of the World at Large this will bring about revelations and maybe even an epiphany if you're lucky. If you create a state you deem worthy of repeating, sometime you may wish to anchor it.

Variation: If you should find yourself stuck in a broken-down elevator with a stranger and wish to pass the time by offering them the gift of enlightenment, you could find out their name and treat them to a 'vertigo of meaning' using this technique by simply repeating their name again and again.

Awareness is needed for labelling — once labelling begins it disrupts the usual thought train !!!

Chapter 8

Learn how to control your thoughts using the Bubble Meditation

An intellectual is someone whose mind watches itself.
Albert Camus

This exercise is probably the second most important exercise in the entire repertoire. Somewhat like chess, it takes minutes to learn and a lifetime to master and you will never be perfect at it. That is as is should be. The exercise utilizes the mind's propensity to loop thoughts, and begin to control that process. It is particularly good for anyone who 'suffers' obsessive, circular or intrusive thoughts.

In the exercise, you are asked to visualize various images; don't worry if these images are not full Technicolor hallucinations, the vividness of the imagery is not directly connected to the effectiveness of the techniques. Your brain will be holding these concepts in many different ways and the images will be there, but not necessarily at the front of your consciousness. Some people may even experience total blankness or other images/thoughts. Don't worry that's OK, simply follow through the exercises. Remember it's OK to be Not-OK and also ponder the thought that it is often the changes that we are not even aware of that effect us the most.

1. Sit down and relax (use a quick progressive relaxation if you wish by simply relaxing each muscle in turn from your feet all the way up to your head), close your eyes if you wish. Imagine yourself to be sitting at the bottom a pleasant lake.

2. Now clear your mind as much as you can. This clear mind is

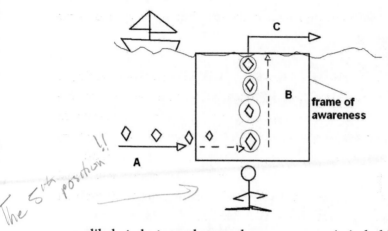

unlikely to last very long and as soon as any 'mind-object' (any awareness, thought or sensation) pops into your frame of consciousness (A), notice how the mind-object seems to come in from outside yourself. Put a bubble around it and freeze the mind-object and allow it to rise out of your head.

3. Allow the bubble and its contents to rise towards the surface of the water (B). Notice how the mind-object in the bubble will try to morph, twist, expand and pull in other associated thoughts and feelings as it is rising.

4. Keep the mind-object fixed and as pure as it was when you first bubbled it. This is not easy at first, but if the mind starts to wander gently guide the mind back to its path.

5. Allow the bubble and its contents to slowly rise. The bubble should take a few seconds or so (perhaps ten but do not count these seconds) between leaving your head and reaching the water's surface. As the bubble breaks the surface (C), let go of that mind object immediately and without reservation.

6. For a scant moment your mind will be blank, it will not remain so for long. Just take the very next mind-object and repeat the

process of freezing it within the next bubble as it rises to the surface.

Notes: The term 'mind-object' denotes any awareness, anything at all that ventures into your frame of consciousness. If you are aware of it, then it is an awareness that is worthy of freezing in the next bubble. An awareness can be a thought or sensation, picture, sound, feeling; absolutely anything you're aware of!

As the next awareness pops into your mind, you must endeavor to be completely unselective about which mind-object you freeze, it should be the very next one.

When each bubble reaches the surface and pops you let go of the mind-object contained within that bubble immediately. The exercise actually utilizes the circular thought processes that normally take us away from consciousness to push us back into consciousness. This is an unparalleled exercise for those with circular or intrusive thoughts.

Benefits:

1. Trains acceptance in *what is*. (A)
2. Helps to clarify the actor/observer distinction. Notice in the diagram that the observer sits outside the frame of awareness, notice also that the mind-objects seem to come from outside the frame of awareness.
3. Trains the mind in letting go of mind objects instantly at will. (C)
4. Trains the mind in holding mind-objects steady. (B)
5. Increases ability to 'bracket' experience (B) - that is to say you'll be able to 'chunk down'. Perceive smaller and smaller experiences as singular mind-objects.

Sooner or later the mind will start to monitor its own observations. This may happen visually as in the diagram below.

It may happen verbally:

> *"I just thought a thought. Wait! That in itself was a thought; should I put my thoughts about my thoughts in the bubble? Does it count?"* (The answer is yes you should – remember <u>anything</u> that comes into awareness should always be frozen for this exercise.)

or

> *"Who is the 'I' that is watching these mind objects?"*

or

> *"I'm thinking about the bubble, can I put a bubble in a bubble? Oops now I've thought about putting the rules relating to putting bubbles in bubbles – can I put that in a bubble?"* (YES)

or

> *"My mind is blank. Now my mind is not blank, as it contains the thought 'my mind is blank' – which should go in the bubble?"*

This will demonstrate that your sprites, that is to say the directions of your conscious attention, show mischievous and restless tendencies most of the time. Every thought that you have seems to collect hangers-on, freeloaders, stowaways, whose aim is just to spend as long as possible basking in your conscious awareness because it gives them life. The only exceptions are mind-objects that are reflexive (self-seeing and circular), they can either free you up or completely bog you down.

You can only ever see a reflection of yourself in your mind; the observer will never observe itself. In its attempt to perceive itself, the observer can only ever watch the actor as the actor pretends to be the observer.

Heads Inside Heads Inside Heads

The difficulty of finding an observable-observer is known as the 'homunculus problem'. It appears whenever we try to treat a facet of ourselves as if it was a little person (a homunculus), because if our model of a mind is one that is fragmented, then each of our fragmentations will have its own fragmentations.

Have a go at this thought exercise, it will show you why the observer can never be observed and it will also locate the workings of your mind as the very centre of the universe (at least for you). If you get a good vertigo of reality during your experience, you may wish to anchor this state so you can easily access it again later.

Be wary as this exercise can cause some strange sensations of vertigo, a bit like standing between two parallel mirrors and seeing the reflections reach out into infinity, but persevere. Some readers may find the state this exercise produces as undesirable that is fine, you will still learn something by producing it even once.

The exercise:
1. Just look at the world around you. In fact, sense it in every way; smell, taste, touch and hear the world. As you do this,

become aware of how your mind is locked inside your head and only has contact with the World at Large through the nerves, like little wires carrying messages into the brain.

2. When you have this feeling, hold it until you begin to get some sort of gut-validity, so you actually feel it to be the case, or at least feel it could be the case.

3. Now notice that your consciousness is locked away inside you head. In fact, notice how the entire world - the entire universe - is simply a model; a simulation running inside your head.

4. Begin to ask yourself now, as you perceive that the whole world is, in fact, a model within your head, exactly where is your head? This is an easy enough question to answer normally; it's just there in the world, yes that's fair enough but we have just seen that the world is only a model within your head and so on.

5. Now, as you sense the world around you and see it to be just a model inside your head, you will notice that your head itself must be *inside your head* and there will even be another head inside that head.

6. If you now go *out* instead of *in* and start to look at the sky or as far out 'into the world' as you can see, and know that all of it is inside your head. Try to conceive of this giant head that you are living inside. It's your head, yet it can only be conceived of inside another head.

7. From your perspective, you are at every position inside your head, inside your head, inside your head, ad infinitum and outside your head, outside your head, outside your head, equally, ad infinitum. Whilst you begin to realize that you will

never step outside of this system, it will occur to you that there is nothing special, nothing more valid about any of these positions you conceive than any other. The whole universe is yours yet you are trapped inside a little skull, with only a few crude wires running in and out to connect you to the World at Large.

8. Keep playing with the idea until you begin to feel it is 'the way things really are' and set your anchor. You can use this anchor now every time you wish to feel yourself located, not only *at* the centre of the universe, but *as* the centre of the universe. Know that existentially (phenomenologically at least) this is not an illusion and is a completely valid conception of exactly where you really are!

Chapter 9

Knowing your true Wants and Values

All things are subject to interpretation, whichever interpretation prevails at a given time is a function of power and not truth.
Friedrich Nietzsche

Earlier we looked briefly at some ways you can work towards goal achievement, which is all well and good once you have set a goal and you are determined to achieve it. The setting of that goal is quite another thing, however. There are probably plenty of things you would know exactly how to do, but have no particular desire to achieve. Now we'll look at how to decide what exactly it is that you do want, focusing once again on our ultimate goal of enlightenment.

Traditional notions of enlightenment conjure pictures of monks having given up all belongings and, beyond their basic physical needs (that they service ascetically); we assume they pursue higher *spiritual* matters. Perhaps this is *absolute* enlightenment. On reflection, this position seems to be very extreme and only available to a minority of people within a society. In the real world, it unrealistic to abandon all the trappings and structures of society, but this does not stop you becoming and remaining *practically* enlightened.

If you were to ask yourself right now, "would I like some money?" or even, "do I like money?" the answer will probably be "yes." This is quite predictable because, within our society, money makes things happen; it can get things done in the World at Large.

If you imagine yourself to be stuck in the desert with a huge pile of cash, temporarily away from the monetary system, you will require a few things, none of them actually being the pile of cash you are sitting on. Water, shelter, food, transport... These will likely be your most basic requirements. It will be no particular surprise when I tell you that nobody wants money, only the things it will provide. Perhaps more illuminating for you, will be the realization that you do not even want the things that money provides, only the values those goods or services answer.

Imagine that you are back here in civilization now and you have a windfall of a considerable sum of money. Think about one of the first things you would like to buy; a new computer? A house? A car? A holiday? Plastic surgery? Jewelry? A library in a university? A charitable donation? Land? A dog? Gifts for others? A peerage? Your name on a star? More food than is nutritionally necessary? Home furnishings? A party?

Do these thing possess value in and of themselves or can you see how these things will all ultimately answer deeper (or should that be 'higher'?) values?

Let's look at the computer, for example; we will have a look at just one possible value hierarchy. A value hierarchy is a chain of values, where one leads to the next; it helps us to discover the more fundamental driving forces behind what we want. It is built up by just questioning, "Why do I want that?" we do this until repetition begins to happen.

More money may buy you a faster, bigger (smaller?) computer, but what does that computer buy you?

- Well, it might be that the computer helps you work faster.
So, why work faster?
- It will let you get more done.
But why would you want to get more done?
- To save time.
Why save time?
- To do other things (more leisure time).
Why have more leisure time?
- To enjoy yourself more.
Why enjoy yourself?
- It feels good.

Why feel good?
- It's comfortable.
Why be comfortable?
- It's comfortable.

Handwritten note: "Could ask what is the intention (purpose) of x")

'Comfort' is at the end of this value hierarchy and seems to hold its own inherent desirability without any deferment to a further value. Often, it will happen that a person wants something just in and of itself. If they can't relate that back to the core psychological values that it addresses, we call this a *'Confusion of Wants'*. It is not rare; most commonly, an object or 'magical state' is desired with no real insight as to the shadowy associations that are attached to that. Dissatisfaction is likely to result because the superficial desire is unlikely to really reflect the underlying desire. So dissatisfaction is certain to arise when the car does not provide status, when the deodorant does not make you attractive, when the thinness does not bring confidence, when the brand of beer you drink does not bring you the lively social circle you saw on the advert, when the money does not bring an end to all your problems. If you are not aware of your *hierarchy of values* then you will be vulnerable to the *confusion of wants*. This will result in the disappointment of forever chasing the end of the rainbow because you don't know what you want. No one likes to hear this but, by and large, people do not know what they want.

It could be argued that if you could find cheaper, easier or quicker ways of satisfying the values of comfort and enjoyment, the buying of the new computer, in the example above, would no longer be necessary. It could be argued that if there was a way of enjoying your work or being comfortable with the discomfort of work or getting away with doing less work then the comfort-drive could be satisfied through a different value hierarchy. The same destination may be arrived at via a different path.

Most people, when asked, would not give up their car. The reason is because they see no better alternative for the needs it fulfills – which actually, in turn, only serve other needs. For a lot of people, the car is necessary for their job but why is that job, with its long hours, high pay, high status and high pressure really necessary? From an absolute sense it certainly isn't! From a relative sense it probably isn't necessary either! When offered the theoretical alternative of a Star-Trek transporter/helicopter/magic carpet, many people are more than happy to forego their previously precious car; those who are not are still clinging to some secondary benefit that their car provides, extra to being a means of transport. You'll notice as you look around now that not many people will buy a product for its actual value, but for an unconscious hierarchy of deferred values. The car, for example, is status, a pastime, control, a diversion, a distraction; no longer just a means of transport. Often people will get into debt for a newer shinier model. How has this happened? Because of an unawareness of the hierarchy of values; that is to say a 'confusion of wants'. Can you see how a hypothetical and instant, worldwide removal of the confusion of wants might devastate the car, home furnishing, jewelry, confection, cigarette and shoe industries, to name but a few?

Whenever we construct a value hierarchy (above the level of pure survival), judgments and values come into place and words like; more, faster, better, bigger, smaller, nicer, easier, newer, shinier and higher (higher up what, the slippery pole?) seem to start popping up. If we concentrate on only the more superficial elements of a value hierarchy then we attempt to change our situation in the World at Large, when it may often be easier and/or quicker, cheaper, nicer, faster, more possible, more plausible, more feasible, more lasting (and so more useful) to begin to accept our freedom to question, and control, the meaning we give to our current situation. There will always be more not-OKs within the World at Large round the next corner. The only way to break the trap is to reject the position of; it's not-OK to be not-OK, and embrace the idea that it's OK to be not-OK.

Authenticity

The word 'Authenticity', as I use it in this book, refers to Authenticity in the existential sense. *Existential Authenticity* describes a position where one is aware of one's own freedom of thought and action. Freedom of thought includes the freedom to assign meaning to the World at Large. Freedom of action is often constrained by conditions in the World at Large, but is never constrained by our thoughts unless we freely allow it.

Authenticity in an individual is a lack of ignorance about the facts of the World at Large; including the 'fact' that it is each of us who assigns meaning to the world for ourselves. It is also knowing that all the meanings we project onto The World at Large are subjective and could easily have been different because they are no more valid than anything else.

It is often said that "Ignorance is bliss." Let's expand this well known phrase to, "those who are unaware are happy." So does that make the Authentically-acting individual, in as much as they are aware, unhappy? Well if *happiness* is defined as encountering no discomfort at all then the answer is yes; the authentic individual will be unhappy. Yet if we define happiness as not allowing discomfort to *operate upon us* then the answer is no. Authenticity, and the awareness that comes with it, does not rule out happiness. Perhaps we need a better definition of happiness then.

Happiness is a continuation of happenings which are not resisted.
Deepak Chopra

If we can encounter discomfort, yet *not let it operate upon us*, then we can be happy *and* authentic. How would we go about this? Simply by understanding that we can be comfortable about discomfort. Another way of putting this is: It's OK to be not-OK.

Absolute vs. Practical Authenticity

As with many of the concepts we've discussed, *Authenticity* has its purest meaning as an *absolute concept* and it has a softer meaning as a *practical concept*. We have already seen that any attempt to impose absolute concepts onto the World at Large collapses into paradox and this applies equally to the concept of *Authenticity*. Each attempt at pure, absolute *Authenticity* will always collapse into some sort of *Inauthenticity*. So we must content ourselves with practical *Authenticity* or to put it another way, *Authentic-Inauthenticity*. We can do this because it's OK to be not-OK.

In fact, the application of pure authenticity, if it was possible, might end up being a little disturbing. *Authenticity* is not about honesty in the moral sense; it's about honesty in one's choices and in the assignment of meaning to the World at Large.

The thief who says he steals because of his background, his upbringing, or society, acts *Inauthentically*. He plays the victim role. The thief that steals simply for greed, knowing it is 'wrong' (in the agreed social sense), and who knows the value hierarchy(s) driving that greed, acts *Authentically*.

Likewise, the charity volunteer who cites, to themselves and to others, wholly altruistic motives for their actions is acting *Inauthentically*.

In this particular example, the charity worker has not enquired far enough along the hierarchy of values that they hold with respect to their charity. If we continue, we are likely to find that they derive some personal and private benefit from their actions. They are likely to feel good in helping others, and that's all very well but we must recognize that they are exercising their own freedom and their own pleasure principle in defining 'helping others' as a condition in which they allow themselves to feel good. In order to embrace *Authenticity*, the actions need not change, just the understanding of the motivations. And the motivations need not change either; it is enough that they are understood to be arbitrary and subjective – and yet still freely chosen.

Even in the ultimate altruistic example of someone laying down his or her own life for some cause, we would be able to find the pleasure-principle in action. Whether it is the case that they could not live with the discomfort (guilt) of acting against *their* chosen values, or the belief in some eternal reward, the comfort-approaching, discomfort-avoiding drives are the motivating factors that drive the person to act as they do*.

If I'm two-faced and I know I am acting that way and I know why I'm acting that way then, ultimately, I am acting *Authentically*. The acceptance of my freedom requires no necessary consistency in my action or in the meanings I assign to the world. Thus, a freely chosen change of allegiance or change of goals is authentic, although to choose one goal over another is to buy into a sense of subjectivity and, therefore, *Inauthenticity*. So, how can we reconcile this?

Whatever I am doing it is OK to be inauthentic by acting on subjective values, as long as I know that I *am* doing it and I know *why* I'm doing it. Yes, because it's 'OK to be not-OK'. This is an *Authenticity* of kind, it's called 'civilisation'. Civilisation is based upon the transference and deferment of one value to another and so we end up treating something like that which it is not. Money is a good example of this; it's just paper or numbers. We are agreeing here that we can approach *Authenticity* simply by knowing how and why we are acting *Inauthentically*.

Authentic
Inauthentic

This *Authentic-Inauthenticity*, is the most we can hope for and we call it *practical Authenticity*. And so this position comes about through an intense honesty with our selves about the dishonesty we practice through our self-delusions. There is no reason to go and live up on a mountain in order to step out of the game of civilisation. In fact, you may be able to become all the more adept at the game of civilisation for being able to see it now from the outside as well as from the inside. And see the arbitrary nature of the rules of that game, and make an active choice whether to buy into those rules or not. No choices are forbidden to the enlightened individual, but the enlightened individual is ultimately aware of the hierarchy of values, which drive any choices they make. The enlightened individual may ultimately make the same choices as the pre-enlightened individual and for similar reasons but, most importantly, for reasons that they are aware of. We could call this an 'informed choice'.

Reinforcers

Money is a strange thing; almost any individual will find it reinforcing (rewarding). Money acts as the universal reinforcer. The power of almost any other service or object can be represented very liquidly in money. This will only happen at a certain level of higher intelligence. You can't train a dog with financial reward as the incentive. A dog will react only to the 'primary reinforcers', these are food, shelter, sex and thirst. 'Shelter' covers a wide range of things, including, protection from attack, breathable air, and other suitable conditions for our homeostasis, such as temperature, baric pressure etc. Many of these we take for granted until they fall outside of reasonable parameters.

Even in a dog pack, 'social behaviors' will come down to the control of these primary reinforcing elements. It is the same with us, despite our complex value hierarchies, our drives are ultimately derived from these primary reinforcers. This can be why a lot of our plans fail, because the rewards (the reinforcers) are too abstract or too disconnected from the actions that will bring our plans to fruition. Likewise, some of the big killers of our time are too far removed from their causes in time, and so the consequences can, all too easily, become divorced from the actions: smoking, over-eating, and sloth figure most notably here, but there are plenty more.

Try making a list of a few things you want; they don't all have to be consumer goods, it could include positions, relationships, achievements, services, anything.

Now make your own hierarchy of values for these things; you'll notice that, as you get higher, you will be pulling out the primary reinforcers, or something like them. Look at the list again: sex, thirst, shelter and hunger. All the primary reinforcers are driven towards survival of the species** through the individual's personally experienced drives.

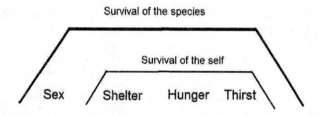

Notice how everything you want, or can imagine wanting, or imagine someone else wanting, ultimately boils down to some very basic instincts. Theoretically, every want above the survival level is a vicarious, fetish-ized convolution of the basic physical needs.

Imagine that you have your consciousness downloaded into a robot body. There is no need to drink, have sex, eat or find shelter; you are immortal, but now what do you do? After a certain period, apathy will set in and you'll sit down, do nothing and just exist. Our motivations to act lie in our most basic physical makeup and we can't change that, but we can, at least, acknowledge, and work around, it. This is the biggest reason why the enlightenment we seek must be *practical* and pragmatic, not *absolute*.

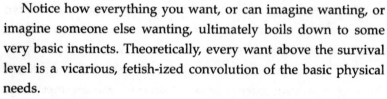

The Conflicts and Confusions of Wants

We have defined enlightenment as being in Uptime as a default and only, by choice, dropping into Downtime as an option to help us with the practicalities of life. One major obstacle that stands in the way of doing this way is internal conflict. It can sometimes seem that 'part' of us wants something different to another 'part' of us, and so an internal conflict is present within us. If we look at the whole value hierarchy, however, we may see that, actually, both 'parts' want the same thing but believe they have to go different ways about achieving it.

We will often feel conflicted about what we want, and it is common to use the metaphor of having different 'parts'. There are no parts inside of us really; just conflicting beliefs and values about *what* we want or *how* to get it. Sometimes, these parts even show up as *devil* and *angel* in cartoons. Let's have a look at an example.

A says	"I want to smoke."	(Devil)
B says	"I want to stop smoking."	(Angel)

Part A believes that smoking will be a move *away from discomfort*.

Part B believes that stopping smoking will mean more health and money and that, in turn, *is a move towards comfort*.

Imagine that you and I are business partners and we sell one product in this country. I want to increase the product range within this country and you want to sell our one product worldwide. At the level of *what* we want, 'to expand the business' we are in agreement, but we are in conflict as to *how* to achieve that aim. Anytime you feel any sense of internal conflict a similar process is at work within yourself. In our smoking example above, the two parts want the individual's comfort but disagree as to how best to do this. One part prizes short-term comfort and the other long-term comfort. The two parts hold an identical aim, but differing beliefs of how best to go about achieving that goal.

The following exchange is not uncommon in clinical practice and is a classic example of a time when one does not really know what they want because they have not thought it through. This is a 'confusion of wants'.

Client: I want to lose weight.

Therapist: Are you sure that's what you want?

C: Yes.

T: So if you lose weight and remain the same shape that's OK?

C: No.

T: Why not?

C: I want to be slimmer.

T: Well hypothetically, if you had to make a choice and you could be either:

the same weight and slimmer, or

the same size and lighter,

Which would you choose?

C: I'd be slimmer and weigh the same. (This is by far the most common response.)

We see here that weight loss is actually not the real goal, slimming is.

T: Ok, so slimness is a more important value to you than actual weight loss, that's great. That's OK, but can you tell me what's so good about being slimmer?

C: I'll feel better in myself when I am thinner.

T: Oh, what about being thinner means you will feel better in yourself?

C: I'll have more confidence.

There is no logical connection between being slimmer and being more confident.

T: How will being thinner give you more confidence?

C: How do you mean?

T: What is it about being thinner that will mean that you'll have more confidence than you do right now?

C: It will make me more confident.

T: How?

C: I just know it will.

T: OK. Can you describe what the word 'confidence' means to you?

C: You know - confidence.

T: Yes, what is it?

C: I just want to have more confidence.

Confidence, as is the case with so many 'traits', means different things to different people. It is not something you *have* or *are*. Confidence is not a noun, it's a verb. It's something you *do*, you act confidently. There is no magic trait, but those with no conception of what they want may think it can be magically given to them. The idea of 'confidence' is prized here despite the fact that this person has no idea what it really is (or more accurately, *how it operates*).

T: OK, let's try another angle; when you are feeling more confident what will it do for you?

C: I'll be happier.

T: How will having confidence make you happier?

C: I'll just feel better.

T: So your ultimate goal in all of this is to feel happy?

C: Yes.

T: You want to lose weight in order to be slimmer, in order to feel happy?

C: Yes.

T: So, hypothetically again, if you had to make a choice between being happy and being slim which would choose?

C: I'd rather be slim.

Wait! What? If slimness is prized because it will provide happiness, then why is it this person would rather, if they were forced to choose between the two, be slim than happy? Whatever situation this person finds himself or herself in; there will be disappointment afoot of some kind because value-confusion exists. The situation in the World at Large is not what needs addressing here; it's the belief structures, the value hierarchies. Of course the major belief that needs addressing here is that our situation (the 'facts' of the World at Large) dictates our feelings.

This belief that drives an intense focus on changing the World at Large is an extension of, 'It is not-OK to be not-OK'.

It's Not-OK to be Not-OK and Discomfort Distractions

Taking the position of *It's not-OK to be not-OK* leads one, quite naturally, to attempt to remove discomfort by changing one's situation in the World at Large. If the discomfort cannot be removed or tolerated, then a distraction technique may be adopted to avoid the perception of discomfort.

Let's look at a classic example, cigarette smoking (the exact same process applies to emotional eating, gambling, tranquilizers, drinking, shopping addiction, nail biting and a host of other things too, so this is bound to be relevant to you somehow, some of these activities contain drugs, some do not – it doesn't matter. The psychological processes easily outweigh the physical chemical component of any drug, which will soon subside upon disuse). Consider the smoker, and as you do so be aware of your own discomfort distractions. Within 'the smoker' internal conflict arises when part of him wants to stop and another part wants to smoke. Smoking is much like money in so far as, people don't want to smoke per se, our bodies certainly don't, but people do want the things which smoking pretends to provide. Imagine that the smoker finds, as one of its functions, smoking helps them to alleviate that scourge of the modern age - boredom.

Boredom is a vital problem for the moralist, since half the sins of mankind are caused by the fear of it.
Bertrand Russell

I believe that the intolerance of boredom is the biggest killer in today's modern world. Much like a psychological tranquilizer or a painkiller, the cigarette takes away the discomfort of boredom by masking it, yet underneath the same process (the same boredom signal) will still persist. Just as pulling the leaves off a weed is a short term measure, this underlying process will reassert itself as soon as the effect of the cigarette wears off.

Let's take a moment to look at the mode of action by which these activities distract our minds from other concerns. Go back to planet X. If all your sprites are wandering aimlessly and frantically, either inside the house or outside, you will feel fragmented. Now this fragmentation seems to be uncomfortable in and of itself. Cigarettes, and the other above activities, focus all your sprites and calm them down. This is why these activities help us to focus. If you only have limited ways of calming down your sprites, your mind can only choose between these few alternatives. No way of satisfying these needs are right or wrong, you'll just have to decide the usefulness and the cost of each method for yourself. Some of these activities, such as smoking, can actually focus the mind on the immediate sensations of the moment; they can facilitate concentrated Downtime, or even concentrated Uptime. If only there was another way to get all that, but at a lower cost!

Whenever we look for solutions we need to look at the balance between short and long term gratification. Imagine that I am cycling down the road and I have a slow puncture; if I fix the puncture it may initially be more of an effort and take longer, but it is the 'right' solution. It only needs applying once and this is one of the hallmarks of a 'good' solution. Instead of doing this, I may decide to stop and pump the tire up every mile or so. This is a 'bad' temporary solution. I am too lazy or stupid to stop and fix the puncture; it's a false economy. Notice that if it is my only choice (I have no puncture repair kit) it is actually a good temporary solution because it's the best I've got available. Yet it is ultimately still my fault for not equipping myself with more options and, therefore, more choices from which to select a solution to this problem. Can you see that in the second solution, I am going to end up 'chain pumping'? This is completely irrelevant, however, because there is absolutely no similarity between this and 'chain smoking'. All smoking is chain-smoking, by the way, it only depends on how long the links are.

As I continue on my stop-start bike ride, an inconsiderate driver knocks me and I break my leg. It hurts. When the ambulance gets to me, they administer a strong painkiller - Great! After all, there was no meaning behind that pain, was there? Everything's fine up to this point, but let's fast forward two months into the future. I was impatient, things needed doing, so I kept taking the painkillers; after all, there was no meaning behind that pain, was there? Now I'm walking around on a broken leg; things are not looking good, but things need to get done; the rat race is pulling me back in. I was so wise to dull those messages of pain. Not all messages have a meaning behind them, do they? Besides, a message ignored is a message answered, isn't it?

This is all completely irrelevant, however, because there is absolutely no similarity between this and smoking, is there? What can the smoker do though? Boredom comes along and there is certainly no way anyone could tolerate much of that, is there? So the smoker has taken the frame that he is uncomfortable about the boredom. If we see boredom for what it is - a form of discomfort - we see that the smoker has taken the frame that he is uncomfortable about his discomfort.

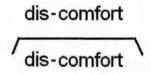

Or to put it another way, he has embraced the position of, 'it's not-OK to be not-OK.'

not-OK

not-OK

If we feel uncomfortable about boredom then we are naturally compelled to try to annihilate this symptom. But there is a way of imposing the 'it's OK to be not-OK' frame over this situation and, in doing so, reconciling the internal conflict.

The smoker begins with this internal conflict:

Part of me wants to smoke; it helps to address the discomfort of boredom by distracting me from it, which makes me feel comfortable (or more accurately *not-uncomfortable*).

vs.

Part of me wants to stop smoking, it will make me richer and healthier and fitter, and this will, ultimately, make me comfortable.

Both parts are moving towards the same goal by different means. Both parts are interested in your highest level comfort, yet their beliefs about *how* to do this conflict with each other. One part is thinking about long term comfort, whilst the other is interested in short term comfort. Neither is 'right' or 'wrong', the long term goal is what most people would swing towards, but an ex-smoker in front of the firing squad is maybe 'right' to have a cigarette. Likewise, if a meteor were destined to hit the earth in a million years, it would be absurd to start trying to find a solution to this today. It's a question of balance. If the smoker has chosen that his long term gratification is the more important, he decides to stop smoking. Even though he has sided with one of his parts (the angel), the other part (devil) will still operate at times and so internal conflict is still present. The 'it's OK to be not-OK' frame will help to resolve the internal conflict and implement the decision.

To begin with, the smoker holds the, 'it's not-OK to be not-OK' frame regarding the discomfort of his boredom and this is a common attitude. Ask a few people you know for ideas about how to deal with boredom. You'll, no doubt, get a variety of imaginative and fantastic answers, some involving a lot of effort and cost. In the pre-enlightened individual, boredom is seen as an enemy to be fought and annihilated, that's actually fine if you find yourself in a position where you can affect action in the World at Large. Sooner or later though, you will eventually find yourself bored, you can rely on it. What this mind-set invites us to do is to see the situation of having nothing you want to do, or no suitably novel stimulus to distract us, as a problem.

Remember the Acceptance – Amelioration – Annihilation process.

Acceptance first - Dare yourself to tolerate boredom.

You can feel comfortable about the boredom.

You can feel comfortable about the discomfort.

It's OK to be uncomfortable.

It's OK to be not-OK.

Great, now the discomfort of the boredom has been reconciled, there is nothing pressuring the 'need' for that distraction activity anymore. You are free to allow the stop-smoking and keep-smoking parts to pursue their common goal of your highest level comfort.

Remember though, that this is not all about smoking. I have only been using smoking as the classic example of deferred gratification: 'solving problems' through distraction or through unnecessarily complex means. As I stated earlier, it applies to many other behaviors too. Allow yourself to become aware that if you smoke, or engage in any other distraction activity, it may not be just for boredom, it may be for many reasons; maybe a different one for each time that the behavior is expressed. It could be anger, upset, tension etc. Each message needs addressing separately. The beauty of this way of resolving these internal conflicts and deferred gratifications is that it attacks the root of the problem, so the problem will not re-surface in another area of your life. For example, a lot of people who stop smoking will put on weight. Someone who does this has not addressed the underlying issues that drive the behavior so the same mechanism has begun to drive emotional eating instead. If they stop the emotional eating somehow, we may find them playing the fruit machines or compulsively shopping, or self harming or...?

Many authorities would have you believe that the behaviors above are very diverse problems that require very different treatment methods, but this doesn't have to be the case. If you see that someone is simply using a distraction activity to resolve discomfort instead of addressing the source of that discomfort then no matter what that person's distraction/vice is, the only problem is the belief that it's not-OK to be not-OK.

You can label people as drug addicts, compulsive gamblers, chocoholics, binge eaters, self harmers, smokers, OCD–ers, reckless drivers, etc, but these labels are not very helpful at all, as they define a person as having a problem, when, in fact, the 'problem' is really a dysfunctional attempt to address another situation in that person's life which is *operating* problematically through their belief systems.

Let's take the so-called 'chocoholic' for example. It looks like this person's problem is that they eat too much chocolate, but this is not the case. In fact, this person has simply fallen into over-eating chocolate as a method for distracting themselves from discomfort. When we look only at the behavior we miss the fact that it is an attempt to address another 'deeper' problem. In these cases, where the attempted cure has become worse than the dis-ease, it's the attempted cure that is mistaken for the whole problem. So actually our chocoholic is attempting to cover feelings of discomfort. It is feelings of discomfort that are operating as a problem for the 'chocoholic'. But those feelings of discomfort will only operate as a problem within the beliefs that this person is holding. Namely the belief that discomfort, at every level, must be avoided at all costs, because it is intolerable, i.e. it's not-OK to be not-OK. And the belief that every level of discomfort may be avoidable is faulty; there is always a payoff, always a price to be paid. Of course, the distracting behavior (eating chocolate) leads to its own discomforts; in this case, weight gain, rotten teeth, etc. These discomforts themselves can actually become drivers of the behavior itself and so 'it's not-OK to be not-OK' sits at the very center of the vicious spiral that goes something like this:

"I feel fat."

"I feel unattractive." (This doesn't necessarily follow outside the logic of society's fashion.)

"I feel uncomfortable." (Another value judgment, it doesn't have to follow.)

"These feelings of discomfort are intolerable." (Alarm bells! This is the real problem variable.)

"Therefore, I must suppress the feeling of discomfort through my chosen means of distraction."

"I must eat some chocolate."

"I feel fat."

I'm sure this is a very familiar, problematic situation for a lot of people and there are many areas at which we can intervene. For example, some people like to be fat, some people like others to be fat. This is fine if you are happy to find yourself in some strange sub-culture, but the chances are that you have chosen to buy into society's values. This is fine as long as you know why you have made your own very definite choice on this matter.

The situation above that arises from thinking, 'it's not-OK to be not-OK', has resulted in a 'damned if you do, damned if you don't' arrangement. Now a lot of people in this situation will tell you that if they could just stop eating (too much) they would lose weight and be comfortable, or if they could just be comfortable they could stop eating. The error comes in defining comfort. An immovable demand that all feelings of discomfort should go away is going to keep them in the trap. This demand follows from the following link in the chain of belief: 'These feelings of discomfort are intolerable'. AKA: 'It's not-OK to be not-OK.'

The very best level of intervention will be to shift to the belief, 'I would prefer not to have these feelings of discomfort but I can tolerate them'.

AKA: 'It's OK to be not-OK.'

As much as the first belief will spiral, snowball-like, to make things worse, in the latter belief, the very same mechanism will operate to make things better, the better things get. *"The rich get richer and the poor get poorer."* So when you begin to realize that all these disparate problems can be traced down to one process; one core belief, the labels (chocoholic/alcoholic/addict, etc.) can be seen to be actively keeping the 'problem' alive.

Instead of labeling someone as a *'chocoholic'*, it's much more useful to think of them as *'someone who believes that it's not-OK to be not-OK, and therefore uses discomfort- distraction behaviors; in this case, the excessive consumption of chocolate'*. This term is not catchy, nor does it help us to condemn those around us by thinking about them in a simplistic way, nor does it help the 'sufferer' to abdicate their responsibility through the inauthenticity of the victim script. For these reasons I have my doubts about this term ever catching on, but you don't always have to speak this way to think this way (to hold the conscious beliefs). Even more important than thinking in this way, though, is acting in this way (to express the behavioral beliefs).

On holding Yourself to Your Decisions

It seems a common human trait to 'not follow through' on decisions and agreements. Simply, by holding yourself always to the standard of following-through, you can raise yourself in an instant from the masses of do-nothings to take your place among the few achievers. Rise from the conflicted to the authentic. If you want something and you know why you want it, then don't ask whether it's going to be easy.

Instead, ask yourself, "is this possible?"

Imagine that, as you move through the world, you can step out of yourself and watch yourself as an outside observer. Is that person you are watching someone you would trust to keep an appointment, to make a decision and actually act upon it?

Do you want to live in a world where your decisions, your commitments to yourself, mean something or nothing? When you know what you want and you know why you want it there is no conflict. You have made a decision according to you true motivations, and whether you are flying along, or suffering setbacks, you'll be happy to find that you ALWAYS FOLLOW THROUGH

As you get into the habit of always following through and make it a part of your 'personality', you will begin to trust your future selves and free yourself up to living in the only place you'll ever be - In the Here and Now.

Stress Revisited

So far, we have looked at how we move toward certain goals and how those goals may conflict with each other, yet the situation can become more complicated. Not every drive will manifest as a moving-*toward*; it can often take place as a moving-*away*. If a lion chased you, for example, you would try to run *away* from the lion (away from danger), and this will mean that you are happy to run in any direction as long as it puts enough distance between yourself and the danger. This example carries through to everyday life in many things and if your desires are characterized by what you *don't* want, you'll find yourself moving in any direction, as long as it is *away* from the thing you don't want. It could be argued that, as you run *away* from the lion, you are running *towards* safety, but this is secondary, as your main motivation is to get *away* from something you don't want. This becomes clear if we consider another example: imagine you are in the desert and you are thirsty, you know there is an oasis five miles west so you move in that very specific direction. Again, it could be argued that you are moving '*away* from your thirst', but it is still clear that, in fact, you are moving *towards* the water. It is all a matter of whether you choose to motivate yourself by focusing on what you *do* want or by what you *don't*.

This difference can cause a whole host of problems if we don't understand and control how we motivate ourselves to go in particular directions. Let's have a look at the mechanism by which stress can come into our lives. We've already seen that the English language can hinder us by not letting us see the difference between the situation in the World at Large and our reaction to it, but there are further factors at play. In the diagram below we see a donkey on a hill, this donkey is motivated by a carrot (something it *does* want) 'pulling' it towards the top of the hill.

An alternative motivation for the donkey could be the stick, as seen in this next diagram below; here the donkey is 'pushed' up the hill by avoiding something it *doesn't* want.

Again, we will find it more useful to characterize the two types of motivation not along the lines of *good* and *bad*, instead we need to consider the pluses and minuses of each type of motivation, and come to our own conclusions about where each type of motivation may be appropriate. So let's see where each motivation style is *useful* or *un-useful*.

When the donkey moves itself away from the thing it doesn't want, first we could surmise that the donkey will not be motivated to move to the top of the hill, but only as far as it has to go to escape the stick. Unless the stick-wielding man moves up the hill as the donkey moves away, we can imagine the donkey will only take a few steps up the hill. It may even have charged off rather enthusiastically at first, as the stick really hurt and it found itself quite far away from the man with the stick, but the donkey may begin to slide down the hill and will feel no motivation to move up the hill again until it gets to the bottom where the man (who hasn't moved) waits with the stick. Counter to this, when the donkey moves up the hill to get the carrot, it is motivated to keep going until it reaches the top. This is a general rule: if you want to use 'away-from' motivation, you must keep moving (modifying) your 'motivator' as you make progress.

Other factors affect the system here as well; the donkey's strength to move, the steepness of the hill, the size of the carrot, and the distance between the donkey and the carrot, will all play a role in the equation that will govern whether or not the donkey moves. These factors all play a role in the away-from motivational style too, except the size of the carrot is replaced by the painfulness of the stick. Now I should probably mention here that I have never hit a donkey, but I would imagine that a donkey would be more motivated if I hit it with a heavy iron stick than one made of foam. And I also imagine that the donkey would be more motivated to get a bigger carrot than a smaller one.

The donkey moving towards the carrot may be more consistently motivated if we cut the carrot into bits and spaced-out the many pieces all the way to the top. This would equate to us creating many smaller goals, and a quicker reward for each of

Zaizen ! (

these, instead of one big goal.

You may now find yourself motivated to search inside yourself to discover which motivational style you find more effective for you (either by wanting to eliminate less effective patterns, or by wanting to install more effective ones). It's worth mentioning that you may find different styles effective for different situations, so don't judge yourself to be motivated more effectively by only one style or the other across all situations. Even a judicious combination of both may be appropriate at times.

Although I champion neither of these motivational styles above the other, it will be worth considering that the stick (the 'away-from' style) causes discomfort all the way up the hill until the goal is reached.

Now let's see how this relates to 'stress'. In the diagram below, the donkey cannot move forward as there is a boulder in its path, yet it is still motivated to move forward as the man behind is still hitting it with the stick. It is stuck between the proverbial 'rock and a hard place'. In psychological terms, the donkey is in a 'double bind'.

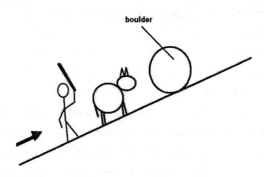

boulder

How does this relate to our lives? Well, first let me tell you something: you are the donkey, but not just that: you are man with the stick, you are the carrot and, to some degree, you are the steepness of the hill. All these factors are within you. To motivate yourself in these ways you must split your mind into separate entities, you must feel yourself to be the donkey in order to allow yourself to want the carrot or to hate the stick (both of which you have also created inside your mind but have perhaps not realized it).

Why does the man continue to hit the donkey? Well the truth is that the boulder is invisible, so the man has not realized that there is something ahead which is preventing him from controlling the movement of the donkey. If the boulder becomes visible and is judged to be small enough to be climbed over, then increased motivation may overcome the obstacle.

Imagine, though, that the boulder is completely insurmountable and invisible. Higher and higher motivation (more blows from a harder stick) are meted-out, yet no one has realized that an insurmountable obstacle is preventing any control over the outcome. This is the point; many people will believe that they do not control the man with the stick or the carrot, but that they should be able to control the boulder. ← outside world

Things in the World at Large - situations 'out there' - neither stress, nor please us unless, by previous agreement, we give these situations permission to control how we feel.

The average pre-enlightened individual may be heard to complain:

"I have a lot of stress in my life, it's no wonder I am stressed." (Notice here the confusion – the lack of space – between the cause and effect.)

The individual with a little more understanding may say:

"If I feel under pressure, then it is the result of the choices I have made in deciding how to motivate myself and also in deciding how to assess what is (and is not) within my control."

It's never the case that events stress us; it's more the case that we stress ourselves. If you want to stress yourself about something then the perfect formula for you to do so is to assert, and demand, that you cannot feel alright until everything goes your way. In other words, just hold in your mind the belief that 'it's not-OK to be not-OK'.

So, stress is a result of trying to motivate yourself by causing yourself pain so that you will move *away-from* an undesired situation. And in doing this, you unknowingly continue to attempt to move in a direction which is blocked.

Deconstructing Emotions Exercise

Constant exposure to dangers will breed contempt for them.
Lucius Annaeus Seneca

As humans, we have the capacity to experience many different emotions. We can never know that how we experience a specific emotion is how others will experience that emotion, the same may be said of almost any experience. Some linguistic theory supports the view that a suitable language is a necessary precursor for any experience, and particularly the representation of that experience. To label a given experience certainly has implications for how we choose to respond to that experience of emotion and, in that labeling, we are the very creators of our experience. I talked earlier in the book about various techniques that can be used to directly affect the situation in the World at Large and what follows is one of those techniques:

We shall use as our example the emotion of 'Anxiety', but the same theory can be applied to any emotion. It's very easy to write off 'anxiety' as a direct experience but it is not; it is the labeling of a direct experience. So when one reports 'anxiety' they are, in fact, perceiving the accumulation of a given set of sensory experiences as a single experience to which meaning is assigned. If this takes place without awareness then a certain amount of authenticity and freedom have been sacrificed. If one perceives a collection of bricks to be a house then the house becomes the mind-object, yet the meaning 'house' has actually been projected onto a given arrangement of bricks.

The way emotions are created is that events outside or inside us invite us to hold certain thoughts, and these thoughts create certain reactions in the body. The way in which we label those reactions does not just signify the emotion, but it actually contributes to the creation of the emotion itself. Emotion does not lie outside of cognition. Soon the reactions that constitute that emotion begin to trigger the thoughts themselves and so a self perpetuating cycle can come into existence that has lost any connection to the original event. This book is full of ways to address those thoughts but, in the face of overwhelming emotion, the mind may become so inert as to not be able to make use of those techniques. In those cases, and others, it can be useful to dissolve the 'overwhelm' of the emotion before any measures are taken to address cognition. In a sense, we are putting the cart before the horse and this is very effective in breaking viscous circles of causation.

The technique:

1. First of all, decide on the emotion you would like to deconstruct (anxiety here) and split it into its physical symptoms (sensory components). The 'sensory components' are only experiences of your senses; for example, hot hands, achy back, stiff neck, the smell of tar, the taste of sugar, hunger, etc. Beware of listing other emotions in this list of symptoms; things like panic, fear, sadness, worry, apathy etc. They are labels for groups of symptoms, not direct experiences.

2. Next make your list of symptoms.

3. Make a second list. For each symptom find a memory of a time when you felt that emotion but it was OK (it may still be unpleasant, but you felt OK about it).

4. Close your eyes and drift back to the first memory, begin to see what you saw, hear what you heard and allow the feeling you felt back then to increase. As you experience that symptom again inside your imagination, label it with a code-word (one that you can use to quickly bring the event back.) Repeat for each symptom.

5. Now, quickly recall each symptom fully as you go through your code-words, faster and faster until all the sensations begin to overlap.

6. Repeat until your neurology has begun to learn a new way of perceiving that collection of symptoms in a way that is OK (even if it is not necessarily preferable or pleasant).

7. Optionally, once you have modeled this new way of feeling, you can project yourself, in your imagination, into a situation where you might have felt the emotion (so in our example that would be any situation which causes anxiety).

symptoms (make sure these are physical symptoms, not thoughts or feelings)	memories of when/where that symptom has been OK
jelly legs	(after cycling) walking up my stairs
heart racing	(driving fast) Snake Pass
fast breathing	(whilst running) Castle Hill
'butterflies' in stomach	(theme park) Atton Tower
hot / cold flushes	(sauna) Hopefarm gym

* In this case, it seems that *comfort* is operating as a higher value than *survival*, but the individual's belief in values that survive in a sort of metaphysical level after one is dead, or an after-life, simply put the meaning of the value of survival at a higher level than the conventional level of simple survival of the individual body. Also, survival of the species may seem, according to the convolution of the personal value hierarchy of this individual, to be best served in some way by one's own demise. Is this *virtue* or *inauthenticity*? Is there any difference?

** Survival of the species may be driven by some even greater need, such as existence itself. Why existence is considered to be so wonderful we can't really discuss, it just seems to be axiomatic in that it requires no other reference. Existence could be seen then as a 'prime mover', something for which no meaning beyond itself is needed. This is beginning to sound a little like description of God. Yet it is interesting to note that the most fundamental religious question is 'does god exist or not?' So it appears within this question that *existence* is a value that can operate (or not) upon God(s). Or is this argument just some terrible linguistic error?

Chapter 10

Identification with the Myth of the Self: Recognizing who you really are (and who you are not)

I think, therefore I am.
Descartes

We have already seen that objects have no necessary boundaries and that even our wants and values are built on less than stable ground. Given that we objectify each other and ourselves in our own minds and that our sense of self is derived partly from our values and preferences, where does this leave the idea of our 'self identity'

We have many different ideas of ourselves, including:

A. The self we present in everyday life to other people (this may shift and conflict as we interact with differing others).
B. The sense of 'who we are' as reflected to us in other people and how they interact with us.
C. The sense of self we present to OUR SELVES.
D. The self we would like to be.
E. Some sort of process that compares C with D and forms a judgment – usually that C is lacking.

We all have some kind of idea of who we are. The mind creates a myth, a tendency towards some sort of consistency of acting and thinking. Many people will never even consider this sense of self in any real depth but they still hold beliefs about it in an unconscious, unchallenged way. These beliefs are likely to be along the following lines: "My sense of self is…

a) who I am."

b) unchangeable."

c) necessary." (Could be no different)

d) teleological." (Leading towards some inevitable meaning)

e) predestined." (Created in its entirety before our birth –perhaps in some sort of cosmic waiting room)

f) sacred/unique/special/important."

g) essential." (Has a single reality)

h) consistent."

Naturally, if these beliefs remain unquestioned, or even unacknowledged, then we can't help but be ruled by them as we relate to our sense of self and the outside world. In the same way, we find it difficult to understand concepts without recourse to their opposites so it is with the self. 'Hot' does not exist unless in relation to 'cold', likewise we have recourse to our conceptions of others in order to help us define ourselves.

This has lead to a conflict of interests and confusion of wants innumerably throughout human history. Let's take a look at a few examples: The 'Mods' and the 'Rockers' (rival gangs or 'tribes' in 1960s UK) seemed, *prima face*, to be sworn enemies and often fought with each other viciously. Yet a recognition of both of these groups as sub-culture tribes, who define themselves through the choices they make, would show they have far more in common with each other than it would first appear. Despite the fact they have made different choices at the bottom level, they have all made the same choice to define themselves according to the same variables (drugs/drinks of choice, music, clothes, style of motorbike, vocabulary etc.). So, despite the apparent rivalry between the two groups, they needed each other as negative reflections of themselves with whom to dis-identify with and so create their own identity just as much by who they *weren't* as who they *were*. This process can be seen time and time again in many groups and individuals so much so that entire groups or individual identities can define themselves, first and foremost, by what they are not. The anti-Nazi league, teetotalers, the celibate, the virtuous and vegetarians are but a few groups who derive a reflected identity. Even our choice of religious beliefs is defined through contrast.

Atheism is a move in a game whose rules are defined by the believers.
John Gray

It has been suggested that the creation of mental illness is just another form of imposing 'us and them' categories on people. It is desirable, necessary even, for society to have the 'insane' to help the sane define who they are. The faithful, the law-abiding, the fashionable, the important, the good, the non-smoker, the beautiful, the happy, the winners, the well-adjusted, and the useful all need to subjugate some other 'out-group' to sit in opposition to help solidify their own position. The real trick is to convince everyone, including yourself, that you hold the default position, thereby consigning the opposite position to your own as the one of deviation. All armies like to believe that God (and right) is on their side. Consider that in the 1940s the only no-smoking areas were probably near flammable materials but, as opinions have changed over time, more and more non-smoking areas appeared until the gradual flip around. Now, in more and more spheres of life, non-smoking is taken for granted and the no-smoking area is disappearing to be replaced by the 'smoking area' as the minority. It's the power to determine what is considered to be the default and the deviation that belies the power to create reality.

Consider this simplistic scenario: 5% of the population is insane. For some reason the insane 5% disappear from society. Now the least sane 5% of the remaining population become the new insane; it's all a relative judgment. If this second 5% disappear then the lowest 5% of the remaining population slip into the category of the insane just as before. This would continue until the eventual annihilation of the population. This is why it is actually undesirable to eliminate criminality, insanity, unhappiness and so on. I heard an ex-founding member of a green movement speaking recently about why he left his own organization. It appeared that the mainstream acceptance of some of the group's goals encouraged many members to become unnecessarily radical in response, because having no goals unique to them would mean a loss of their identity. As mainstream politicians took environmental concerns firmly into their agenda, pushing for carbon limitation and other measures, the green group began to lose it's ownership of it's own agenda and so, in reaction, the group began making more and more radical demands in order to stay marginal.

The environmental group satisfied some psychological needs in some of its members who were much less interested in the supposed agenda of the group. It was suggested that in the past a lot of these radical members had been proto-communist until the collapse of the Russian and Chinese communist agendas. Once this had happened then a new cause had to be found that was suitably marginal. For these individuals, an underdog cause, a devil to fight, was obviously a more important need than the attainment of any political or environmental goals. This is a confusion of wants and, therefore, represents some degree of inauthenticity. A negative-identity has been created, that is to say, an identity defined more by what one *is not* than what one *is*. This could simply be a matter of semantics, and to have oneself or one's group defined by what they are not gives the opposition group power, so a whole double vocabulary springs up as competing groups try to legitimize their position as the positive identity and not as the deviation. So, the freedom fighter who is at war may be known by others as a terrorist. The anti-abortionist can shrug off their negative identity by becoming a pro-lifer. Accordingly, within that mind set, 'pro-choicers' now become 'anti-lifers'. Each opposing side attempts to assert their reality over the given situation, to gain the positive identity and, therefore, more control over the agenda.

This 'us and them' approach to defining ourselves, whether as part of a group or as an individual, can seriously limit our reality. I met someone who believed that because they were 'creative' they were excluded from being 'practical'. This binary-opposite way of defining traits led to such strong beliefs within this person that, to their mind, any move towards becoming more practical would equal a loss of their creativity. This is a reality that will actually operate upon them if the belief has enough conviction and this then becomes a self-fulfilling prophesy. This is just one example of how a fixed and unexamined sense of self can operate as one of the two factors limiting our freedom – the other being the intolerance of discomfort. Incidentally, the creative vs. practical example, above, should be setting off very loud 'inauthenticity' and 'diva-complex' alerts within your own mind. Leonardo De Vinci certainly did not believe that practicality would cost him his creativity; he was incredibly talented in both areas. The idea of *practicality* actually bears no logical opposition to *creativity*, at least not in the way that hot is naturally opposed to cold. It would be equally valid for us to suppose that *creativity* is opposite to *destructivity* or even simply *un-creativity*. How many of your beliefs about your 'self', about 'the kind of person you are', are holding you back from embracing the freedom of thought and action you already have within yourself?

The Creation of, Uses and Abuses of, the 'Self'

Authenticity and enlightenment, as existential ventures, are greatly focused upon the doctrine of 'becoming what (who) we already are'. The Myth of the Self is a model we carry around in front of us; it's as if we were invisible but we carry around a small avatar (a bit like a doll or puppet) in front of us. We expose certain facets of this avatar to certain other people (although we almost never see other 'consciousnesses', we only see other 'personalities' walking around the world – that is to say, other avatars.) The irony is that we do not just use this *Myth of the Self* avatar in order to relate to others, but we can also use it to relate to ourselves. We can use the *Myth of the Self* avatar to define and remind ourselves of whom we are. Again we may only expose this avatar to ourselves from certain angles.

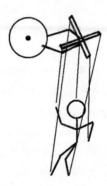

Of course, this implies a split between 'I' and 'me'. To look at one's sense (myth) of self, one must step outside of oneself, and so the separation of observer (I) and the actor (me) is developed. So many people will only ever recognize themselves as the 'me' and not the 'I'. The 'I' can never be seen in and of itself, because however much the avatar (me) changes in order to represent the 'I' (the point of true, pure consciousness and experience), the avatar will need to be observed by something, and that will always be the 'I'. This actor /observer split compels the pre-enlightened individual to attend primarily to the infinite needs of the Myth of the Self and to identify with it.

Many common phrases belie this split;

"I hate myself."

"I am very pleased with myself."

"I have surprised myself."

"I am outside myself."

"I don't feel myself."

"This isn't really me."

"But I am not really like that."

If there is conflict between one's actions and one's *myth of the self*; that is to say, if we act outside of our fixed idea of who we are, this causes a 'vertigo of identity'. A gap is opened that must be closed; this is known as *cognitive dissonance*. All sorts of inauthentic strategies are developed in order to close this gap. We will not go into the specifics of those strategies here, apart from to say that they all involve deception and inauthenticity of some sort.

The Myth of Self (the 'me') is made up of worldly associations that only serve to obscure the 'I' (the 'true self', the experiencer; the monad of consciousness). Common ingredients that constitute the *Myth of the Self* are likely to include ideas of possession, roles, profession, social groups, bodily characteristics, social position, thoughts, language, feelings, concepts, philosophies, relationships and so on.

Character 'traits' will also make up a lot of the *Myth of the Self*; it greatly helps these traits to solidify if others will recognize and validate them. We can get others to legitimize our sense of self through our own self-promotion and, thereby, control our *Myth of the Self* as it exists in the minds of others. Alternatively, we may find ourselves in complicity by acting consistently with a personality that others define for us. A lot of our social interaction may be considered to be the battle for the acceptance of competing versions of who everyone is. More often than not, the inauthentic position of a cease-fire compromise is agreed where we might agree to accept other's versions of 'who they are' in exchange for them agreeing to legitimize the self that we are promoting ourselves to be. This complicity could last a lifetime, but it is only likely to last until the opponents' positions change and if one player suddenly gains an advantage; a re-arrangement of 'who's who and what's what' might be instigated by one of the combatants. This constant re-negotiation can lead one to feel that their sense of identity is shaky because the *Myth of the Self* is in constant flux.

Beware of others who deign to tell us who we are. The initial creation of the *Myth of Self* will not have taken place in a vacuum; your sense of self will have developed greatly in the shadow of the agendas of others. Beware of the inertia and incumbency of your current myth of yourself, particularly with respect to how it will cause others to feel anxiety if you act 'out of character'. For them, it will be a natural reaction to want to perpetuate the status quo in order to alleviate the anxiety they may feel if you step outside of their idea of who you are.

"You don't normally do X."

"But you don't like Y."

"Now we are seeing your true colors."

"Is this the real you?"

"That's not like you, what's wrong?"

"You are lying to yourself."

"Drop the pretence."

"You are in denial."

"You haven't been acting yourself lately."

Pigeonholed!!!

The primary prerogative of the *Myth of the Self* seems to be to serve itself (this comes from an insatiable appetite to become everything – but more on this later.) The purpose of the *Myth of the Self* may be to provide a sense of consistency that, no doubt, plays a role in learning, social interaction and survival. Our consciousness can take on any content, just as a TV screen can take on any picture, yet the TV (the frame around the screen) remains constant and likewise, at some level, the mind needs to impose some sort of constancy too. The complicity of accepting and promoting different selves will eventually break down as re-negotiations start again and again; it is this that led Sartre to declare that "hell is other people." Yet, this need not be the case if we can identify some other consistency with which to identify.

It is the *Myth of the Self* though, with which we are conditioned to identify, and in order to give it some semblance of consistency, defense mechanisms and games must take place. The need for a consistency of our sense of self comes, in part, from its ability to prevent anguish, the anguish of the free. It will invite great anguish for you to know that you may, in the future, act in absolutely any way at all and that no assertions, promises or contracts can absolutely guarantee that you will act tomorrow as you would have yourself do today. Notice that it is a concern with the future (one of the Downtime dissociations) that drives the need for a consistent self concept. Yet from where (or when) can this *Myth of the Self* be created? Well the future does not exist yet and contains an infinite possibility so it's obviously not there. In the pure present moment, no actions take place and no meaning to events is assigned so no self can be found there either. A sense of consistency can certainly be inferred from finding patterns in our behavior in the past and it is these patterns that we use to build our personality or 'our character'. When we act it is a fluid process, but personality traits are treated as if they are structures and, as such, they are seen as solid and unchanging. The uncertainty regarding our future actions leads us to create a self (a *Myth of the Self*) out of our past actions. We then project that self into the future to give the future some sort of predictability, and this allays the angst of uncertainty, but at what price? It can cost us our freedom, spontaneity and authenticity. We can derive from this discussion one of the basic existential tenets: anxiety arrives in direct proportion to one's freedom. To feel anxiety, is a sign that you have the option of acting freely. To tolerate that anxiety is the key to embracing that freedom. Life can only be understood backwards, yet it must be lived forward.

From the point of view of *absolute* enlightenment, it seems to be desirable to eliminate the *Myth of the Self* altogether but in reality, this would cause obvious problems. *Practical* enlightenment is the art of managing what we have; in other words, it is the feasible optimization of the human condition through authenticity. So, because we need to be pragmatic, our intention is to be aware of the ways and devices of the *Myth of the Self* and to minimize its impact on how authentically we live our lives and relate to the universe. We have seen that mind-objects have no true boundaries, and that boundaries may be set large and wide (chunking-up) or small and narrow (chunking-down). To have a large and wide view of the self, a view that accepts contradiction and change, is to embrace a flexibility of action and thought. Again we come to the importance of knowing what we want and why we want it. Authentic-inauthenticity through the knowledge of our value hierarchies can forgive us for even the most frivolous or petty motivations – as long as we see them for what they are. So a connection with our pure consciousness is not to be confused with an awareness of the contents of consciousness; awareness of consciousness, as a process, is the most vivid reflection of the core-self we can ever experience. Even the most fundamental of our mental faculties are just tools to use; vehicles through which we navigate the social and physical world, then we need not strive for a completely permanent separation from that apparatus so much as a sense of dis-identification with it and control over it.

Return to the Woodchopper

Let's return to our wood-chopping friend. Earlier he told us that after enlightenment he chopped wood and carried water, but there is another version of the story that retains the idea that enlightenment is everyday but makes another point in addition. In the second version of the story, when he is asked what he did after enlightenment he answers, "before I was enlightened I chopped wood and carried water, after enlightenment wood is chopped and water is carried." In this second version the self, the 'I', appears to have been taken out of the equation; here is thought without consciousness of a self or a thinker. On Planet X the situation would look something like this.

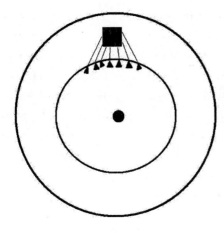

Here we see all the sprites collecting on the edge of the boundary to direct their cameras at one object of attention. This could be the ultimate in uptime. The entire content of awareness for this persons mind is a single object, so there is a complete lack of any self consciousness at all. This maybe 'the zone'.

Planet X

Above, we see a complete absorption in the sensations of the task at hand; of course the attention can be split between various outside stimuli but the above represents the purest Uptime possible. This state is equivalent, I think, to *The Zone* - a state of mind and body when everything seems to just gel together and the individual feels themselves to be almost an observer of their own automatic actions. This is commonly associated with sports, but can be readily applied to any performance. One common report of *The Zone* is that the one who experiences it has little or no recollection of the experience. It seems likely that under 'normal' circumstances, a small portion of the brain's executive power must be reserved in Downtime in order to encode, and therefore store, memories. To make sense of things, to give things meaning, is what allows us to remember them. Meaning may be imposed upon the world through the labeling of sensory infor- mation. So at some level of Downtime, if the wood chopper looks at the wood and labels it as brown, then he may remember it later, but at that time, he also washes much of the complexity of the shades and textures out of his perception and he then experiences the world only through his concepts. This is rather like looking at a Liechtenstein, where all the colors are flat as opposed to some renaissance painting, where the complexity is represented more deeply. Concepts digitize our world and so we lose definition but gain, perhaps, a wieldier model of the world. This wieldier model is more useful for survival and social interaction. We don't have to choose one or the other, though; we can flick between them at will. And we have already set the a-conceptual (analogue) viewpoint as the default.

In *The Zone*, if all of the mind's attention is directed purely to the raw incoming sensory information then there is no part of the mind attaching meaning to the outside events and sensations. It is for this reason that those in *The Zone* have no memories of the experience. So, as our wood chopper chops his wood and carries his water then his attention is directed so purely to the task at hand that his own conception of himself as the doer, the toiler, in these tasks, disappears. In *The Zone* there is no self and so no problems.

In his famous dictum, "I think therefore I am," Descartes seeks to prove his existence through the observance of his own thought. He is saying that the very ability to even ask the question, "do I exist or not?" provides proof that he exists. He says, because he has thoughts there must be a thinker and so, where thought exists a thinker must exist. This is all well enough from the perspective of a general singular grand truth, yet from each individual's own personal perspective it doesn't stand up so robustly to enquiry. To begin with, the very first statement, "I think," presupposes an 'I' that is doing the thinking; this is no good as it is presupposed upon no grounds at all other than the thought itself. The first statement, "I think," would be more accurately replaced by, "there is thought." So "there is thought therefore I am" does not logically follow. "There is thought therefore a thinker exists" is much more like it, but it does not prove a self; only thought.

There is thought and there is the content of those thoughts. If you think about yourself or you think about your thoughts then a self is created (not encountered). If thought does not contain itself or its origin (a thinker or self) then there is no sense of self operating in the mind at that time.

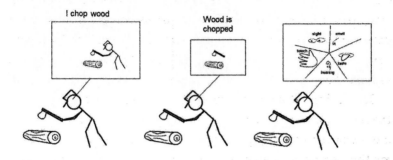

In the above diagram, our first man is a 'wood chopper' in all the sense of the term, as he is in reflexive consciousness, and aware of himself and his actions. The second man is in unreflexive consciousness; he has deleted himself from his own experience and so all that exists is the task at hand, yet still the substance of wood and the act of chopping are labeled and therefore reduced to categories. Our third man has deleted all concepts from his experience and so has lost sense of time, self, place, action and so is purely within the moment and within the incoming raw analogue sensory information. Even though, from our outside perspective, the third man is fully in the moment, he, himself, feels no sense of being 'in the moment' as he has let all concepts relating to time slip away momentarily. None of these positions is desirable, in and of itself, outside of any assessment of usefulness with respect to one's situation and goals. I suppose if enlightenment and authenticity are our highest goals then we would seek to move as far to the right as our situation at that time will allow. I think our wise man, in the quote, really intended to convey this third position but, due to the extent that language is intertwined with our 'reality', he overlooked the fact that he is still labeling his experience to some extent. Likewise, if you will remember our raspberry-eating cliff-faller, I mentioned in the introduction, and how a thought went through this man's mind.

The thought was not in words but I could only convey to you in words, "This raspberry is delicious." As he is a model of enlightenment for us, I like to think he didn't even label verbally his enjoyment of that raspberry but that he was purely within his sensory information in the moment.

Earlier, I outlined the intention I had a few years ago to switch myself off mentally during mundane chores as a way of escaping the drudgery of the toil. You'll see in the diagram below on the left what I had originally conceived. I didn't know at the time but it was an escape into Downtime, but this position is inauthentic and is also likely to result in a half hearted, clumsy job. How much better to be in Uptime (lower right)? Notice how, in Downtime, there is still a sense of self located centrally, and through which the Downtime dissociations are experienced. In Uptime there is no sense of self and so there are no problems.

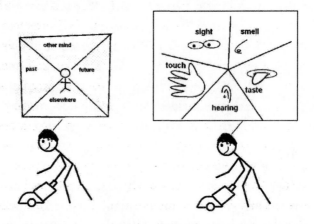

Why Does the Self Defend and Promote Itself?

The self defines itself on an 'us and them' basis, where to contrast is to define. So the self can desire to be more than it is only through the precondition that it divides the universe up into *self* and *other*. The Myth of the Self defines itself through relative judgments. I am smart because you are scruffy, I am quick because you are slow, I am old because you are young, (not always directly logical, e.g. "I am honest because you are rich"). Anyway, an uneasy love-hate relationship exists between the Myth of the Self and what it considers to be *other*. The Myth of the Self is making the best job it can of rearranging it's own value hierarchies around to come to terms with it's status of *other* to everyone and everything but itself. So the Myth of the Self seems to have a tendency to act as if it wanted to grow and begin to subsume what is *other* into what is *self*. It might be said that boredom is the protest by the Myth of the Self that this venture is not moving forward quickly, or definitively, enough. So boredom moves us to frantic activity to discover new and available means of increasing the self/other ratio.

In social life everyone wants to fit in, yet everyone wants to be an individual and so an uneasy balance is created; particularly when negotiations are at their opening and most critical point - adolescence. Interestingly, this need of the Myth of the Self to be unique is a type of insurance; it is a move in the battle to oppose its own death. One trick that the Myth of the Self will play upon us is to fool us into thinking we are unique and therefore important and special. Cold-readers will play upon this, and so many people will see themselves in a tarot reading or a horoscope. Ironically, it is the individual who recognizes how entirely ordinary, how entirely unremarkable, how entirely mundane they are, who is truly approaching uniqueness.

So the Myth of the Self, like a black hole, tries to pull in all that is outside and so moves towards the annihilation of the self/other distinction by the consumption of the other. This is why the unchecked human condition is one of infinite wants.

Running parallel to the logic and practice of destroying wants at the source and not through consumption, so the Myth of the Self can be satisfied by stepping outside its conditions, we can realize that that self/other distinction, whilst it has to be managed on a pragmatic front, is itself illusory in as much as it is unnecessary. We are not saying it is absolutely false, but that it is unnecessary, it is contingent, it could be otherwise. As much as you allow the self/other (object/subject) dichotomy to operate, then it *is* your reality and in this sense it is a true distinction. The rules of any game are agreed, and any choice to abide by them is an act of freedom, and so it is when we use the distinctions of self and other yet know them to be contingently imposed.

The Myth of the Self is inextricably linked with the search for meaning. The self endeavors to project a veneer of meaning onto the World at Large and this is not possible without being able to make distinctions and therefore define relative relationships, comparisons and contrasts. However, a more insidious logic may be at work because not only does the Myth of the Self require meaning, but also meaning itself requires the self/other (object/subject) distinction. We have a vicious circle as the path of causation runs both ways. Similarly, if we are happy we smile, but if we are in no emotional state then smiling can cause us to feel happy. So meaning and dualism are both cause and effect to each other. The search for meaning, whether that meaning is believed to be a discovery or a creation, is the search for an annihilation of existential anxiety (or more generally, any discomfort, i.e. anxiety, depression, paranoia or discontent). A sense of time and place are prerequisites to both Meaning and the Myth of the Self. Accordingly, to move away from the need of a self or meaning is a move toward the fullest appreciation of the present moment and place without recourse to other times or places.

How do we go about resolving the apparent needs for both a *self* and for *meaning*? The need for a self and the need for meaning are both palliatives for existential anxiety in as much as they try to address our demand for certainty. Then it seems that an acceptance of the anxiety innate to the human condition, as opposed to a demand for its annihilation, is the answer. But how do we accept existential anxiety? We simply realize that it's OK to be not-OK.

Finding Ourselves in Others

Everything that irritates us about others can lead to an understanding of ourselves.
Carl Jung

Whatever one of us blames in another, each one will find in his own heart.
Lucius Annaeus Seneca

Perception is projection; there is nothing in the outside World at Large that you do not perceive through yourself. As you begin to recognize the Myth of the Self you will begin to see it in other things, in other people, the difference is that you will be able to look past it as now you are no longer searching for it 'out there'. To begin to realize this is a move towards interconnectionism, as your perception begins to move towards perceiving existence-at-large in its complete entirety. The whole outside world you experience is actually a model within your own head; yes, it bares some resemblance to the World at Large as far as physical matters go. Yet, even though you may infer that you share some common meaning with others, it is ultimately always your mind that projects meaning for you onto the 'mad dance of atoms' outside.

When we see traits that we find undesirable in other people, and we begin to judge them, it is often the case that it is those traits within ourselves that we also find undesirable. This is a popular idea and it is based upon the doctrine that 'all perception is projection', this is the idea that any meaning is not actually 'out there in the world', but is really created in our minds. Have another look at the face/vase illusion in chapter 3. The meaning of the image is created by your mind; it is not 'out there' in the world (in the page). The very same thing happens when we see traits in other people; those qualities are, in fact, within ourselves. This provides another excellent opportunity to become aware of our unconscious processes and to begin to understand how we create a lot of our own 'problems'. *Projection* is one of the original psychodynamic defense mechanisms. The mind will project on to other mind's or other objects its own traits. It's yet another way for the Myth of the Self to continue its existence.

When we see these traits and apply them to ourselves, it shows us what we really need to change in ourselves in order to become more accepting of ourselves and of the world. If you know someone you judge to be petty then, perhaps, you are petty sometimes; perhaps it really means that you are too flippant and need to move more towards pettiness, bringing you to a more balanced position. When you apply what you see in others to yourself, there are several ways of doing this. You may have the same trait you see in others, you may actually be jealous of a trait you see in others and are lacking in yourself. Anything that annoys or upsets you in any way always has an element of yourself in it.

The ways we seem to project onto the world are not always the same. Our language has many formal logic structures in it and this determines how we create meaning within our lived world. Using a technique of putting our *other-downing statements* (statements we use to criticize or 'down' others) into a simple sentence structure allows us to further deconstruct what our projections onto others might be saying about ourselves.

We only need to make an other-downing statement about someone else and find the other logical permeations.

So if I say, "*My **boss** is too **stingy** towards **me**.*" Then we have the three necessary elements necessary. There is the **boss**, **me** and the function **stingy**.

So we can extrapolate the sentence to make a demand:

"*The **boss** should be **less stingy** towards **me**.*"

Now we have all three elements but it will be easier in this case to take the negative out of the function, so we end up with:

"*The **boss** should be **more generous** towards **me**.*"

Now we can use these elements within a Cartesian logic coordinate table. If you'll remember, Cartesian logic dictates a theorem and three types of 'opposite': an *inverse*, a *converse* and a *non-mirror image reflection*. The way students are always taught to remember this is that the theorem (the initial statement) is just like a glove, i.e. you can have the other hand in that pair, or you can turn that glove inside-out or, finally, you can have no glove at all. In logic notation they look like this

(++) (-+) (+-) (—).

Of course the Cartesian coordinates need a non-dualistic paradigm within which to operate. A lot of readers will not be familiar with these ideas of duality, although they are operating for us all somewhere in our minds. The dualistic paradigm is so embedded in our thinking and our language that it seems hard to perceive.

Try this exercise; fill in the question marks at the end of the series…

(AB) (BB) (BA) (??)

The reason it is so easy and obvious is that we take duality so much for granted that, like the proverbial goldfish and his water, we don't even see it.

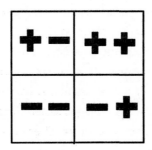

So, after our first statement, "The boss should be more generous with me." Let's see the three other rearrangements:

"I should be more generous with the boss."

"I should be more generous with myself."

"The boss should be less generous with me."

These opposite statements may help to identify better ways for you to be and even some errors in the reasoning you used to come up with the theorem initially. If so, you can back track and ask yourself what the reasoning was that led you to your initial other-downing statement.

As we dis-identify with the Myth of the Self, there is no need to self-down or self-blame regarding what this exercise may bring to light, it's all a learning experience, and you will track down some errors in your reasoning and attributions rather than any 'fundamental character flaws'.

The uneducated man blames others;
The partly-educated man blames himself;
The educated man blames no one.
Epictetus

One important thing you should be aware of is that you may have to chunk up and down on the particular action contained in the statement in order to apply something to yourself. For example, a woman says of her husband, "I think he spends too much time in the snooker club." Now because this woman does not play snooker she will have a hard time relating this back to herself. But snooker is a game. So she might expand (chunk-up) 'snooker' to 'playing games', now she can easily run this theorem:

"If you ask **me**, **he** spends too much time **playing games**."

Through the three other Cartesian coordinates, the inverse, converse and non-mirror image statements can be produced. Now if this woman we are discussing here happens to be a keen bridge player, which is one of the many games people play to help them structure their time, then she can be more specific when relating this to herself with regard to her bridge playing. She has chunked up from snooker to games and back down again to bridge. Now there is no problem for her to continue with the exercise:

138

A Stoic once gave the advice that when taking a walk with someone we should try to foster any good qualities we see in the other within ourselves and try to correct any bad qualities we see in them within ourselves.

Reassess Beliefs about the Self.

In conclusion, have a look again at all those unquestioned beliefs about the self and see if you can find a more useful and open set of beliefs regarding the self. No need to go back in the book, here they are again for you.

The *Myth of the Self* is:

a) Who I am
b) Unchangeable
c) Necessary (could be no different)
d) Teleological (leading towards some inevitable meaning)
e) Predestined (created in it's entirety before our birth –perhaps in some sort of cosmic waiting room)
f) Sacred/unique/special/important
g) Essential (has a single reality)
h) Consistent

To be able to recognize the machinations and ways of the Myth of the Self begins to reduce the extent to which it demands to operate upon us. In letting go of this self-orientation, we also let go of many of the reasons our awareness was pulled away from the Here and Now.

Chapter 11

The secret to letting go of your Past and Future selves

I contradict myself. I am large. I contain multitudes.
Walt Whitman

We have already looked at how various behavioral beliefs drive our attention into the four dissociations away from the Here and Now. There is one grand behavioral belief that drives many other sub beliefs and behaviors and it, when written, would be something along the lines of, *"I must be consistent."* Much social coercion exists to bring us into line if we step outside this most unchallenged of beliefs, such as; *"you are two faced," "you are a hypocrite," "practice what you preach," "I don't even know who you are anymore," "that's out of character for you,"* and so on. Such is the endemic belief that we need to be consistent. As soon as we internalize this belief, and we do so at an early age, then we need to create some form of structure (or bundle of processes) to remain consistent and we call this 'The myth of the self'. If you watch your actions, you are not consistent though, so the myth of the self is employed not only as a blueprint to tell you who to be and how to act but also to facilitate self deception in order to iron out any inconsistencies. The method it uses to do this we call 'cognitive dissonance'. It would be a mistake to think that the Myth of the Self imposes this grand, *"I must be consistent"* belief upon us. The Myth of the Self is the *result* of that belief.

We can often get pulled into the future because we think we would like to act a certain way when we arrive there, so we go there in our minds (Downtime) to plan and rehearse those actions. Likewise, we can also get pulled into the past to learn, or even to help us figure out who to be and how to act. The illusion of a continuous self, the Myth of the Self can need to be constantly rehearsed to keep the congruence and continuity; this helps us deal with the anxiety of having a completely free choice of identity and action in the future. This apparent need within ourselves is the drive behind the pre-enlightened tendency to have Downtime as the default. This chapter contains the exercises you can use to help to resolve this anxiety regarding your future action and also the tendency to slip into the past. This frees you up to live in the Here and Now.

You are going to go into Downtime in order to remove a few mental pieces of elastic that may be pulling on your attention; this will be a very good example for you of Useful-Downtime. Of the three exercises in this chapter, the first exercise is the ideal of being able to let go of past and future, the second exercise allows you to begin to let go of the past, and the third exercise allows you to plan for the future and to extend a new style of your sense-of-self there whilst remaining free in action and behavior.

Try the first exercise a few times, and if you get it then great! But if, as you go through life, you find your attention being pulled into either the past or future and you need to concentrate specifically on that, then try the appropriate other exercises here. Once you have completed these, return to the first exercise - *Timeline of Selves*.

In the exercises, you are asked to visualize various images. Don't worry if these images are not all full Technicolor cinema experiences, the vividness of the imagery is not directly connected to the effectiveness of the techniques. Your brain will be holding these concepts in many different ways and the images will be there, but not necessarily at the front of your consciousness. Some people may even experience total blankness or other images or thoughts. If this is the case don't worry, simply follow through the exercises. Remember it's OK to be not-OK and also ponder the thought that it is often the changes that we are not even aware of that effect us the most.

Timeline of Selves Exercise

1. Sit down and relax (use a quick progressive relaxation if you wish by simply relaxing each muscle in turn from your feet all the way up to your head), close your eyes if you wish. Imagine yourself to be standing on a big line running along the ground from behind you to in front of you, a bit like standing on a deserted motorway.

2. As the line runs to the front, begin to see all your future selves out in front of you; these are all the selves you will be in the future. Be aware that all the selves standing behind are your past selves. Now float out of yourself up above the line to a point when you can see the whole line; all your future selves and your past selves.

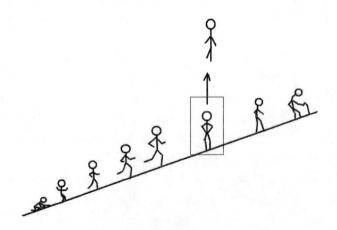

3. From this vantage point you can see all the selves you have ever been, and will ever be and the self you are right now. Notice how all the selves, even the yesterday self and tomorrow self, are different, in at least some small way, to your present self below. These differences may be physical, in the knowledge they possess, the context in which they find themselves or the preferences they hold.

4. As you experience your sense-of-being as just a series of momentary selves, how do you become aware that there is a connection of sorts between all of yourselves? What color will you visualize the 'string' that connects all of these selves? This connection is not a continuation of consciousness that is turned off and on every 24 hours or so. Any sense of a continuation of consciousness is 'downloaded' every 24 hours, when you wake up after sleeping. The connection is one of action. <u>All your selves are connected by a single fact: that every self you are, have ever been, or will ever be will always make the best decision for you within that context, with all the information they have at that time.</u> How soon will it be before you begin to enjoy the implications of this fact? You can absolve the present self from any connection to past events and selves and also have faith in the ability and behavior of your future selves.

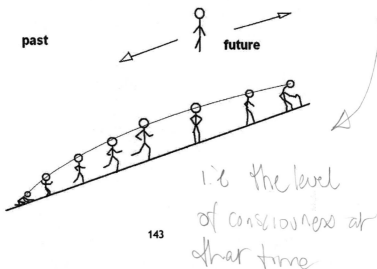

past   future

i.e the level of consciousness at that time

5. Understand your new sense of disconnection with the past and future. Where (when) does this leave you? In the present!

6. Re-associate: once you have felt all the energy and attention that was being pulled into the past and the future returning to you now in the present, just be aware of your attention and energies being more fully in the Here and Now; notice the different ways this feels much better. Become aware of how you know it is possible to feel like this all the time.

Timeline of Selves Exercise - Reconcile with Past Variation

The mind, at some level, automatically and unconsciously makes its own decisions about where (and when) to go and, often, it is all we can do to provide it with as many choices as possible and sometimes to guide its default choices using techniques from the behavioral school (the Uptime anchor exercise is an example of this). Yet at other times the mind will pull itself into the past to relive some experience or other.

It seems the mind has got into a 'habit' and the way to break a habit is two-fold. Firstly, you reconcile the reason, the meaning, behind the habit. Secondly, you behaviorally de-condition the habit. So, if the Uptime anchor exercises are the de-conditioning element, then this exercise is the reconciliation of the meaning behind this 'habit'. This technique is useful if the Uptime anchor is not working out too well for you to begin with. Firstly, use this technique to address any reasons your mind may have to drag you back to the past and then return to the Uptime anchor exercises. Remember my example of the money burning habit? How, once the underlying reason was eliminated, the habit just dissolved? This is exactly the same. Once the meaning of the action is resolved, the habit is free to disappear.

You are going to review a past from other perspectives to extract any useful information that may be lurking in that event.

The event may be pleasant or unpleasant; a world shattering change of direction or just a mundane everyday thing – it doesn't matter, all those labels are arbitrary illusions anyway – just go with it. In every action or event there is a positive higher value being expressed, even if you are not aware of it, just trust that it is there.

Repeat the exercise as many times as needed for as many past events as your attention feels pulled back towards.

1. Sit down and relax (use a quick progressive relaxation if you wish by simply relaxing each muscle in turn from your feet all the way up to your head), close your eyes if you wish. Imagine yourself to be standing on a big line running along the ground from behind you to in front of you, a bit like standing on a deserted motorway.

2. As the line runs to the front, begin to see all your future selves out in front of you, these are all the selves you will be in the future. Be aware that all the selves standing behind are your past selves; maybe even turn your head around to see them. Now float out of yourself up above the line to a point when you can see the whole line, all your future selves and your past selves.

3. From this vantage point, you can see all the selves you have ever been, and will ever be and the self you are right now. Let yourself float back into the past until you are floating above the time in the past that your mind keeps on returning to. Identify this event as clearly as possible.

4. Float back to just before this event then allow the event to play itself through again in your imagination, as you watch from above now absorb any learnings; any positive information you can about that event. Stop or even replay the event if necessary until you have sucked all that is good from the event. You may

even replay the event from other perspectives such as from the point of view of other people who where there, or just a different camera angle or whatever, just experiment. (It does not matter whether the event was pleasant or unpleasant it will still contain some important positive information – perhaps something you haven't learned.)

5. As you suck all the learnings from the scene below you. You may or may not be aware of what these learnings might be. You might find it easy to imagine this visually as you see all the color drain way from the picture and into yourself. Check to satisfy yourself that you can draw no more positive information from this experience by checking all the color is drained out of it. Now decrease the size of the picture of the event beneath you until it becomes a tiny spec; almost invisible on your time line.

6. Take all these new learnings - the colors - back with you to the present and drop back into yourself on the time line in the present. Imagine all the colors dispersing through your body, finding their own way to exactly where they need to be. Take a moment to allow these learnings to become an integral part of you.

7. Re-associate: once you have felt all the energy and attention that was being pulled into the past returning to you now in the present, just be aware of your attention and energies being more fully in the Here and Now. Notice the different ways this feels much better.

Timeline of Selves Exercise - Reconcile with Future Variation

Never let the future disturb you. You will meet it, if you have to, with the same weapons of reason which today arm you against the present.

Marcus Aurelius

Is it cynical to understand that if things are not going exactly how you expected (that's not-OK) then everything is as it should be, the universe is always working perfectly (so that's OK then)?

The mind can find itself pulled to the future as easily as the past, partly from concern over the outcome of future events, and partly to re-affirm the Myth of the Self in the future. Sartre thought that one our greatest fears, as we struggle to balance our freedom with the anxiety it fosters, is that we make an appointment with our self in the future only to find that, at that time, we no longer want to keep the appointment. We can make no cast iron guarantees about our future behavior or the conditions in which we will find ourselves. The Myth of the Self can help to quell this anxiety, but at the expense of our freedom of action. Quite often we find ourselves in future-Downtime inside our minds to rehearse our reactions to future events, yet things rarely turn out as expected leaving our rehearsals a somewhat obsolete waste of time and energy.

If your rehearsals were more focused on creating a flexible self in the future, with less set rules or direction at the lower levels and just a few higher levels with which to concern yourself, then you are allowing your future self to have a freer range of actions whilst still keeping to your wishes. This will take into account the nature of the future as ill-defined and open. As a result of this, going into future-Downtime during this exercise will be less absolute so just go with it. Let your mind fill in the blanks. Trust your mind, during this exercise, to be able to take you to a vague event, time or place and to later apply any new behaviors and attitudes at the right time and place. The unconscious processes will take care of all the details automatically, allowing you to just let go and enjoy the Here and Now. Our conscious processes are not suited to micro-management and if you try to push them into that role you'll find yourself overwhelmed and stressed.

Repeat the exercise as many times as needed for as many future events as your attention feels pulled forward to.

1. Sit down and relax (use a quick progressive relaxation if you wish by simply relaxing each muscle in turn from your feet all the way up to your head), close your eyes if you wish. Imagine yourself to be standing on a big line running along the ground from behind you to in front of you, a bit like standing on a deserted motorway.

2. As the line runs to the front, begin to see all your future selves out in front of you; these are all the selves you will be in the future. Be aware that all the selves standing behind are your past selves. Now float out of yourself up above the line to a point when you can see the whole line; all your future selves and your past selves.

3. From this vantage point you can see all the selves you have ever been, and will ever be and the self you are right now. Let yourself float forward into the future until you are floating above the time in the future that your mind keeps on returning to.

4. Notice your conception of this event; how do you see it? As vague concepts/pictures? Moving/fixed? How much color and so on? As you watch the event unfold, see it as you would like it to happen. Change any of the events, and/or your conception of those events, until you feel it is realistically going at its best. Even if the events unfolding are unuseful or unpleasant, let your reactions in behavior and thought be the ones you would choose to exhibit under those circumstances. You can watch this 'film' over again until you are happy with it.

5. From above this event, look back to the present and look

forward on your time line to make sure everything leading up to the unfolding of that particular event fits in (is 'ecological') with all the other things you would like to happen. Now assess the future consequences of your actions closely.

6. Find the overriding values that are driving this event in the way you would like it. The higher you can go on these values the better.

7. Now allow yourself to drop down into this imagined future event and feel yourself to be in it; see what you see, hear what you hear, do what do you do, feel what you feel as everything goes as you would like it. <u>Be particularly aware that you are allowing your higher values and drives to dictate the eventual meaning of your actions but not those actions themselves per se. You are acting in a way in which all your selves agree; thus, freeing your mind up for living in the Here and Now (in Uptime) and acting flexibly and freely as this event unfolds.</u>

8. Drift back up above yourself whilst remaining aware of your higher driving values, and then drift back to the present. Now, in the present, your future self in that situation, and others like it, will be acting not in a robotic or fixed way, yet still in accordance with your highest benefit.

9. Re-associate: drop down into your present self. Once you have felt all the energy and attention that was being pulled into the future returning to you now in the present, just be aware of your attention and energies being more fully in the Here and Now; notice the different ways this feels much better.

Chapter 12

Freeing yourself from Identification with the Myth of the Self

You are a little soul carrying around a corpse.
Epictetus

A lot of our sense of self is located in so much of the 'machinery' of living in the real world. Perhaps we have come to locate our sense of self in our social position, our bodies, possessions, thoughts, abilities, language, roles, and, of course, our past and future. In order to conceive ourselves in this way we have to mentally step outside ourselves to get this sense of reflexive consciousness. One thing is for sure; our ideas of ourselves are unlikely to agree with other's ideas of who we are anyway. Of course other people who 'know us' don't all get together at a meeting every week to discus and agree on an idea of who we are and we can be certain there is no general consensus amongst others of who we are. We step out of ourselves and into Downtime to generate a working model of our personality constantly, and this is to some degree necessary for practical matters. For anyone who has ever found the conception of them self (wherever that conception may be held) restrictive or unuseful, the following exercise will come in handy. The exercise is designed to decon-struct the way our lives, brains and bodies masquerade as our self. We are attempting to uncover the deeper sense of consciousness at our core, thereby increasing our flexibility and giving us a perspective from which we can begin to choose who we really are. Our roles, intellect, bodies, memories, and language are just tools, much in the same way we might drive a car, use a computer, and wear clothes. Our ability to step back from our feelings, wants and thoughts can help to reveal the most vivid reflection of our centre of pure consciousness available to us.

Again, a complete Technicolor apparition, during this exercise, is not necessary at all and the exercise can be done at any time you wish. You may wish to set another anchor for this liberating state of disidentification with the Myth of the Self when you get there. Perhaps you could use a word you can repeat or squeezing one of your earlobes as the anchor?

As you identify each 'facet', visualize or feel it just the way that seems right to you; a little like peeling an onion or taking apart a Russian doll. As each facet drifts away and disperses into the universe, just feel safe in the knowledge that if/when that facet is needed for any practical purposes, it will automatically drift back into place as you choose. Imagine yourself to be floating in space.

You may need to allow each facet to drift away bit by bit, especially at first and with the 'deeper' levels. So, for instance, instead of letting go of all your possessions in one go, let go of the watch, then the TV, then the car, then the house and so on.

1. Sit or lie down, relax your body*, close your eyes, drift into your mind.

   Find your conception of your possessions; your house, car, clothes, watch, the size of your bank account, your credit cards, your holiday later this month, your computer, the books you own, etc. You are not your possessions. Let that facet (your conception of those material goods) just disconnect itself and watch as it defuses and drifts off into the distance. That facet will look after itself, let it go completely.

2. Find your conception of your friends and family, acquaintances, colleagues; your wife, boss, son, the man on the train, the character from the novel, the author of the book you last read, etc. You are not other people. Let that facet just disconnect itself and watch as it defuses and drifts off into the

distance. That facet will look after itself, let it go completely.

3. Find your conception of your roles and labels; mother, husband, cynic, old, lawyer, hero, barman, son, carer, neighbor, Irish, white, philosopher, animal lover, handyman, creative, fat, leader, mindfulness seeker, artist, female, alcoholic, Christian, good sport, cool dude, worrier, honest man, unique individual, loser, winner, stamp collector, the better man, survivor, victim, etc. You are not your roles. You are not your labels.

    Let that facet just disconnect itself and watch as it defuses and drifts off into the distance. That facet will look after itself, let it go.

4. Find your conception of your behaviors; your breathing, your blinking, your smoking, the way you walk, your daily training of Uptime as default, how you dance, the pattern of actions as you get into the car each morning, the order you get dressed everyday, etc. You are not your behaviors. Let that facet just disconnect itself and watch as it defuses and drifts off into the distance. That facet will look after itself, let it go completely.

5. Find your conception of your feelings; worry, confidence, despondency, tiredness, warmness, hunger, strength, weakness, anger, happiness, contentment, nothingness, something, etc. You are not your feelings. Let that facet just disconnect itself and watch as it defuses and drifts off into the distance. That facet will look after itself, let it go completely.

6. Find your conception of your thoughts; your philosophy, your first language, your obligations, your sense of time passing, your sense of spatial location, your memories, your plans, your rights, the words you use, the pictures you use to think, let them just drift. You are not your thoughts. Let that facet just

disconnect itself and watch as it defuses and drifts off into the distance. That facet will look after itself, let it go completely.

7. Find what you are as all these facets drift away endlessly into the void. If there are any other facets; anything else that you know can just drift away, allow it to just drop away and let it go now. It will look after itself, so you can let it go completely.

8. Find what you are now; experience yourself as what you really are; an endless expanse of conscious awareness, a core of will, the unmoved mover, the primary cause, the centre from which you direct everything else. A singularity which utilizes so many tools for practical day to day living yet remains constant and unchanged as all around changes. Keep this awareness as long as you like and anchor if so desired.

Now it's time to reintegrate all the facets into a whole once again. There are two ways you may wish to experiment with in doing this.

9a. Reintegrate the parts now. Allow all the facets to just float back. They are all parts of your 'self', so they will all return in some form or other, but notice the different arrangement of the facets, notice the different way each facet arranges itself around your core of consciousness. Each facet can now be seen in its true form as a tool, a device through which the consciousness interacts with the outside world. Now open up your eyes and see how that perspective of true consciousness still lingers on. Notice how the relationship between your 'self' and the world seems much different.

Or:

9b. Just open your eyes, get up and move around the world from the perspective of your central core of consciousness.

153

Allow yourself to become aware of how all the facets, (the ones that dispersed out into universe earlier in the exercise) come back. Be aware of the way that it is the world around you and the social world especially, that demands the re-attachment of these facets, not the simple fact of your existence itself.

Halo Exercise

This exercise is one of deeper experimentation than some in this book.

The halo has been a convention in art for many years. Apparently, its adoption by those creating Christian iconography was relatively recent, but more interesting is the idea that it has come about independently in the art of many separate traditions. It seems that the halo may be archetypal. The hovering ring, which is the more common modern day conception of the halo, originates with the use of perspective in art. Another theory is that the Greeks or Romans sometimes used to put big metal discs over statues to prevent bird droppings befouling them. This actually has nothing to do with the halo whose interpretation into sculpture is more likely to be shown as something approaching the crown that is worn by the Statue of Liberty.

The older way of depicting the halo was as a circle (not a ring) behind (not over) the head. As the old-style art is very flat, it would be a mistake to think of the halo as flat; in fact, it is the two dimensional depiction of a three dimensional cloud of luminescence; it only appears to be 'behind the head' as an artistic convention to allow us to see the person clearly.

The halo itself is normally depicted around the head, but the halo is only a subset of what is known as an Aureola, which is a luminescence that surrounds the whole personage. Sometimes this Aureola is split into two parts; one for the body and one (the halo) for the head. Does this represent some depiction of an early mind/body dualism? Could it be that separate traditions had all tapped into something universal in their depiction of the Aureola as a cloud that surrounds the entire body of an enlightened individual? Isn't the full Aureola much more representative of what we would expect to see as a depiction of a more pantheistic or mystic relationship to the cosmos.

What I am suggesting is that once you have transcended the Myth of the Self, and are able to feel that sense of interconnectedness, then your depiction of that event becomes one of a kind of luminescence shinning outwards. That is an Aureola. Your awareness in-and-of-itself, cannot depict this experience, either to itself or to others. So the interconnectedness becomes 'dumb-ed down' as the mind tries to comprehend this interconnected awareness. The processes of the mind can only use sensory metaphors with which to conceive of this event and so we get the Aureola. When the mind begins to remember and conceive part of any experience, then it begins to build up the entirety of that experience, as if the whole was holographically contained within each part. This happens through the same mechanism as when a smell triggers a host of memories and feelings. To recreate, even if from an atavistic memory, part of the interconnected experience is to begin to recreate all of the experience in its entirety. So, as we let the mind fully perceive the projection of an Aureola, this paves the way to allow the awareness to begin to feel the indescribable feeling of interconnectedness.

With this exercise we are only seeking to foster the conditions within the mind from which awareness (which lies outside the processes of the mind) will find it most easy to spontaneously make the leap to the indescribable experience of interconnectedness itself.

The exercise:

1. Relax the body, close the eyes and look inside yourself; notice how you perceive your sense of self, your sense of personality. For example, some people will feel a particular shape and size inside their head, or a face, or a particular color. If you have

been particularly aware whilst falling asleep or in other meditative practices you may have felt the dissolution of this conception of the personality. This metaphorical conception of the sense of self is not *just* a depiction it *is* the sense of self as it manifests within the 'programming language' of the mind.

2. Tune into the color, size, shape and location of this idea of the self. Is it inside or outside your conception of your body? Notice any other qualities such as; is it heavy, is it solid, is it soft, is it warm, does it move/pulsate/metamorphosize... and so on...? Remember that you are not necessarily 'seeking' a full blown technicolor hallucination here. The mind may want fireworks and roller coasters, but the experience may be very subtle. If you can't find this metaphorical self, go on with the belief that it *is* there - it must be. Any absence will not be the absence of this 'metaphorical' sense of self but an absence of sensitivity within your perceptions to perceive it. Don't take this as a reflection of anything other than the fact you need to learn to pick up on more subtle sensations; don't take it as some sort of personality trait or personal weakness. You may wish to ask yourself, "If I could see/hear/feel it, what would it look/feel/sound like?" And then you will have your answer.

3. Now, with each out-breath, as you relax a little more each time, begin to breathe out the color of that self, as you allow the visual aspect of this self to turn into rays of light, a little like those on the 'rising sun' version of the Japanese flag. Allow these rays to extend to infinity and all directions.

4. After expelling all that color, find the next quality, such as the weight, sound or shape of this self and breathe that out too in all directions, just as you did above. If you find it difficult with weights, sounds, shapes, etc. just change them into the color that best represents that aspect and breathe it all out.

5. Continue until all the aspects of the self have been dissipated into the infinity of the universe. If any aspect remains it should be only that of an 'invisible' and infinite extension into the space around you. Relax completely and enjoy the experience for as long as you wish without any attempt to conceive any meaning or interpretation of the experience. You may wish, at this point, to anchor the state in some way.

This exercise can be done at first quietly on your own, but as you progress you could try it whilst sitting or walking even, and you will have the anchor to help to speed up this process and access the state of selfless interconnectedness.

---

* It has been suggested that tension is our way of making ourselves separate from the universe, so it seems congruent to actively relax as much as possible and to expect that relaxation to automatically deepen as the layers drop away.

Chapter 13

TOTEs: What are they? How do they control you? How can you break them?

It seems, in fact, as though the second half of a man's life is made up of nothing but the habits he has accumulated in the first half.
Fydor Dostoyevsky

How do you straighten a picture hanging crooked on the wall?
First perhaps you look at the picture and decide it's not straight, then you label the situation as not-OK for you and so you seek to change the world to a state of OK-ness, and this is fine, it is easily within your power. And you know what you want and why you want it.

Aside from OK and not-OK for a moment:

1. You look at the picture and just decide it doesn't look straight – you have Tested the situation by making some form of measurement with respect to an outcome you have somewhere in your mind.
2. You approach the picture and move its angle. We call this Operation, you have Operated on the picture, you have changed it somehow.
3. Now you step back and look at the picture again. You are Testing the situation again. If the situation is agreeable, that is to say if the picture is straight, you will Exit the task of picture straightening.

However, if the picture is still not straight, you will approach the wall once more to make some more changes to its angle. That is to say you are Operating on the picture again. You will continue these steps until the picture is straight, at which point you will

Exit your picture straightening strategy.

We can see clearly in the picture example, the Operating and Testing stages of the behavior, and it can easily be seen when we want to Exit that picture straightening program. In actual fact, you are using this same strategy in so many areas of your life you would not believe it. This is the concept of the TOTE. You will test A operate, test A operate as many times as needed, seamlessly, until you are at your desired outcome and then you will exit the program.

Our human systems are very good at learning bigger and bigger TOTEs and running them unconsciously. Putting a spoon in your mouth, changing gear in a car, putting away the coffee, flushing the toilet after you've used it, keeping a bicycle upright and shaking hands; these TOTEs are incredibly useful in allowing us to perform sophisticated behaviors without the slightest thought. Without them we would eat like a two year old, drive like a learner driver and generally make a mess of everything. If we want to do something well we drill ourselves to do it again and again. However, much like when we ask someone else to do a task for us, when we use a TOTE, we relinquish some control of how that task is done. TOTEs also have the potential to rob us of our ultimate freedom. When you say a sentence, you use words from the finite amount available in your vocabulary according to various rules such as grammatical syntax and sentence structure. When we choose a car or some clothes, we choose not from an infinite variety, but from what is available.

Light cannot be split into packets smaller than one photon, much as a toy LEGO house can only be split into the plastic bricks available. We can make anything else out of those bricks, but the bricks are set for us. This is the way with the TOTE; our freedom comes from choosing how to link those TOTEs together in a chain of action but we are not normally really free to alter those TOTEs themselves. In fact, being interrupted in the middle of a TOTE can stun us into a sort of trance. This is perhaps why the playground gambit; "Shake my hand! Too slow! Now I'm doing a nose waving. Nah! Nah! Nah!" is so annoying. It has violated a social TOTE, i.e. the handshake TOTE.

Various martial arts deal with deconstructing and/or reconstructing of TOTEs at a conscious level. Would you experience more freedom if your TOTEs were bigger or smaller? I think the answer to this depends in what sphere these TOTEs are operating. If you have unuseful or undesirable reactions to things or get stuck in unuseful loops then to break these TOTEs would be nice.

If you are looking at the TOTEs you use to drive a car, you should expect it might be unwise to mess with these. To build up big desirable TOTEs by combining smaller TOTEs again and again is the art of the sportsman, the dancer, and the musician – in fact, anyone who is good at anything. There is an exception though; in many sports, where the opponents come face to face in play (not taking turns), a 'feint' can be used by one opponent to fool another into accessing a TOTE that is useful. An example of this would be the 'dummy' in soccer, where a player dribbling the ball fools his opponent by pretending to start to go right, then quickly going left so sending him the wrong way. The opponent, upon seeing a movement to the right, accesses the TOTE that makes him turn in that direction. If the opponent is stringing together shorter TOTEs in his response, then he has an earlier opportunity to Exit the unwanted behavior than if he was using one long TOTE. When two separate TOTEs begin with the same actions, but then diverge half way through then, at the point where the actions differ, a choice must be made, and this forces a split of the original TOTE. After this, a single TOTE will constitute the first part of the behavior until the split. Then two separate TOTEs exist for the two differing actions toward the end. So if our soccer opponent had drilled for both contingencies by doing drills for both a real turn and a dummy, then he would be much more responsive to a 'dummy' but at a cost to the quicker and more definite response to the genuine turn. Optimum performance is a matter of balancing these payoffs.

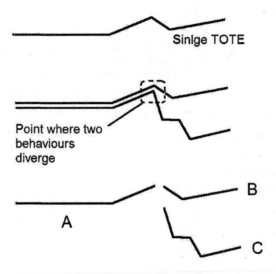

The drilling of a new TOTE is necessary as there will be a neurological lag as it takes our brains time to 'rewire' and get the 'groove' of a new TOTE. Try swapping the hands you hold your knife and fork with to see this in action. So the flexibility of our behaviors can be increased in this way much as house bricks offer more options of possible buildings you can construct with them when compared to large prefabricated walls. Spontaneity is the way we string together our TOTEs and often we need to break TOTEs to give us more choice.

Using TOTE Breaking

Experiment daily with just observing yourself and finding TOTEs that you enact in everyday life. Around the house, mundane chores for example; these are nice places to start hacking into the size of your TOTEs. To begin with, this is simply an exercise in consciousness awareness and the awareness of your freedom of action. You might find that you hold the fridge door open with your foot as you lean to pour milk into your coffee, and when you replace the milk bottle that foot swings round to close the door as you look toward the sugar, just like so many set pieces of a dance.

Do you have a Tango of the toast? Do you do the Samba of the sieve? Perhaps the Da Capo of the dishes? The Conga of the coffee? Maybe the Salsa of the sock removal? The Waltz of the wood chopping? The Calypso of the carrying (of water)?

A little alliteration aside, see how easy you can find it to stop yourself in the middle of these activities and consciously find yourself directing the activity. As you break the pattern, a squeezing of the Uptime anchor may be in order to bring you into intense conscious presence. In fact, a particular stimulus is always present at the start of a TOTE; this is the 'access stimulus'; a signal to begin a TOTE. In our soccer example, it would be the movement of another player in a certain direction. For other situations it may be a facial expression, a green light, seeing a cream bun, a tone of voice, the door bell, opening a door, the smell of a cigarette or many other things. If you can find the access stimulus to a TOTE then you can link your Uptime anchor to it on purpose to allow you a choice at the very beginning. So, if you find that every time a particular thing happens you go into an undesirable TOTE then simply expose yourself to that stimulus whilst firing off your Uptime anchor, until the stimulus alone begins to automatically fire off Uptime for you.

TOTE breaking will come into play in breaking the behavioral associations left over once one has addressed the meaning behind a habit. How often have you made a cup of coffee then suddenly looked up to find you had boiled the water to cook with? This happened because once the first piece has been initiated and you're not paying enough attention, you just go through the motions of the TOTE which is strongest i.e. the path of least resistance. If you become conscious halfway through, then you can find it very easy to stop the set behavior halfway through. There are language-based TOTEs and thought-based TOTEs, as well as behavioral TOTEs. Are there some stimuli that set off thought-chains, emotions or automatic phrases for you?

The 2nd Error

Beware the '2nd error'; once you know the concept you will see it everywhere. It acts as if it were an invitation back into the Downtime, into circular thoughts, it is driven by the Myth of the Self's need to perpetuate itself and be in the foreground. If you proceed with good intentions regarding anything, and hit a less than perfect outcome, then your next reaction to this event is probably more critical then the previous set back. So, one error will spur on another second one, whose effect is now compounded. The 2nd error is an error of categories, where one becomes fixated at a single level of value or meaning to the detriment of other levels. To invest our sense of self in an ends-goal so fully that the means-goal happens to be completely counter productive is the primary mode of action by which the 2nd error occurs.

The seminal example may help to illustrate: Imagine that I have been drawn into discussing a situation in which I allow myself to get agitated, by becoming overly defensive towards a perceived slight against my 'self' for example. Shortly after my agitation I review the outburst in my mind and label it as not desirable, I can then worry about my lack of progress toward a more enlightened state of being and worry about the likelihood of my getting agitated in the future. This, itself, can now cause agitation on a different level. If I do this, I have totally missed the opportunity to just be in the Here and Now in the moments directly after my agitation. If I have failed once in being more enlightened and stepping back from automatic, archaic reactions to events, then any further grief I give myself about the situation is the 2nd error. It would be more enlightened of me to accept what has happened instead of worrying about how to ensure lasting enlightenment. This has happened through not accepting what has happened and then judging my in-acceptance itself to be less than acceptable.

This leads us to another insidiously ironic practice; the 2nd 2nd error (again this is an error of categories - of levels). If a person identifies themselves to be making the 2nd error, then they will say: "I have been wrong in making the 2nd error," and/or "I must not make the 2nd error again." Again an opportunity has been totally overlooked to just be accepting of what the present holds. The Myth of the Self is trying to drive conscious learning from the past and motivation for correction for the future. So the Myth of the Self, in order to perpetuate its illusion of being constant through time, pulls the attention out of the Here and Now.

Imagine a person finally makes that decision to sort out their weight problem once and for all, so they resolve to throw away all the 'bad' foods in the cupboards. Once the pile of food is assembled on the table the individual thinks it will be a waste to throw the food away, yet wants rid of it. So the individual decides to eat the food in one go. Ironic!

Imagine that a person decides it really is not useful for them to be downing themselves by holding their whole selves harshly to account for their behaviors or thoughts. The person finds that after an initially promising start, for whatever reason, they find themselves engaging in self-downing behaviors. That's the 1st error. The 2nd error is in downing their self about downing their self.

The perfectionist, the finisher (the closure maniac), the non-quitter, the quitter; these are just a few of the 'traits' that can drive the 2nd error. The solution to the 2nd error is to first be able to identify it. Next you must break your state and this can be done by squeezing the Uptime anchor so as to access the Uptime state - thereby escaping the Downtime state where the 2nd error takes place. Another anchor you can give yourself is simply to say to yourself in your mind "2nd error," and, at this point, STOP! Stop thinking, stop talking, stop acting, stop feeling.

Allow the whole arrangement of ideas, values and concepts

that go into the creation and continuation of the 2nd error to just drop away. To practise inactivity for a moment or two, as you reassess what you really want, is they key here. The 2nd error is typically the reaction to a first error and so creates a pendulum effect, just as when a car begins to speed wobble and each correction only increases the divergence from the chosen line. This can happen in behavior too. Consider the person who has tried to control their eating to control their weight and has ended up in a binge/starve cycle. The starve compensates for the previous binge and then the hunger gets too much and another binge is on the cards. The solution to the past error necessitates another error. The response to either a binge or a starve should be an average feed. If you swing to the right, don't compensate with a swing to the left, just return to the middle. Our car driver needs to just lock the steering wheel in order to bring the speed wobble under control.

The voice inside one's head is a strong platform for the 2nd error to assert itself. The voice constantly chatters away pretending it is you. It is actually the Myth of the Self constantly striving to ensure its survival, and, as we know, this requires the past and the future to be brought into the equation. The trick to dealing with this incessant voice is never to answer it inside its frame. This is also a good technique for dealing with other people whose Myth of Self seems eager to validate them by 'hooking', then locking, horns with your Myth of the Self. You may be wondering what I mean by 'never answer the inner voice inside its own frame', well I'll give an example.

Suppose someone calls me 'stupid' and my response is to launch into a counter attack or simply a refutation of the assertion that I am stupid. I may be able to make the most water tight, compelling and convincing argument in history so that no one could possibly believe I was stupid, but it doesn't matter. Why? Because I've already lost control over the reality being asserted (the frame). I've deemed the comment worthy of an answer and have already, therefore, 'lost' by losing sight of the level that 'the game' is being played on.

It is exactly the same with the voice we hear in our head. So long as we continue to identify with it, the voice inside our head is always compelling us to search for certainty in the future. It seeks reassurance of the integrity of the body, relationships, even its very sense of self. I've seen exactly the same thing time and again with people who are operating phobic patterns. Let's consider the hypochondriac because it clearly demonstrates the problem and the solution that can operate in all of us. See if you recognize the actions of your own inner voice in this example.

The hypochondriac is constantly on the look out for new symptoms, like a new mole, a slight unevenness or a change in colour. For each symptom he/she must seek reassurance from an authority such as a doctor. Eventually, the drive for certainty brings a distrust of the authority figure and so a second or third opinion is sought, and so it goes on. The hypochondriac believes it is the physical symptoms that need to be addressed and reassurance given. He/she believes that once reassurance is given then he/she can relax and so more and more reassurance is needed until each reassurance begins to lose its value. He/she will only be rid of this cycle when he/she realizes that the need for reassurance needs to be denied. The need for reassurance is an anxiety avoidance; it is driven of the Myth of the Self's need for certainty. The Myth of the Self (sometimes manifesting as an internal voice) has an insatiable need to know that all will be OK in the future, but of course the World at Large will never oblige to these demands, sooner or later something in the future is going to be not-OK. The only way we can make the future OK is to know that, even if not-OK, when events happen, we will be OK about them.

Much as we try to step outside of the frame of the Myth of the Self's voice, in retaliation, it too can attempt to hook the awareness back in by shifting frames so we end up asking ourselves;

"What if that voice needs to be listened to?"

"What if it has some vital unconscious information?"

"In ignoring the inner voice am I suppressing some psychic material that may catastrophically erupt later?"

But these questions and needs for reassurance need to be ignored, just as every other statement or question does because as you listen to these questions you'll begin to realize that the voice who is asking these questions is not your own, but the inner voice (the Myth of the Self) again, and so it lays its trap to, once again, attempt to ensnare you.

My dear brothers, never forget, when you hear the progress of enlightenment vaunted, that the devil's best trick is to persuade you that he doesn't exist!
Baudelaire

As you learn more and learn to do less, the very act of saying in one's mind "2nd error" will become an auditory anchor for thought stopping and clear-mindedness. A confusion of wants is often an integral part of the arrangement of thoughts that go into creating a 2nd error; this is why a reassessment of what you really want, and why you want it, is prescribed here.

The Application of TOTE Breaking

TOTE breaking is also useful for breaking the quick associations that drive the 2nd error and knee-jerk reactions. At first, you may begin to observe knee-jerk reactions in yourself that are 2nd errors or just simply unwanted reactions. It may be that every time something 'goes wrong' you find yourself automatically looking around for someone or something else to blame. Your mind starts tracking back; building a list of suspects from those nearby or having any loose connection at all to yourself or the situation. You will now have the opportunity to say, "Now look what you've made me do," to the other entity you wish to blame. If you are very quick and very perceptive (you've been practicing the bubble mediation) you will find it is possible for your mind (at the 5th position) to catch these processes at work.

Assuming you find this behavior undesirable, you might initially wish to eradicate (Annihilate) the reaction entirely. This would be a mistake as you have demanded the *ends* but without understanding, or taking ownership of the *means*. Acceptance of the original knee-jerk reaction will allow you to take control by catching the behavioral TOTE and then the thought TOTE and reducing it in duration and in magnitude (Amelioration), then, perhaps, you might get spontaneous Annihilation of the reaction. This breaks the TOTEs that comprise this reaction into smaller and smaller ones. At each break between one TOTE and the next, conscious control can be exerted. You can see how helpful this is to address reactive behavior (including anger management) eventually you can even prevent the unquestioned judgements around which that behavior used to hinge.

A Strange Practice

One more practice that may be of use to the adventurous TOTE breaker is a strange form of dynamic meditation I have heard of but have no name for. The meditation is simply that you must try to be spontaneous in your actions, without repetition. The major benefit of the practice must be the illumination of just how much of our actions, and accordingly our thoughts, are no freer than a train on a track. When I heard of this mediation of the no-repetition, I wanted to see it in action so I could have a go, until it struck me that to see this either never or a thousand times would make no difference; it's only constancy is change. Upon reflection, the requirement of no repetition in this meditation really calls into question the chunking size of the TOTE and one's focus. Surely breathing, moving, living and a hundred other things must remain constant throughout the practice, on the one hand. On the other hand, consider the idea that the enlightened individual does not recognize such a thing as an 'ordinary moment'. Given these two points, it seems that with no boundaries set as to the chunking size of the actions, everything and nothing is an equally valid manifestation of this no repetition meditation. Anyway, give it a go.

A Word on Habit

Plenty of people will insist that 'habit' drives their thoughts or behaviors. I'll tell you now what a habit is. A habit is just something you do time after time. <u>A habit contains no power other than the meaning behind the actions</u>. If you can address the meaning underlying a particular habit, then all you have left is the behavioral shell. Habit can dictate *when* a behavior happens, but not *whether* that behavior happens or not.

Imagine that we have a deal with each other, I come round to your house each morning and if you burn one five dollar bill, I'll give you a fifty dollar bill.

"Should we do it again tomorrow?" I hear you say. "You bet!" I answer. Fast-forward twenty years from now. Everyday for twenty years you have burned a five dollar bill because you expect to get a fifty. You have developed 'a habit'. Now, one day, I come around to your house and explain the deal is off. They are carting me off to jail because I've hit a cyclist with my caravan or something. Anyway, whatever the reason, the deal is off. How many days are you going to keep up the habit of burning a five dollar bill every morning? Not many, because the *meaning* behind that activity has disappeared, and the 'habit' is certain to dissolve in days. The TOTEs of a habit can be caught and broken very quickly once the meaning is addressed.

Even if your habit involves some form of deferred gratification that involves a drug of some sort this still applies. You may have some extra physical discomfort from 'withdrawal', but that's OK (remember it's OK to be not-OK).

Chapter 14

Quietening your Inner Voice

The Myth of the Self has many ways of asserting its position and, above all else, its goal is to survive and ensure its future survival. This goal probably existed as some form of survival mechanism in our collective pasts, yet if the Myth of the Self takes on certain beliefs about how it will perpetuate itself into immortality, then it may rarely even force actions that lead to the death of the body. For example, the belief that one's name will live on 'in song and story', may lead a person (driven by their Myth of the Self) to take reckless, even suicidal, actions to gain a certain notoriety. The Myth of the Self may believe that it is better to be a dead somebody, than an alive nobody. This kind of decision takes place within the dissociations of *Other-minds* and the *Future*, maybe also with a little *Elsewhere* tacked on. The Myth of the Self, in this case, has prized its existence in other people's minds (who, it assumes, will live on after it) more highly that its true existence within the mind and body of its 'host'. It can be seen then that the very idea of 'The Self' can become more prized than the true awareness that lies behind the Myth of the Self.

Other conceptions of what happens after death, such as some form of afterlife, may lead the Myth of the Self to believe that it will live on and, accordingly, this reckless behavior may be seen again.

These are both just extreme examples of how the Myth of the Self will assert itself at all costs. To most of us in everyday life this doesn't operate in such an extreme manner, yet that may just be an illusion, as the above examples simply required certain beliefs to be in place for them to come about. You are (that is to say, your Myth of Self is) acting just as strongly, as in the above examples, the only difference being, that it is acting according to a different set of beliefs. It is much harder, in today's society, to give credence to any sort of afterlife, and the Myth of the Self may try all the harder to assert itself as a living reputation during this life. It wants to become an idea in the minds of others.

Once there is good evidence that an idea of our-self is held in others' minds, it gratifies us only when we go into *Other minds-Downtime* and imagine that all these other people in the world know of us. So once again, we have set up, in this example, a situation where we look for evidence in the World at Large to give us permission to imagine something inside our heads (In Downtime) that we can then feel a particular way about. A decline in the realistic possibility of an afterlife (at least one where the Myth of the Self is preserved) goes hand in hand with people's increasing hunger for worldly fame. Because the deadline has been brought forward, the Myth of the Self seeks to assert its reality and immortality in a more down to earth form

The method that the Myth of the Self can use most effectively to shape its host's behavior is to assert a system of punishments and rewards that operate much along the same lines as we have seen in our earlier examination of the mechanisms of stress.

In order to gain maximum effectiveness in shaping the host's behavior, threat of punishment should be ever-present, and the rewards should be short lived, semi-respites from an ever-present, shadowy anxiety. This 'ever-present anxiety' is the Myth of the Self's fear of its own demise. The Myth of the Self can contort (sublimate) this fear into all sorts of small fears. For us as living bodies, death only comes when the body actually stops functioning. Yet for the Myth of the Self, death or some portion of death can come bit by bit in many forms; a small sleight by a friend, a loss of reputation, the feeling of insignificance, the realisation of your ordinariness, the loss of status, the loss of a possession, someone wandering on to 'your territory', the feeling of powerlessness both in the World at Large and (perhaps more importantly) the lack of the power to persuade others to join you in your 'correct' interpretation of the World at Large, someone forgetting your name... and so on.

If we take an existentialist view of ourselves, we can see that we have the capacity to act entirely spontaneously; for example, what assertion can I make today to myself or others that I will not suddenly decide to burn the house down, or to go on a gambling spree, or even to decide to kill someone or myself? These are all things I would not agree with today*, but how can I trust the 'tomorrow me' to concur? Ultimately, there are no assurances, yet if I have acted consistently in the past, and I can extend my sense of self into the future, then I can have some degree of assurance, or at least the illusion of assurance. Is it true then, that we accept or even generate this Myth of the Self in order to mask our own spontaneity from ourselves? If we do, then we deny *that which we are* - thereby generating inauthenticity and alienation.

In order to create the most fertile breeding ground for a stagnant, entrenched and inflexible Myth of the Self, we need two things; the denial of what Sartre called our 'horrible freedom' (the thing that makes some people fear they may jump as they look off a tall bridge), coupled with a distrust of the motives and actions of a future self that is in any way different from who we are today**. This type of Myth of the Self may need to suck an enormous amount of energy to fulfil certain subtasks to keep its position; to keep all these balls in the air. The subtasks often include, rehearsing positions and actions, reliving or redefining past events, internal conversations, a constant parrot-like repetition of one's values today in the hope that tomorrow they will live on in the 'tomorrow me'. To try to assert values on to one's self seems a fallacy; your true reactions (which reflect your true values) will be authentic to who you are at that moment and the prevailing conditions of that moment. In a film I saw, a man asks a woman if she would promise not to react badly if he tells her something. She refuses to promise on the basis that her reactions will be her natural reaction and he must take his chances. She thereby demonstrates a belief and trust in her future self that she refuses to have suppressed. She strikes a blow for her own authenticity. I can't remember what it was he had to say, or if she took it badly or not.

I don't sit here and think, "I may drive to the shops later, let's just sit and rehearse the entire journey a few times." In fact, if I did this and followed through on my rehearsals then my reactivity to prevailing road conditions would be a shambles because (Ooops!) my rehearsal did not take account of that child running out into the road. Of course, to try and rehearse these kinds of things is absurd, yet if we take the view that all must be OK in the future on every level, then we demand certainty of the future and this can lead to habitual rehearsal. Sometimes we may overtly find ourselves rehearsing conversations, or sometimes the Myth of the Self, much like an attention seeking child (who is, by the way, just manifesting externally this exact same process), constantly clatters away through the use of our imaginative and language systems. The child allows the experience to externalise as overt behavior, yet we adults are not so much more sophisti- cated simply because society has conditioned us to split our mind and allow these things to go on internally.

No one can deny that we all have a lot of extra unnecessary noise going around in our heads, whether it is nonsense or semi- directed thought. Our names for these experiences betray our feeling that our true core of awareness is somewhat dissociated from these ruminations; they are often described as 'intrusive thoughts' or 'circular thoughts'. When robot-men on films malfunction, this is often depicted as them getting 'stuck in a loop' of behavior; repeating phrases, presumably from their past or, in one film I've seen, a robot misses the door and keeps bumping into the wall next to it, like a fly against a window. We are very much like these robot-men as we go through the same lines of thinking again and again during 'circular thoughts'. 'Intrusive thoughts' necessarily require a degree of dissociation within the mind in order for us to feel that they are somehow coming from outside, or not under our control. It could be that, as we begin to separate our awareness from our Myth of the Self, it begins to fight back by using these 'intrusive thoughts' as a disincentive to having any space between 'I' and the contents of thoughts. The Myth of the Self abhors simple awareness in and of its self; some may suppose that it would like us to believe that in order to be aware, we <u>have</u> to be intentionally aware (that is to say, aware *of* something, to direct our awareness at some *mind object* or other.) This is not necessarily the case; it is possible for us to be just *aware*.

This split between the 'I' (the background sense of awareness we have) and the contents of thoughts is a nail in the coffin for the Myth of the Self, and is bound to provoke some of its defence mechanisms.

Incidentally, I should mention that we could experience the 'inner voice' in many ways, not just as a voice in the auditory modality, although this is by far the most common. You could experience pictures or symbols for example as the expression of the inner voice. It's conceivable that the deaf (especially those who have been deaf since birth) may experience the inner voice differently. One could easily conceive that the imagined feeling of the hands doing sign language (or the imagined sight of watching sign language) could easily be the inner voice of a person who is deaf, and their 'thinking out loud' or 'talking out loud to themselves', which we all do from time to time, would be expressed as hand movements.

We have already covered not answering this voice in 'its own frame', yet we take things even further by enlisting the action of the conditioned response to make this 'denial of the inner voice's frame' more automatic. Let's have a look first at a traditional Cognitive-Behavioral method of thought-stopping before moving on to a few other variations. Notice as you look at the exercises that we are seeing the management, instead of a complete eradication, of the inner voice. Remember Amelioration comes before Annihilation of a symptom. You'll remember, of course, that before Amelioration comes Acceptance; you'll have covered this as you watched (and accepted) the thoughts as they go by during the *Bubble meditation* exercise. In fact, during that exercise you'll already have begun, to some degree, to Ameliorate.

Actually, even the simplest thought-watching meditation creates this base of Acceptance, and as soon as Acceptance begins Amelioration is bound to follow.

You can experiment with the first three exercises simply for fun, and to build a base for the fourth exercise the *Marble Dropping Mediation*. Ultimately though, the practice of the *Marble Dropping Mediation* is the most important.

The Taped 'STOP' Method
The traditional cognitive-behavior-based, thought-stopping exercise goes as follows:

1. Get a tape recorder and record your self saying "stop" every few seconds or so for perhaps a period of twenty minutes.

2. Play the tape back and as you listen to the tape, and in the blank spaces, allow whatever thoughts you have coming into your mind to just exist. When you hear the word 'stop' on the tape, allow all those thoughts within your mind to just drop away. Repeat this for the entire length of the tape.

   The word 'stop' becomes an anchor that is associated with simply dropping thoughts out of your mind and letting go. The word can then be used later if you are plagued by unwelcome thoughts or pseudo thoughts.

Changing the Qualities of the 'Voice'
In Neuro linguistic Programming (NLP), it is explained that the important factors in our internal thoughts are not so much the

content of those thoughts, but the very structure of the process by which those thoughts manifest. These are known as 'sub-modalities' and include all the qualities by which our sense-perceptions can be categorized. That is to say with regard to the voice; its pitch, rhythm, tone, speed, accent, volume, the direction the voice seems to be coming from and even who the voice sounds like. With respect to any visually-based thoughts, these qualities would be color, contrast, movement, size, brightness, and so on; basically, all the things that you would control if you were the director of a film. Normally, the more 'real' these qualities are, the more that thought appears to operate upon you

Simply allow the little voice (or visually-based thought) to go about its business as you observe it in your mind, ignoring the content whilst taking note of its qualities. Experiment by actively changing these qualities and noting the differences that those changes make to the operation of that thought. So, for example, if a thought comes into your mind that is voice-based, change the volume, the tone, the pitch, everything about that thought. Pay particular attention to the direction that the voice appears to be coming from and move it around. Generally, notice how much control you have over these qualities and how that profoundly affects the power those thoughts have over you (or not).

The White Noise Method

The white noise method utilizes our language-making devices and short-circuits the way that the Myth of the Self hijacks these mechanisms in order to plague us with incessant thought-chatter. You may have noticed, as you observe seemingly nonsense-based thought-chatter, that this internal noise still appears to have some form of structure. I believe this is because we have in our heads, almost like a separate tool, a device for making language which controls how we put sentences together; syntax, grammar, and so on. It is this device that is often employed by the Myth of the Self to create the sometimes intelligible, sometimes unintelligible, noise. We consciously control this device, however, whenever we engage in conversation. Yet, if left alone, the Myth of the Self can tap into this device. Some people may have accidentally come about crude strategies for preventing the Myth of the Self from carrying out this hijacking procedure, and in doing so, have been able to release themselves from this internal noise to some degree. Such strategies involve constant conscious control of the language-making device by singing, humming, chanting, whistling, or (when in company) talking incessantly about nothing in particular. In this list we could even include some superstitious rituals such as obsessively-compulsively counting things which don't need counting, or reciting prayers. Another use of this 'radio jamming' style of strategy, and one that also takes us into Uptime, is the contemplation of some form of external stimulus. Waves crashing on a beach, the wind, the rain, cars driving by, music, crickets in woodland, even the static of an un-tuned TV or radio, these are all examples of external white noise. If we focus in and concentrate on this type of white noise it 'jams' our tendency to otherwise listen to the Myth of the Self and all of its ramblings. These stimuli are all auditory and this is congruent with seeking to drown out the auditory 'inner-voice', yet jamming stimuli can be found in the other senses. Tastes, smells, kinesthetic feelings and sights could all plausibly be used as distractions; the most notable example would be the taste, smell and feelings associated with unnecessary 'comfort' eating.

Interestingly, for some people this kind of effect is disturbing, especially if it comes at a time, and in a form, they are not in control of. If you find yourself in the midst of some chaotic noise like, for example, a playground full of screaming, yelling children, you may say to yourself, "it's so noisy I can't hear myself think." This, and any attendant anger, frustration or anxiety, is your Myth of the Self asserting a defense mechanism and you might be tempted to leave the playground and find somewhere 'more peaceful' in order to allow the Myth of the Self to rehearse its story. In return, it will reward you with the withdrawal of the unpleasant feelings. It is a similar story with regard to many of the exercises in this book; the Myth of the Self may see them as an attack and then, in order to pull you back into line, give you unpleasant feelings along with thoughts such as; "it's not working" or "I am missing out on something more interesting or more productive" or "if I dissolve any of 'myself' I may not able to relate to others, nor them to me." (I.e. "I owe it to others to be 'who I am now'; it's expected; they won't thank me; nobody likes change.") All of the Myth of the Self's little jibes come from the four Downtime dissociations (Past, Future, Other-minds and Elsewhere). It can never use any of the actuality of where you are right now and what you are doing right now to scare you into 'towing the party line'.

Many, if not all, of the above techniques using both external or internal 'white-noise' could conceivably be called forms of meditation, but a lot of the above strategies involve unnecessary effort, side effects, or rely on some type of external setting. Let's see then how we can use this effect more independently, actively and directly.

The exercise:

1. Simply notice how this language-making device puts together the stream of noise in a way that we instantly respond to; the speed and rhythm of this noise mimics normal conversational talking. It may be making sense. It may not be making too much sense; a little like hearing people on the other side of the wall having a conversation but you cannot make out the words, or hearing someone speaking a foreign language.

2. Now it's time to take back control of the language-making device. Simply allow the flow of noise to continue in the form that the Myth of the Self is sending it. Now begin to insert

random words into the flow, (keeping the same rhythm and syntax), even, perhaps, inserting some nonsense words.

3. Speed up this process until you can no longer find the words to insert. Keeping the rhythm and syntax intact and simply speed up the process until there is absolutely no way that you can make any sense of the flow. Now, allow it to speed up until it becomes a white noise in the background.

   You can consciously drive this white noise faster as if adding more and more momentum to an ever-quickening flywheel, until eventually the stream of white noise becomes quite automatic and begins to blend into the background.

The Marble Dropping Meditation

This exercise is a combination and extension off all of the exercises above and will also utilize the now (Uptime) anchor that you set up earlier. You will need to buy a bag of marbles, or if you wish, you may use pebbles, nuts, chickpeas or whatever. The exercise, as with all the exercises, not only functions during its practice, but sets up powerful cognitive chains that will become the automatic routes your brain will take as you go about your daily business.

1. Take the first marble and hold it as lightly as you can between your finger and thumb; use the same finger and thumb as you used earlier for your now (Uptime) anchor. Now just allow any thought-form to appear in your mind as it will.

2. Change the qualities of that thought-form (the speed, voice, tone, etc). Pay particular attention to moving the location of that thought; can you send it outside yourself? From the back of your head to the front? Into your chest, down to your toe? Move it around, quicker and quicker, until it just becomes incomprehensible. It has now been transformed into an

abstract form.

3. Now send it down to the marble; collect all of it and send it all down to that marble, until it only buzzes around inside the marble.

4. Gently squeeze the marble from behind until it fires out from your fingers, at which point allow the finger and thumb to come together in a loop and squeeze them tightly; just notice how, at the very same moment you let go of the marble (and the thought-form), you have found yourself squeezing the Uptime anchor, bringing your awareness into your senses.

5. Release the Uptime anchor and remain in Uptime for as long as your awareness remains there. As soon as another thought-form comes along, pick-up another marble and repeat.

Fractionation for Insomnia

This exercise is adapted from two hypnotic induction styles to relax both mind and body and is particularly good for clearing the mind to help you fall asleep, although if it is not practiced until its conclusion it can produce a nice trance state. In the first half you are relaxing the body, in the second you are relaxing the mind. When relaxing the body, it may help you to know that relaxation is always there underneath the tension; once the tension is released you don't then have to relax, it's just there. You know if you chopped your head off and looked at your body it would very relaxed (please don't try this at home, this is just a thought experiment), what does this tell us? It tells us that to be relaxed is the default state of the body; you don't send nerve messages to relax, you quieten the messages that are saying 'tense-up', and you relax automatically. This tension does not actually want to be there; it is trapped like a prisoner by messages coming from your brain and actively wants to go; you want it to go too, so it's a win–win situation for you both. I have not included it within the exercise, but if you can begin to breathe as if you were asleep right from the start of the exercise, then this will help you greatly. Listen to someone else asleep when you get the opportunity; notice the quickness or slowness of the in and out breath; notice the gap (after the out breath) between breaths. If you're getting to sleep in the presence of another person who is already asleep, you need not match their pace, but if it suits you can do so. As soon as you can, allow the unconscious processes to continue this breathing without your effort as you concentrate on the two parts of the exercise.

Relax the Body

1. Send your awareness down to your feet and concentrate on relaxing them; just allow all the unnecessary tension to drift out of your body through your ever-relaxing breathing. Some people can even imagine this unnecessary tension leaving on each out-breath as a sound or colour. Notice I said unnecessary tension; don't expect or demand complete 100% relaxation – that will only make you tense! In fact, you know that at some level you can feel relaxed about being un-relaxed. As only the *unnecessary* tension is going, you could actually do this bodily relaxation anywhere, even when running/cycling etc.

2. Move to your calves and let them relax too; let them release all the unnecessary tension.

3. Move through each muscle of your body, relaxing it, until you get all the way up to your head.

4. Now your body is relaxed. If you'd like a deeper relaxation just start at the feet again and repeat the process.

A variation on this can be to tense each muscle group for twenty seconds or so then let go and allow it to relax before moving onto the next group. This can break those stubborn pockets of tension too.

Relax the Mind
The second part of the exercise relaxes the mind, slows down and interrupts the tendency of the mind to repeat thoughts, rehearse, or simply to rattle away endlessly.

1. Pick a spot somewhere in the room. It may be a spot on the wall, a bit of light, whatever you like, but just choose a point where, as you look at it, your eyes will be looking upwards, not with your neck looking upwards but with your eyes slightly upwards in their sockets. Stare at the spot for a few seconds, becoming intensely aware of the focus of your attention on that spot.

2. Just notice how your eyes get more and more tired, and when you are ready to let your mind relax, just allow them to close.

3. Now your eyes are closed, begin to count on each out-breath down from a hundred, thinking to yourself "let go" (or "drift away") between numbers. So, "100 let go, 99 let go, 98 let go…" And so on. As soon as the mind falters even slightly in knowing the next number, just let all the numbers drift away completely as you just drop deeper into a relaxed mental state. The very moment even an inkling of a thought comes into your mind, open your eyes and stare at that point on the wall for a moment, sending all your attention back out there to it.

4. After a few seconds, let yours eyes close and repeat the whole cycle.

Just a couple of points - the intention is to repeat this process until your mind wanders, of its own accord, to sleep. It is easy to count down from a hundred to one, but if you watch the mind carefully, you'll notice the slightest hesitations; just a few numbers in, take these as your cue to allow all the numbers to drift away. Have faith that you will suddenly find yourself (though you might not be aware of it) falling asleep. The mind will not necessarily respond in a constant manner to each cycle, so do not necessarily expect yourself to get a constant amount of progress from each cycle. It is common to feel 'nothing is happening' and after only a few more cycles to be completely unaware that you are now drifting into sleep.

Finally, this technique (just like the Bubble Meditation) if practiced just before sleeping, can sometimes lead one into lucid sleep (being asleep and yet aware that you are asleep, often being aware within dreams). If you find this happening and find that it is enjoyable, then that's fine. If you find yourself sleeping lucidly and feel it is not for you, then discontinue using this method.

---

*I use the terms 'today' and 'tomorrow' here just for illustration, there is nothing particular about the unit of time that is known as a day. I might well have used the terms the 'now me' and the 'next-minute (or even, next-second) me'.

**the exercises in chapter 11 are designed to mollify this potential distrust of one's future self.

Chapter 15

The Downtime Anchor: Extend control of your direction of attention through choice

The other side of the Uptime anchor equation is obviously the Downtime anchor and there are times when a Downtime anchor comes in useful. We have only covered the Uptime anchor so far because, for the majority of individuals, a default drift into Downtime is much more likely. It is desirable to be able to escape unuseful Downtime by returning to Uptime using the Uptime anchor, to come to one's senses so to speak. Another desirable application of the Uptime anchor is its ability to be used in conditioning Uptime as the default. Let's remember though that both Uptime and Downtime have their time and place. The desirability of any state is really governed by the usefulness of the state; no state is better than any other per se. The enlightened individual wants to find himself or herself in Uptime as a default position, only to choose to go into Downtime as an option when it becomes more useful than the Uptime in a given situation. This will be either for practical matters or to escape an unpleasant Uptime.

There are many uses for the Downtime anchor, and its role will become more important as Uptime becomes your default. As you begin to find that the effects of the Downtime anchor seem more powerful than the Uptime anchor, it is a very good sign that you have begun to set your default as Uptime. The Uptime anchor will seem to become less effective if it is only inviting you into a state you are already in. As Uptime becomes your default, the Downtime anchor will become more noticeably effective as it is inviting you into a state that you are not finding yourself in as much. The times it can be useful to use your Downtime anchor are times when you are finding it unuseful, or less useful, than the Uptime alternative.

Conventionally, the strength of external stimuli would govern the mind's decision about whether to be in Uptime or Downtime. Many people experience everyday life as boring and so the outside world offers them no novelty or strength of stimuli to attract their attention. The boredom of everyday life is just a creation that is the result of quickly generalizing stimuli into large categories that can be dismissed all too easily as 'ordinary moments.' It's a self-perpetuating process, where the perceptions drive the attitude and the attitude then drives the perceptual tendencies.

If they've seen one, they've seen them all. How easily we can become accustomed to, and jaded with, even the most exotic novelty whilst we let the complexity of the world slide by as we wait for a bus, drive on the motorway, do the washing up, carry water, chop wood...

Everything has beauty, but not everyone sees it.
Confucius

This is the mechanism by which the 'been there, done that' attitude of the world-weary will typically install Downtime as the default. We will have a more in depth look at exactly how this happens in chapter 18. If they are caught up so much in the web of socially-constructed meaning, there seems for them so little time to be in Uptime, except for when a problem or an emergency demands their attention in the outside world. This can lead to the perception that the outside world is only full of unpleasant things (emergencies and problems are rarely pleasant). This will increase the tendency to want to spend more time in Downtime to escape the 'harsh world', and so the viscous spiral continues. The person who has 'been there, done that and bought the T-shirt' is creating their own boredom. James Joyce said once that he had never met a boring man; a statement that said more about his attendance to the complexity and novelty that can be found anywhere in the World at Large than the character of the men he met. I suspect Joyce might agree that there are no ordinary moments.

Some strategies may have been developed, in the pre-enlightened individual, to indirectly utilize the mechanism of the mind that directs attention toward novelty or extreme sensation. The most extreme of these occasions is demonstrated in the self-harmer. The severity of the extreme sensory experience of cutting oneself, for example, will be a persuasive contender for one's attention. It can easily draw the attention away from the past, the present, the future and other minds.

I knew a man who was 'depressed'; one day he dropped a brick on his toe. For the entirety of his toe-throbbing experience, he forget to be depressed; he forgot he 'had depression', and for good reason; for those few minutes he had literally not 'got' depression. Things like depression and anxiety are not something you *are* or even something you *have*, they are something you *do*. Anyway, when the pain subsided he remembered to be sad about feeling sad again. The pain of the toe had no deeper meaning, it was nothing to get sad about, so despite its discomfort, it was a case of feeling OK about something that is not-OK. This can serve as a powerful model for those who are willing to take control and responsibility for the contents of their attention but, of course, you don't need to drop a brick on your toe to get into Uptime. The extremity of the self-harmer situation makes the implications of that type of slippery-slope behavior transparent. You may still be exhibiting this kind of pattern in a subtler form; be mindful and you may find times when you engineer a situation in the World at Large in order to force your attention into Uptime, see examples below (1). Another similar strategy to escape unpleasant Downtime can be the flight of one kind of Downtime to another (2).

1. *Behavior with the purpose of forcing your attention into Uptime only*

as a means of escape from an uncomfortable Downtime: Gambling, smoking, driving too fast, learning a new skill, being in a new place, eating (when not hungry) or other types of activity that demand one's full attention. Risk-taking forces the awareness into the moment. Sensory stimulation forces attention into Uptime too. Even an escape to an uncomfortable Uptime is desirable if the Downtime is more uncomfortable; self-harming is a good example of this. Some demanding activities can be functional, some less so. It is entirely a judgment call on your behalf as to whether, and on what criteria, you deem these palliatives as useful or not.

2. *Behavior with the purpose of forcing your attention into a less un-useful Downtime*: Watching TV is a good example, as is reliving the past and worrying about the future. A particularly dysfunction manifestation is the 'drama-queen complex', whereby small day-to-day matters are blown into major crises in order to avoid more long term, more important, matters. Downing others through criticism, either directly or in private, is also an attempt to shore up the uncomfortable Downtime of low self esteem, by pushing the other person(s) into the foreground; thus, forcing one's own shortcomings into the background.

Remember that (much like with money) we do not really desire, in-and-of-itself, any of these activities. We really desire what these activities will do for us and the questions they answer. Having a direct means of accessing Uptime, via your Uptime anchor, will render these other convoluted strategies, to a lesser or larger degree, unnecessary.

These behaviors, and many more besides, reflect an escape; a running *away-from* an uncomfortable/unuseful Downtime, instead of the more desirable situation of actively going *towards* a more useful Uptime for its own sake, because you are finding it a more useful state at that time. You will notice that an escape from one Downtime to another is often just a jump from one uncomfortable state to another state that is still uncomfortable, only less

187

so. The less uncomfortable Downtime is more useful, relatively speaking, but still remains 'the lesser of two evils'. The same can be said for the flight away from uncomfortable Downtime into an uncomfortable Uptime.

Typically, the pre-enlightened individual may take great delight in their ability to multi-task as they drop inside their mind to 'optimize the use of their time' by over-planning, over-reviewing, over-rehearsing and so on. No time to stop and smell the roses.

The enlightened individual's sensory acuity is high; they attend to the senses, to just existing. The trust of the future and past selves allows them to avoid being pulled into trying to operate upon things where or when they are not. The enlightened individual chooses to create the reality that 'there are no ordinary moments', and so can further reinforce Uptime as the default.

There are still times when you will want to be in Downtime as a conscious choice, to plan learn, and so on. Perhaps you merely need to escape unuseful Uptime. For example, some unuseful pain could be escaped by dropping into Downtime. A marathon runner trying to push through the discomfort signals might find the Downtime anchor useful. This will augment the runner's decision that it's OK to be not-OK, with respect to this discomfort. The values associated with finishing the race outweigh the values associated with the short-term physical comfort of quitting the run. At the most extreme end, the escape from an uncomfortable Uptime is useful for surgery, either with hypnosis or anesthetics.

Long grueling activities can demand a distracting stimulus to concentrate on. Sea shanties, cotton picking songs, chain-gang songs and even the seven dwarves' tendency to 'whistle as they work', exemplify an attempt to distort time and to generally bring the attention away from a specific drudgery, whether physical, mental or both. Again, this can be either functional or dysfunctional. I personally like to listen to music of the right type whilst running or cycling.

Do you find it difficult to drive, wash-up, or eat without the radio on? Distraction from where we are and what we are doing is so endemic that, when forced away from these distractions, we will often whistle or sing. The shower or bath is a perfect example, it is a well deserved cliché to sing in the shower and this is because it is the place most likely to have no distraction such as a radio or television. Do you own a waterproof radio in your bathroom? Why?

It is common practice the world over for children to put their fingers in their ears and loudly chant "La! La! La!" in response to something they don't want to hear, or something they don't want to admit that they hear. The 'mental patient' suffering uncomfortable auditory hallucinations (a misattributed internal voice) could be seen using the same strategy in the extreme by shouting, continuously and loudly, often nonsense. This can give a logical strategy the appearance of complete insanity. The extremity of the patient's situation and the immaturity of the child in the playground make their strategies quite obvious. See how many ways you can observe in yourself, and in those around you, of disguising this strategy as it manifests in its more sophisticated adult form.

Trying to work, or read, in a noisy environment is another possible time when the Downtime anchor will come into use. To be able to drop down into internal focus and not let the strength or novelty of external stimulus pull one's attention away is a skill I am sure you will not find difficult to think of many applications for. The Downtime anchor is simplicity itself, but is only really worth installing when you have already begun to make Uptime your default.

Installing the Downtime Anchor

1. You might find it easier to close your eyes, as you just allow your mind to drift into internal sensations.

2. Pick a memory or an imagination of the future; see the images inside your mind; hear those sounds; feel the feeling of being there.

3. As your conscious attention focuses more intently upon the internal representations inside your mind, you may begin to find that you are beginning to drift away from your direct sensations (smell, taste, sound, feeling, sight) even more.

When you find your focus completely directed into Downtime then it is time to squeeze your Downtime anchor. Simply squeeze the first finger and thumb of the opposite hand to your Uptime anchor.

Break the focus of your attention once again and attend to any external sensation, such as the temperature of the room, sounds outside and so on just to bring you back into your default of Uptime. Squeeze your Downtime anchor and notice if you pop into Downtime. If you do then this is fine. If not, simply repeat the exercise as necessary, making sure you only squeeze the Downtime anchor when your attention is firmly and purely within your internal representations.

Chapter 16

The Cycle of Wants: Freeing yourself from the control of false desire

Wealth consists not in having great possessions, but in having few wants.

Epictetus

Wants are only actualized upon their destruction. Often we construct these wants according to values that we are not even aware of. A want is not a pleasant thing; it irritates like an itch until it goes away. Wants are created only to be destroyed; in fact, to 'want for nothing' is synonymous with ideas of happiness and satisfaction. A want is something to be avoided yet we seem to be in the ironic business of generating so many of them.

In fact, paradoxically, <u>what we really want is to have no wants.</u> This demonstrates that we can never be entirely free of wants. But we do have a freedom to manage our want cycles. When we want something, what we are actually saying is that our current situation is unacceptable. We are essentially saying that the situation at the ground level, in the World at Large, is not-OK. This want, this judgment of the situation as 'not-OK' expresses a preference that doesn't have to be changed, yet we can still diffuse any sense of dissatisfaction that holding this preference creates.

When our situation is not-OK then we can create feelings of discomfort in order to motivate ourselves to act. In order for this to happen, we must hold the position that it's not-OK for things to be not-OK. If I feel bad about being overweight, for example, then this bad feeling is beneficial in its function as a motivation to get slimmer. I am, in effect, causing myself discomfort over my present situation so as to force myself to move away from an uncomfortable situation. It's a simple and sometimes effective motivation strategy, yet you might get what you want and, when you do, you may begin to consider that you have 'paid too much' for it.

When we have affected change in the World at Large and then our want disappears, we come to the position that it's OK for things to be OK; this is, of course, an entirely logical position to find oneself in. It's a good place to find oneself feeling OK about things being OK, yet there is still a hidden position within us that can begin to operate problematically. If we create the reality for ourselves that we can only feel OK about things being OK then there can be an anxiety about the future whereby, if the situation in the World at Large becomes not-OK then we will be not-OK about this. As this represents a threat in the future, it can encourage the mind to be drawn to the future, both to plan and to experience genuine discomfort about a situation that hasn't happened or may never happen. By this means, the tendency to drift into unuseful Downtime can creep back in. If the position before the want was satisfied was that it is OK for things to be not-OK then we can have confidence that our position will be the same in the future should the need arise. That is to say, we have no fear of not-OK situations in the future because we have confidence that if this should happen, we would be OK about it. So at the situational level, we can express a preference without the need for discomfort. Furthermore, if we want things we cannot have this will cause indefinite discomfort, yet by knowing it's OK for things to be not-OK, we can remain satisfied even with unmet preferences and aspirations for the future.

To be without some of the things you want is an indispensable part of happiness.
Bertrand Russell

There is one final and seemingly illogical position, and that is to find that it's not-OK to be OK. This is the most unfortunate position of becoming jaded to the degree that we are not sure what we want. An example would be to move to your dream home, or find yourself at your dream weight and then become aware it was not as good as you thought it was. It can lead to a feeling of not getting any satisfaction from anything, not really knowing what you want, or not to be able to know where the major feeling of dissatisfaction comes from or what to do about it. This is the most ironic of positions; the *windfall millionaire*, the *spoilt child* and the *burnt-out party animal* can most dramatically fall into this category. Once we get what we had wanted in the World at Large and found it did not address all the other values we had semi-consciously attached to it, then hopelessness or apathy can occur. 'Not-OK to be OK' is likely to occur due to an unexamined, or inaccurately examined, hierarchy of values and, of course, that means that the *confusion of wants* is free to operate.

If you get something that you want, yet it doesn't fulfill all the values you thought it would, you'll be more likely to lose it. The classic example is when someone thinks: "I'd like to lose weight because it will make me happy." Upon getting to their goal weight, they find they are not happy and they still 'have' a lot of 'problems' that their weight reduction did not address. These unrequited expectations cause a sense of discomfort which then leads to a step-back to the old discomfort-distracting strategy of eating for comfort. This is especially likely if being slim now seems like it was not all it was cracked up to be. A few months later it's easy for this person to get back into the "I'm unhappy because I'm overweight" frame. And thus, the yo-yoing continues, and at no point between the swing from one state to another is satisfaction found. This operates because of the confusion of values attached to a want. Let's look at a situation where the logic is much more clear, to see how absurd this can be. Imagine you are in the desert at night; it's cold but there is a fire nearby, so you rush up to the fire; it's too hot so you run off back into the desert where it's too cold, so you run back right up to the fire again where it's too hot and then you run off into the desert to find you are too cold...

Do you know anyone who continuously has to mess with things, like redecorating every room in the house, only to begin again when they've finished? Do you know anyone who moves around a lot; job-to-job, house-to-house, from one hobby to the next? Chasing values that simply refuse to attach to home furnishings is a better class of discomfort distraction if you are in the position to do it I suppose, yet it still, essentially, constitutes as inauthentic a position as the opium addict, whether that opium be 'of the masses' or otherwise. Naturally, to find one's awareness dragged away from the Here and Now can lead to an inability to really enjoy the present.

If thou wilt make a man happy, add not to his riches but take away from his desires.
Epicurus

If we find ourselves at 'OK to be OK' but with a worry that if things change we may become not-OK about being not-OK, then our 'OK to be OK' dissolves into the situation where it's not-OK to be OK because there is underlying anxiety regarding the future. There is no substitute for recognizing that it's OK to be not-OK right now and that we do not lose our preferences or motivation to act within the world as soon as we let go of the discomfort associated with the position of it's not-OK to be not-OK. We need trust in our future selves in order to relinquish the tendency to try and insulate against, or second-guess, the future.

If we take the position of it's not-OK to be not-OK then we postpone feeling OK until some outside event dictates that we can allow it to happen. This is not a necessary state of affairs at all; it may seem ideal to set our ultimate goal at feeling or being OK across the board, but it denies our most basic freedom of being able to choose how to feel in the face of any external factors. Up to now, we have only looked at how to modify our feelings about our feelings, that is to say, we have only looked at how to change the upper half of the equation the 'Upper Element'.

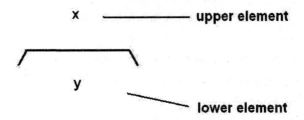

But the Lower Element contains a value 'Judgment' in itself. And though it may be possible to change that, there is sound reasoning behind the choice to operate upon the higher element. The higher element has been chosen because any higher value will necessarily color the Lower Element and also the higher element is more readily and easily changed.

Many people have asked me how they can just ignore something that is not-OK, like physical discomfort for example, but that is not the intention; I am not promoting a form of denial of our preferences, and if we can change the Lower Element situation, then to not do so would be a denial of our freedom also. Enlightened individuals are courageous enough to understand their situation, and are courageous enough to seize their own freedom of choice, whether that is in the World at Large, or within themselves.

The following metaphor will help to illustrate: Imagine a time when the phone rang and you knew who it was (someone you didn't want to speak to) and what they were going to say, so you decided not to pick the phone up. The situation is there, and you are fully aware of it (you know what the content of the telephone conversation will be), but are not fully buying into the whole event. So if *pain* signals (ringing) come from your toe for some reason, it's actually your choice whether it *hurts* (you pick up he receiver) or not. In other words, it is your choice as to whether a situation 'operates upon you' or not.

Outside events in the World at Large (situations) can seem to hold their own inherent values to us. For instance, a cash windfall or a good night's sleep may seem to hold an inherent and obvious OK-ness, as much as a rainy day, or a parking fine, or a bad night's sleep appear to hold an inherent not-OK-ness. The bottom element is not just one element but two: a situation and Judgment about that situation. When I talk of the 'situation' I mean, strictly, the ground level physical facts. This is why we can say that nobody ever encounters a problem or has a problem; instead they are encountering a situation that is operating problematically for them. This is fine as it expresses preferences but that will only be useful as far as they have control over outside events.

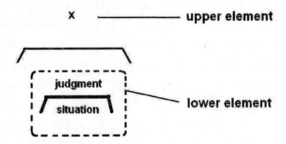

It becomes problematic to try and change the Judgments at the Lower Element level directly because the values and beliefs they reflect are so deep, so taken for granted, so 'unconscious'. It is very difficult, at times, to convince someone that there is no meaning, no essential value, behind the situations they encounter in the world. It can be seen in phobias that physical reactions to any given stimulus (the situation in the world) will happen incredibly quickly, at the behavioral level, before any sense of thinking can intercede. This shows us that the recognition of a situation and its reaction can happen at a level in which we cannot easily intervene; so, even though the Lower Element level has two components, we may as well treat it as a single element. The reaction to a given stimulus may also be seen within yourself as a facial expression. Even when an emotion is not overtly felt by someone, they may infer their reactionary Judgment to a given situation by their own momentary facial expression. These expressions have been shown to be somewhat innate in their meaning across cultures and through time; they are not arbitrary signs to express something, they are part and parcel of the emotion itself. An individual can watch their own expressions, as if from outside, and to some degree observe their reactions to events that are happening before conscious processing has time to intercede at the higher element level. In this way, an individual can become even more self-aware. Care must be taken to correctly infer what that Judgment is actually about. If, for example, I catch myself facially displaying anger for a split second I must consciously guess exactly what that anger is directed at. Is it myself, another, an object, a situation, the transgression of values? Is it something that is happening now, or am I projecting a past event/emotion on to the present? These reactions will very rarely represent a reaction purely to the now. Even in our example of the raspberry-eating cliff faller or the skydiving pig, the bottom element took on a sort of immediate unalterable direction of either OK or not-OK.

The good news is that we can choose how to feel about this at the next level (the Upper Element level) and any other higher level. This can, in time, change our lower 'instinctual' Judgments to situations in the World at Large*. For example, the phobic will have to realize that it's OK to feel anxious before they can hope to start reducing the anxiety at the situational level. 'Anxiety', in this sense, refers to a Judgment at the Lower Element level, namely that a certain cluster of physical symptoms are not-OK.

In the diagram below we can see (in the dotted box) that anxiety at the Lower Element level is really the Judgment or labeling of a given set of value-free physical symptoms that are present in the World at Large. As the Judgment of the physical symptoms is 'anxiety', this means the labeling of the physical symptoms is one of being 'not-OK'.

In the diagram below, the Upper Element is undecided as yet. Should the Upper Element level be chosen to be 'not-OK', there can be no modification of the lower level. Should the upper level be 'OK' then, to begin with, the potentially overwhelming nature of the Lower Element level has been disrupted; the individual is free to see that the physical symptom has been arbitrarily labeled outside of their conscious control. This is ACCEPTANCE.

As multiple experiences of the acceptance level continue, the Judgment of the situation (the physical symptoms) will become less harsh, this is AMELIORATION. Perhaps ANNIHILATION will take place, although this is not guaranteed. The process can be sped up by a number of techniques if you deem it necessary. We've already seen one of these techniques (deconstructing emotions) in chapter 9.

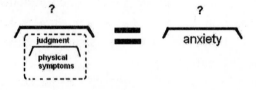

Models of Enlightenment and the Cycle of Want

When I first thought about 'traditional' and popular models of enlightenment (absolute enlightenment), such as the Buddha, I conceived of a being that would find every situation OK in every way. Upon reflection, it seems that to want to, or to attempt to, find everything OK at the lower level is really to hold the opinion that anything else would be less desirable. So Judgments and desires are still taking place, necessitating some distinctions in levels of OK-ness. To feel rich today means that others must be poor and even the recognition that one would judge this situation as not-OK (at the Lower Element) brings in anxiety by the back door.

On my second attempt at finding a model of absolute enlightenment, I imagined a person who could encounter the World at Large (situation) without any values whatsoever.

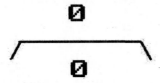

In fact, to be able to encounter the world in a completely value-free way, at the most fundamental level, continuously, may not be desirable, even if it is possible. The odd epiphany accessed by whatever means, in which the veil of projected values is ripped away from the actuality of the physical world outside, is possibly desirable but as a full time prospect it seems a little unrealistic. Things would not happen, stagnation would set in, such a person might be said to be devoid of any personality or sense of self, a drone. Euphoria aside, the epiphany is only a useful experience in so much as we can bring back our learnings to our wood chopping, water carrying, hoovering, cleaning, wanting, shared reality.

The Judgment upon any situation we encounter in the world (the Lower Element) is the deepest expression of our wants. To desire a world in which we would want to have a value-free interpretation of events is, in itself, a position whereby we are really saying we want to have no wants. In other worlds, we value a value-free position. We cannot escape a subjective angle because there is no grand narrative; no absolute interpretation.

The focus of this book is to define and teach a sense of *practical* enlightenment that will work in the real world for real people. I suppose we could call it a sort of relative or pragmatic enlightenment, but to understand that *absolute* enlightenment is impossible, undesirable, or at best impractical is one of the great leaps towards practical enlightenment, in and of itself. *Practical* enlightenment is a realistic and achievable prospect. And, in this sense, is the truest expression of enlightenment.

Unchangeable Responses and the Happiness-Fallacy

We have been talking so far as if all our responses are fluid and within our control but there are a few special cases to be aware of. This is particularly important as an unawareness of these unchangeable responses can lead you into a trap that we call the happiness-fallacy.

We can choose what we value at most levels of deferred meaning, particularly with regard to abstract happenings in the World at Large, or when looking at our own thought processes, but there are two interconnected classes of experience we cannot change the meaning of; the primary reinforcers and the primary emotions. The primary reinforcers (thirst, sex, shelter, and hunger) are reinforcing in and of themselves; they must defer to no other values (except existence itself) as a mandate for their value. The satisfaction of these primary reinforcers is inherently OK and cannot be otherwise, unless there is a conflict of primary reinforcers. The primary reinforcers have an order of immediacy, and it runs -shelter is the most immediate, thirst, hunger then sex. We would not start to think about what to have to eat if a lion was chasing us, would we? Or we wouldn't think about having a drink if we were trapped under the water and suffocating.

The second category is that of primary emotions, and these are fear, anger, sadness, disgust and joy. These emotions happen almost automatically, sometimes unconsciously, and are a direct and very rapid response to outside situations. Fear, sadness, anger and disgust are inherently not-OK and joy is inherently OK.

That is not to say that we cannot feel either OK or not-OK about any of these inherent responses but in and of themselves they are inherently OK or not-OK and this is related to our biological function. They should not be denied.

With regard to the emotions, they are still *post-cognition*, that is to say we must project some cognitive meaning or labeling onto the World at Large before these responses can happen. So if someone rings up on the phone and threatens to kill me in

Chinese I will not feel fear as I have not been able to comprehend the situation (I don't speak that language). If someone points a gun in my face, I feel fear, but if I point a gun at a cat, it does not feel the fear. No event in the World at Large can spark off sadness without your comprehension and your attachments. The point is that if you encounter any of these unchangeable responses, you cannot change it directly, you must simply move to the next level and 'OK' what is happening. Let's take a look at how this works with respect to the primary emotions.

Have a look at the diagram below. At the Lower Element we have a situation in the World at Large along with a Judgment. The Judgment represents our identification of what the situation is and a labeling or meaning that is assigned to that situation. At the middle element an unchangeable response pokes its way in; if it's a primary emotion it is fear, anger, disgust, sadness or joy.

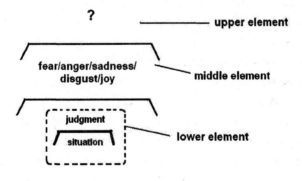

It seem logical to the pre-enlightened individual to try to control the middle element and eliminate disgust/fear/anger/sadness and keep joy there. This is the happiness-fallacy. There are two happiness strategies we would see in this pre-enlightened person:

1. Change the situation in the World at Large (the situation in the lower element).
2. Change the Judgment in the Lower Element.

The first strategy needs no further explanation; the second one will come into play in someone who has, at least, had the realization that it is not the raw situation in the World at Large which defines what they feel. But this person has focused at the wrong level because it is still their desire to permanently install joy at the middle level. We can't control all the situations in the World at Large, and it is very hard to control the Judgments in the Lower Element too. These Judgments lie at the very heart of our preferences, and we cannot have no preferences; we must have some. And even if they could be controlled directly and at will, the Judgments would need to shift as per each new situation. Those who indulge in this second strategy may make untenable demands and say to themselves things like, "this is only a small matter I *should* not be this upset about it," or even "what is wrong with me? I have the big-win/the car/the money/the wife/the children/the health... I should feel happy about this. Why don't I?" These kinds of demands make situations into problems and drive feelings of intolerable frustration. A further likely outcome would be that this person begins to foster some sentiments that are very self in-acceptant.

Now, it is at the Upper Element where we really have control over our peace of mind. Given that we can exercise control, where the question mark is on the diagram above, we can put an OK or a not-OK. However, sometimes, one of the primary emotions may push its way in there and that's fine; this simply means you now have two middle elements. Just concentrate once again on the new Upper Element. It doesn't mater how many middle elements transpire; just keep your eye on the prize - the Upper Element that you can control.

We should never judge ourselves over the initial Judgment at the Lower Element level; it is the knowledge and acceptance of our inability to directly control this Judgment or any resulting unchangeable responses that allows us to exercise control at the Upper Element. It is this acceptance itself that manifests as an OK on the Upper level.

It is not my intention to say that control cannot or should not be exerted at the level of the Judgment; after all, some of the exercises in this book help you to do just that. And as a strategy, it is a useful solution for undesirable reactions (such as a phobia), but it should always come second to the control of the Upper Element (remember Acceptance comes before Amelioration which comes before Annihilation). So control of the Judgments on the lower level can only ever be accessed by exercising control of the Upper Element. To attempt to meddle with the Judgments directly on their own level is akin to the CEO of a company trying to run it from the postal room. To recognize that peace of mind comes from exercising the control we *do* have at the Upper Element, and not the control we *don't* have lower down, is how we escape the happiness-fallacy. Happiness, or more accurately, 'peace of mind' is feeling OK about *what is*, not uninterrupted Joy.

And remember that those Judgments at the Lower Element level, that are directly related to our bodily integrity and which drive many of primary reinforcers and emotions, will be very resistant to change. And even then, they could only be inauthentically tampered with through an extreme and unuseful asceticism (the denial of the body's drives and needs). Asceticism springs from beliefs that the body's functions are not-OK and then the belief about that; namely, it is a not-OK situation.

Inversed Status Seeking

The enlightenment seeker who prizes some notion of *absolute enlightenment* makes the second error, through cognitive dissonance, as they seek to arrive at an endpoint; wrongly conceiving enlightenment to be a journey towards some final and perfect destination. Enlightenment is a process and it is re-indoctrinated from second to second. Enlightenment is as compatible with shallow concerns as it is with the deeper; the awareness of a kind of soft-authenticity is paramount. One might imagine the Sufi in his lion cloth, having cast off all other material concerns in order to become enlightened, yet to some degree his extremism has just brought him a kind of inversed status seeking. This is similar to inverse snobbery, where one receives status through their lack of status. The denial of any materialism, of 'shallow' concerns, is still a want for a strange sort of more:

More of less:

The denial of any material goods makes those goods conspicuous in their absence.
Imagine the two monks on the hill.
Monk 1: "I have given away everything, except this simple cloak."
Monk 2: "So have I, but my cloak is smaller."

A brand of car, at the moment, is being marketed as a brand for those who aren't really into badges and status symbols, just level headed people with something better to worry about. Now to me, that sounds very like a brand proposition in itself. The badge itself now says "I don't care about what this badge says about me."

The Myth of the Self is deriving a high status out of a seeming denial of status itself, or maybe even an identity out of a lack of identity. Even if you are trying to drop to the bottom of the slippery pole instead of climbing to the top, you are still on the slippery pole. What should we hope for then? Try to get to the middle? No that's just another pole in a different direction! Hop off the pole then? No that's another pole too! It's poles, poles, poles, in every direction, as far as the eye can see, each as slippery as the last.

Monk 1: "Our enlightenment wouldn't be so enlightening if it wasn't for all the un-enlightened folk running around down there."
Monk 2: "I don't care about enlightenment as much as you, comparing yourself to others. I've realized that isn't the right

way and that's what makes me more enlightened than you."

Monk 1: "Are not."

Monk 2: "Am so."

The metaphor of the slippery pole is about competition with other people and even competition for the power to define what the winning position looks like. Be just as wary that you don't start to compete with your past and future selves, as you find that letting go of the idea of success or failure in enlightenment is the not-wrong path.

Worry by all means because someone, even yourself maybe, has been able to let go of failure and success a bit more than you!

Did I mention that it's poles, poles, poles, as far as the eye can see?

---

* These judgments are the very expression of our preferences and this is how our preferences can change.

Chapter 17

Beliefs: Rebuilding your map of your world

It takes two to tango.
Popular Idiom

We have already learned much about our choice in interpreting (creating) the meaning of external events, and now we will discover the exact mechanism by which this comes into being. As you begin to understand what dictates how different people are affected differently by the same outside events, the means by which you can begin to rest control away from the chance of your past conditioning will become clearer.

I am sure you are familiar with the phrase "he/she/it is pushing my buttons." The idea of 'pressing our buttons' brings to mind images of switches or buttons that people (or external events) can come along and operate, and then we are powerless to resist some given course of action or reaction.

Below, you can see the notation I have borrowed from electronics for a closed switch (pushed button) and an open switch. As you can see, the information, the direction of which is denoted by the arrow, will only flow across a closed switch.

Switches

open

closed

For example, if I felt compelled to defend my ego every time anyone intimates that I am a little thick, people would have a direct path to initiate the defence mechanisms of the Myth of the Self. Someone might just hint that I am acting a bit stupidly and I would go into my autopilot responses. In the first diagram below the switch at 1 is open; this represents no particular signal coming in. The self/world perimeter represents my perceived interface between the outside world and myself. Think of the self/world perimeter in the diagrams below as the boundary between what happens in the World at Large and what happens within us. We will see how we can easily become confused about exactly where this boundary truly lies.

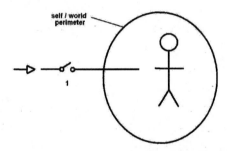

Now below, we can see that the switch at 1 has been closed. This represents the fact that someone has called me thick, and this gets to me at a personal level. Someone has 'pushed my button' and I react. However, the situation below only represents how I feel the world to be when I allow outside events to affect me. The

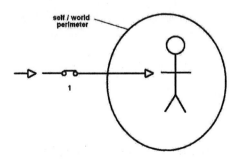

switches are outside my control; after all, I cannot directly control whether people call me thick or not.

In actual fact, as soon as I take response-ability for my own beliefs, the situation is really more like the diagram below. The event can come at me when the switch at 1 is closed, yet I really have another switch by which I can control things. If I am not aware of the switch at 2, my position looks like the diagram above; if I become aware of the switch at 2, my position looks like the diagram below. If I refuse to operate the switch at 2, it may as well not be there and my position is, by my own choice, through inaction, equivalent to the diagram below with switch 2 locked closed.

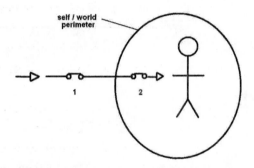

If you are distressed by any external thing (1), it is not this thing which disturbs you, but your own judgment about it (2). And it is in your power wipe out that judgment now.
Marcus Aurelius

I may not be able to affect the outside environment but I can still change the effect the environment has on me. As in the diagram below, if the switch at 1 is either open or closed, it makes no difference because I have opened the switch at 2. I have effectively prevented my buttons being pressed by elements outside myself. I have brought my own buttons inside my control.

This switch (2) does not change what has happened in the world, or even my conscious awareness that is has happened, but

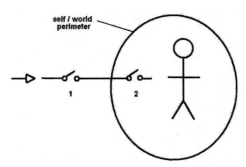

it does change the meaning I give to the situation as it comes in at me. In our example, switch 2 opening is the equivalent of me realising there is no need for a strong and defensive reaction. Perhaps I have come about this new belief through another belief, such as the realisation that the person insulting me has no great validity. Perhaps I no longer feel the need to push forward the Myth of the Self. Perhaps I now begin see an inflation of the Myth of the Self as compensation for some inadequacy or perceived inadequacy

It does not really matter to us here so much about the content of that belief change because this is just one example. What really matters is the realisation that external events can really only affect us in particular ways if we let them, and we let them by holding rigid, unexamined beliefs.

Now a lot of these beliefs will be held outside of consciousness and can be seen only in our behavior. These are the *behavioral beliefs* we discussed in earlier chapters. You can only uncover these beliefs by examining your behavior. You can't perceive them directly. We can't see wind, but we can see its effects in flags and trees in much the same way.

So if a traffic jam 'winds me up', I am holding some 'just-world hypothesis', or some sort of 'easy-world hypothesis', roughly along the lines that: "I should not have to be inconvenienced because that isn't fair and the world should be fair."

If I can affect the world situation (i.e. find a short cut, use a motorbike or make the journey outside rush hour) I am operating switch 1. If I find myself well and truly stuck in that jam, however, I am forced to resort to operating switch 2 by examining and disputing my beliefs.

Multiple Belief Chains

Of course, there are many occasions where one belief is dependent on another. So, for example, if a person holds the behavioral belief that they should get angry whenever someone shows them contempt. First 'contempt' has to be detected and this brings into question what constitutes contempt, or indeed any situation that anyone attempts to detect. If you want to detect a given situation, first you need to have some criteria that must be met. The 'criteria' is the evidence that you are looking for to tell you something is happening or has happened. For example, if you park your car in a no-parking bay and then worry that you may have got a parking ticket then, as you return to the car, you look at the windscreen for a small rectangular object. This is the criteria that will answer the question: "have I got a parking ticket?" Simple!

Now what criteria would you use to detect whether someone was showing you contempt? Well, for a start, if someone calls you stupid, then you can pretty much deduct that they hold you in contempt; easy! But there are many other ways that you could deduct, rightly or wrongly, that someone is expressing contempt towards you. One possibility is that when you see someone looking at you with a certain facial expression (a lob sided smile perhaps), then you interpret this as him or her showing you contempt. So an initial belief comes into play to dictate what constitutes contempt and a second belief comes into play to dictate what the response to receiving contempt should be – in this case, it's anger.

Now the point here is that any behavioral responses revolve around beliefs that could have been otherwise, yet if those beliefs remain fixed through ignorance or the denial of the freedom to change them, this creates the illusion that all your buttons are on the outside. This is the mechanism by which external events *appear* to exert an effect on our feelings and our behavior. In fact, this will only happen if we choose to allow it to happen.

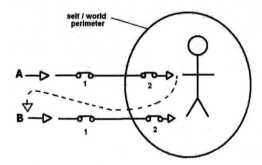

If we stay with the example of the person who responds to contempt with anger in the above diagram:

A1 = Facial expression of other person
A2 = Belief that governs the meaning assigned to A1
B1 = Perception of incoming contempt
B2 = Belief that contempt needs an anger response

Switch A1 is closed, so this is the facial expression of someone looking at our person.

Switch A2 is closed; this is the belief that that facial expression equals contempt (this is actually a social hallucination; this person has gone inside to assign meaning to outside events. They are not keeping their sensory channels clean because they are not just observing outside phenomena; they are going inside their head to label it.)

So as both A1 and A2 are closed, this person *believes* they have been shown contempt. At this point, the B line comes into play; at B1 contempt is, right or wrongly, perceived to be incoming. At B2 is the belief that incoming contempt deserves a response of anger.

These two lines may be operating entirely out of conscious awareness though, and in this case:

At line A, contempt may be perceived as 'out there coming in at me'.

At line B, contempt requires a response of anger - this may well be unquestioned and so obvious in that it is perceived almost as a universal law.

In short, this individual has missed two opportunities to short-circuit what, for them, may really be a response with undesirable consequences. They have perceived the situation in only one way and responded to that perception in only one way. This leads them to feel as if they are being 'attacked' from the outside.

Someone or something has 'pushed their buttons'. <u>This person has willingly (though maybe not fully consciously) given away all their freedom of interpretation and action.</u>

The individual in question could not control the facial expression being directed at them, yet, in their interpretation of that facial expression (at A2), they have determined what happens at B1. So the incoming contempt at B1 is an illusion as much as it lies outside the self/world perimeter.

In the diagram below we can see that, when the individual recognises and accepts his/her own freedom of response to a given situation, the perimeter of what is within and outside one's control looks a little different.

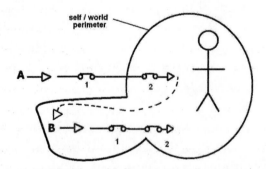

In the diagram above, switch A2 and B1 will both be open or closed at the same time as each other, essentially making them the same switch, giving us the situation below. B1 has disappeared, as it was entirely governed by A2 which is inside the control of the person, inside the self/world perimeter.

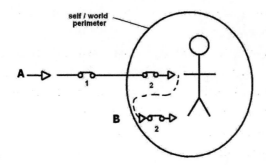

Awareness of control at A2 would certainly lead to a more accurate social interpretation and self awareness. Whilst freedom of control can be exerted at A2, this may conflict with the shared truths of living in a society with others, and a denial of the 'facts' may be a move towards a certain kind of inauthenticity and, at the extreme end, would result in this person not being able to operate in a shared world with others in their society. We are free to deny that something is happening but it will not be a good strategy in many circumstances. If, in this case, a vague suspicion or paranoia is operating it may be desirable to exert control at A2, but if the signs that someone is showing you contempt are undeniable then authenticity requires you recognise it. A reasonably accurate interpretation of events at A2 may force recognition of the situation but it, in no way, prescribes any action. This leaves us with the freedom of control exerted at B2. B2, in our case here, is actually a belief intended to defend the Myth of the Self, i.e. that anger is the response to incoming contempt. We might say the ego is struggling to defend itself against an attack it perceives as a threat to its integrity. This belief that contempt deserves anger will most likely rest on other deeper beliefs regarding the sanctity of the Myth of the Self.

In this chapter we have seen the 'buttons' model explained

using the variables of contempt, anger and facial expression, but it can be extended to any situation you find yourself in, whether that situation includes other people or not. In fact, the model can be expanded to any number of chained beliefs. If, in our above example, the individual had correctly identified contempt on the A line, there may have been an intervening belief governing where that contempt is perceived to be directed.

If you saw someone looking at you and you had correctly identified contempt upon their face, you may have overlooked the fact that that person is looking at someone behind you. The person showing contempt may even be in Downtime and contempt-ing themselves as they replay an internal film of that joke they had told minutes ago that went down like a lead balloon. If you had delayed your anger response and had watched closer you may, for example, have seen them looking past you, or the glassy thousand-yard stare in their eye as they actually looked straight through you (a good indicator of Downtime). One area where the outside/inside confusion operates particularly pertinently is that of stress. How often is it perceived as 'coming-in' from outside when, in fact, it is internally generated according to one's preferences and then projected onto the World at Large?

Much discomfort in life comes from confusion between what is within one's power and what is not. We could blame ourselves for things outside our control or make demands about the weather, or we could refuse to accept our freedom and become victims of things we think we cannot control (when in fact we can). An understanding of what is inside and what is outside this boundary is a very good starting place for authenticity. A reasonable strategy seems to be that you should first assume you can control everything then start experimenting to either prove or refute this assumption. We might call this 'reality testing'; it's a chance for us to test the maps of reality we carry around in our heads for accuracy. As you discover things that are not within your power to change, you can still exercise your freedom to choose how you respond to any given situation.

Examining your Beliefs

Everywhere, and at all times, it is in your power to accept reverently your present condition, to behave justly to those about you, and to exert your skill to control your own thoughts, that nothing shall steal into them without being examined.
Marcus Aurelius

Be brave in finding, examining and, if desired, changing beliefs of any kind, whether they are explicit or behavioral. There are some questions you might ask yourself that will help in this endeavour:

Is this belief justified? (Does it fit with the facts? Are there any other beliefs that could fit with the facts? Are the facts 'correct'?)

Does the belief make sense? (Are you 'socially hallucinating'? Are you giving meaning to something that isn't really there? Are you interpreting the incoming sensory data correctly?)

Does this belief rest on other beliefs? (If so, examine them. What other beliefs do I need to hold to keep this one in place?)

Is this belief useful for me? (Does it get you what you want? Do you know what you want? Do you want contrary things? If so, you are operating out of two different levels of values at the same time and that is the cause of internal conflict.)

What values underpin this belief?

Who does this belief serve?

If you did not have this belief, how would it affect the Myth of the Self? (Is this belief operating usefully in keeping the myth alive, but operating undesirably on the ground level?)

Is this belief too extreme or rigid? (Why?)

Do you believe a belief can be changed? (We have different words in English for feelings and beliefs because they are two different things. Remember a lot of beliefs exist in our behavior. Can you 'fake it 'till you make it', by behaving differently and acting as if your explicit beliefs were different?)

Do you believe a belief should be held because it reflects some 'grand truth', or because it is useful?

Are the beliefs that this belief rests upon imbued with an implicit sense of 'entitlement' or reaction against what is actually the case? (Do any of your beliefs have demands, needs, 'musts' or 'shoulds' contained within them? If so, you are making a map/territory distinction confusion and expecting the world to change to fit in with your interpretations, not the other way around. You are always free to interpret meaning in what you find in the world, but not always free to alter what is found. Be aware of the two types of 'should': one is a demand – "It *should* stop raining"; the other a preference – "I *should* find an umbrella".

There are three musts that hold us back I must do well. You must treat me well. And the world must be easy.
Albert Ellis

To change overt cognitive beliefs (explicit beliefs) takes evidence or intention.

To change behavioral beliefs requires action.

To swap between contrasting beliefs is an inauthentic position if we believe there has to be a single truth out there. However, if we prefer to assign beliefs on the basis of usefulness instead of demanding that they must reflect some underlying truth (and know that knowledge of our inauthenticity on one level is, itself, an authentic position on another level) then we embrace a new freedom. We can be fluid in our beliefs.

Consider this position: you are on the back of a motorbike and the driver is driving fast. You can choose to opt into a temporary belief in fatalism (whatever will be, will be). In understanding that the control of the motorbike is outside of *your* control, anxiety is allayed. But a belief in fatalism, once you are in the driver's seat, would be a dangerous practice[*], however. So when you are driving, a full embrace of your freedom to control the bike is desirable, anxiety (or concern at least) will be present. The anxiety, handled properly, helps to keep you safe. <u>Where there is freedom there will be anxiety, but where there is anxiety there need not necessarily be discomfort</u>. The passenger who buys into the beliefs of no freedom of control is exerting control over their own beliefs; there is always freedom at some level so what appears to be an inauthentic position is actually authentic at the pragmatic level.

* In countries where there are a lot of people who buy into beliefs of reincarnation and fatalism one can expect horrendous accident rates on the road – and this is what we do see.

Chapter18

Just a Moment: Weakening your attachment to time

There is more to life than increasing its speed.
Mahatma Gandhi

How long is a moment?

The short answer is: the same size as a piece of string. Time and space are really the same 'substance'; we know this from relativity theory, and so a small spatially based metaphor will serve our purposes.

Imagine you and a small child are standing on the platform at the train station and a train passes, for you maybe the whole train is a single object but for the child each carriage may be conceptualised as one single object. Perhaps, because you see only the similarity between one carriage and the next you chunk them all together in your mind, but the child may have sorted for differences – that one is green, that one is short, that one is dirtier. The child has experienced the train as a collection of many objects whereas you have experienced it as only one.

Well not only does this apply to spatial concepts but it also applies to time-based concepts. The child has experienced many 'moments' during the passing of that train, whilst you have only experienced one, and the point is this:

Our perceived sense of time, during any event passing, is based not on actual clock time but on the amount of 'moments' we impose upon the World at Large. We are using here the term 'moment' to denote the psychological unit of perceived time.

To make biological survival possible, Mind at Large has to be funneled through the reducing valve of the brain and nervous system. What comes

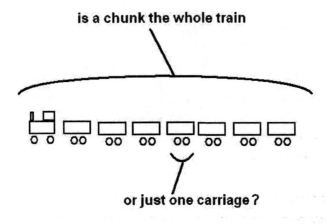

is a chunk the whole train

or just one carriage?

out at the other end is a measly trickle of the kind of consciousness which will help us to stay alive on the surface of this particular planet. To formulate and express the contents of this reduced awareness, man has invented and endlessly elaborated those symbol-systems and implicit philosophies which we call languages. Every individual is at once the beneficiary and the victim of the linguistic tradition into which he or she has been born — the beneficiary inasmuch as language gives access to the accumulated records of other people's experience, the victim in so far as it confirms in him the belief that reduced awareness is the only awareness and as it be-devils his sense of reality, so that he is all too apt to take his concepts for data, his words for actual things.
Aldous Huxley

Aldous Huxley suggests that we all have a 'reality reducing valve' in our perceptual apparatus; this 'valve' acts more like a filter; it reduces the complexity of the incoming stimulus to a level that our finite brains can cope with and so we get only the information that is most important to us. This reducing filter reduces the 'resolution' of reality for us in order to help us cope with the world in much the same way we might reduce the resolution of a photograph in order to more easily and quickly send it across the finite bandwidth of our internet connection. The modes of action of this reducing filter are that it distorts, deletes and generalizes the information coming in. In fact, there is not just one filter, there are many filters in this Huxley valve, and they have been shaped mostly through experiences in our life. The filters have been shaped to reduce information flowing into the consciousness, to allow only the most pertinent information through. For us as social animals, 'pertinent information' will naturally include information relevant to survival and the perception of an agreed social reality*, and may, therefore, predispose us to take agreed social truths as absolute facts. It appears that, in far more dangerous situations than we generally live in today, this filter has evolved to keep us alive. It may be a sad situation, but it is much more important to our survival to be aware of immediate problems than the things which are going well for us with a degree of constancy. In light of this, is it any surprise that many people experience their life mainly through a series of problems or crises? Some people may filter their reality to the degree that problems and crises are actively created in order to bolster the Myth of the Self's existence, this too is a survival mechanism to some degree, as it seems the Myth of the Self may have been a benefit for our survival at one time. It could be argued that, outside extreme survival or warlike situations, in the present day, this process of the mind is somewhat obsolete. Because the Myth of the Self needs stimulation and seeks its own survival as a 'psychic structure' the Huxley valve in each of us may have long ago become biased to disproportionately filter out many 'good'

Huxley valve

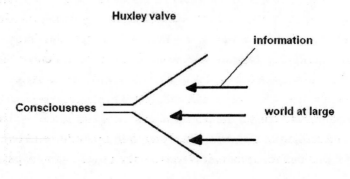

220

happenings, especially those that are around us with a degree of constancy. This process can lead to a kind of 'ungratefulness', where we take things for granted, and plays a large part in creating 'ordinary moments'.

As we get older and we become more habituated to the world and our surroundings, this valve maybe become smaller and smaller, so an adult can write off the passing of a train as a single experience whereas a young child can experience the delights and complexity of each carriage individually. A child experiences the world more phenomenologically (that is to say, the child projects much less meaning and order on what they perceive and so experience things more authentically). The adult, generally, takes much larger perceptual chunks which means they may be able to manipulate more variables and appear more sophisticated, yet for this they sacrifice the immediacy of the child's perception. This creates a distance, an alienation one might call it, between the World at Large and one's perceived reality. This loss of 'perceptual resolution' naturally means there is a reduction in the quality of the adult's experience. Many people may see their sophistication and 'worldly-wise', multi-tasking ennui as a badge of honour or identity, on the other hand, these assessments may be more of a case of sour grapes.

When our Huxley valve is narrow, the larger our perceptual gulps become, the more extensively these perceptual filters are hiding the world from us, and this means the authentic life slips away a little more. In our example of the train, the perceptual filter used by the adult was *sorting for similarity* whilst the child *sorted for difference* amongst the same experience; this is one of many filters that operate within us all. It is the action of these filters that dictate how each of our 'Huxley valves' is set up. To understand how we can affect change over them, let's look at the way our mind creates the perceptions of time and space. Whilst a full discussion of all of the filters and their operation and nature is beyond our remit here, it is worth noting that language pays a large part in the operation and creation of these filters (in Neuro Linguistic Programming, these filters are known as meta-filters).

When we label, we abstract our experience and so put more 'distance' between ourselves and the World at Large, this applies not only to linguistic labelling but to any way in which we seek to represent things through language or symbolism. When we categorise a feeling it becomes an emotion; when we name a colour or a taste it removes us a step further; when we sort cars, butterflies people, etc. into groups our taxonomy masquerades as inherent order 'out there' in the World at Large. As each of these ways of chopping, sorting and representing the world solidifies into a 'Grand Narrative', other equally valid possibilities drop out of our awareness to be replaced by dogma. Bit by bit the representation of each 'thing' (for want of a better word) becomes, and replaces, the 'thing' itself and this can happen to the degree that the entire 'thing-in-itself' is encapsulated wholly by our representation of it. And so on those occasions, we mistake the map for the territory.

The lack of tolerance for the discomfort of the usual, the known, the recognised, is illustrated by the hero of Sartre's Nausea when he encounters the world directly and not through his filters. Roquentin throws words at the objects around him, yet finds they will not stick to the objects (in fact, the very boundaries of the 'objects' are not even constant), and this gives him a great sense of 'fear and trembling'. This 'vertigo of meaning' fills him with fear because he cannot find it OK to be unusual or uncomfortable; the fear comes not from the experience so much as his beliefs about the experience. His beliefs regarding the experience stem largely from a decision somewhere to hold that: 'it's not-OK to be not-OK'. Roquentin's experience shows us that barriers to a more direct and authentic experience (in the form of fear asserted by the Myth of the Self) will persist until one accepts that: <u>It's OK to be not-OK!</u>

The Time Vista

Coming back to our Planet X model, you'll remember that our seven sprites represent the contents of our conscious awareness, and in the diagram below, you can see that if our points of awareness are spread thinly and stretched across more of the past and future, then each moment we experience will be a larger chunk, taking up more clock time. The term 'time vista' denotes the 'width' of our time perception; the very extent to which we 'look forwards and backwards'. When one has a wide time vista (towards the bottom of the diagram below), one experiences a large moment and a lower *time resolution*.

time vista

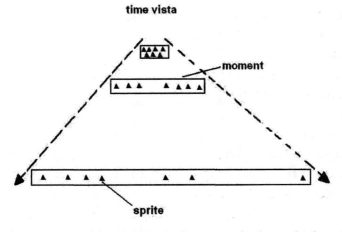

The important thing to note is that not only does a higher time resolution give more quality and authenticity to our experience, it actually extends our experience of time, so the more moments we experience the richer and longer our perception is. In the diagram below, you will see on the top band, where the Huxley valve is wider, more moments are produced in a given length of clock time. On the lower band the Huxley valve is narrower and the incoming information is being screened through more social and survival-based filters.

The operation of the valve is not simply narrow or wide; there are many shades of grey in between and there must always be some filters (some 'frames') through which our view of the world is interpreted, so it can never be 100% open or 100% closed. The widening of one's Huxley valve would, in practical terms, be a switch to a much 'looser' set of filters, leading to a more direct form of experience. We can never really perceive the World at Large face to face (i.e. with no filters), but this loosening of perceptual frames at least represents a move closer to direct perception of the World at Large (a move closer to the widest opening of the valve).

Each style of perceiving has its draw backs and benefits, and pre-enlightened people operate mainly in the social/survival mode (narrower valve) and not many can even chose how wide they would like this valve. How much better would it be if we could choose how strongly this valve operated whenever we wanted? And the good news is that we can do this, but not by our direct intention.

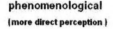

phenomenological
(more direct perception)

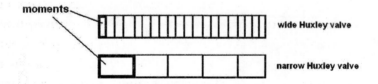

moments

wide Huxley valve

narrow Huxley valve

deleted, distorted and generalised
(more survival and socially biased percetion)

The diagram below demonstrates how people's perception generally changes as they get older. This speeding up of subjective time as we get older is a trend not a necessity. In the diagram, the age groups and moment sizes are nominal and are here just to give a flavour of the average movement towards larger moments (larger chunk sizes of space and time) during the aging process.

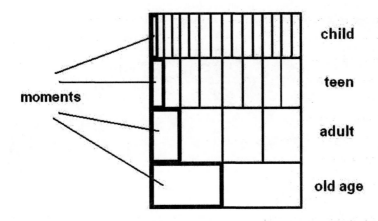

However, even this model has some shortcomings; it is not very often we actually experience moments as jumping from one to the next; although this does happen under certain circumstances which we will come to in a while. More often when we experience a continuous flow of conscious awareness the time vista moves – much like the frame of a film during a panning shot – allowing new information to flow in and old information to flow out bit by bit, not all in one go. Despite the fact that our seven bits of attention jump discretely** from one object of attention to another, most of the time this doesn't happen with all seven bits jumping all at once. Normally, as the seven bits of our attention jump from one thing to another, this takes place in a staggered way giving some overlap. And this is the mechanism by which our brains engage a kind of 'dampening-effect', giving us the experience of a continuity of perception instead of a series of discrete 'pulses'. This same dampening-effect can be seen when we perceive the twenty-five frames per second of a film or TV as a continuous smooth movement.

This can be modelled by likening it to the way blocks were moved around on rollers made of logs in olden times. The rollers from the back are picked up and placed further in front of the block (see diagrams below). There are always some rollers supporting the block. Imagine the rollers here to be the seven bits of information we can hold in our conscious awareness.

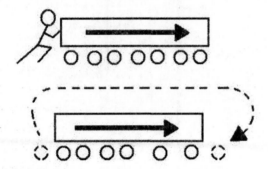

The relative length of each block represents the width of one's time vista, so in the diagram below we see the depiction of a larger time vista than in the two diagrams above. Each roller, as they get spaced out, is taking more weight and providing less support for the block as a whole.

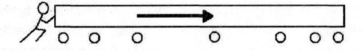

If we were workers pushing blocks around, we would space out the rollers more widely in order to support longer blocks, yet in our actual cognitive processes, the reverse is true. Imagine that the blocks actually expand and contract in response to changes in the spacing of the rollers. In this model, the spacing of the rollers defines the block size, not the other way around.

To bring this back into our model of consciousness, we can say that each individual bit (or 'sprite') of the seven bits of our conscious awareness itself has a time vista, represented by the

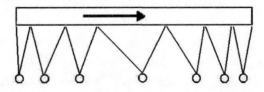

spacing of the rollers here. The combined time vistas of each bit of our conscious awareness makes up the time vista we experience.

Let me add in one more modification to this model; in the roller model, as it would be in a real life 'ye-olde' building site, the rollers would operate on a 'first-in, last-out' basis, where each roller pops out the back of the block in the same order they went in. The actual movement or our sprites (i.e. our bits of conscious awareness) is not constrained by this rule. If you were to watch a man pushing a block where the rollers could sort of swap places and shuffle around underneath the block, this would more closely represent what is happening in the actual cognitive processes transpiring in our minds. The Unseen Watcher controls movement of the rollers and the width of the spacing of the rollers; that is to say, it controls the time vista of each of the seven bits of our conscious awareness.

As explained before, however, The Unseen Watcher's habits are outside of our direction but can be conditioned indirectly through the use of the exercises in this book. The default width of your Huxley valve differs according to many factors and it can be modified through the exercises in this book, but not directly through conscious will.

The roller model helps us to understand the rolling nature of moments and, as stated before, most of the time we do not experience ourselves as jumping from one moment to the next but there are times when this can happen.

One of the times this can happen is when our entire capacity of awareness, all of our seven bits (our sprites) are directed at one mind object. This can happen in either Uptime or Downtime as shown below.

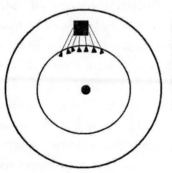

Here we see all the sprites collecting on the edge of the boundary to direct their cameras at one object of attention. This could be the ultimate in uptime. The entire content of awareness for this persons mind is a single object, so there is a complete lack of any self consciousness at all. This maybe 'the zone'.

Planet X

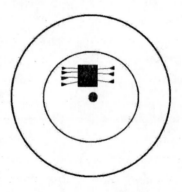

 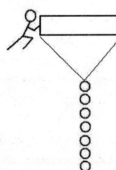

In our roller model, these times might look something like the diagram **left**. Notice how the size of moment may differ, yet on these occasions all the seven bits of our conscious awareness share the same time vista – a time vista only one moment wide.

During these occasions, the experience of the passing of time (from one moment to the next) can appear to no longer operate, although, as we can see from the diagrams above, a time vista still operates to define the size of that single moment. In this moment, that can feel like an 'ever present now'; the sense of self can also disappear. The individual experiencing this will not always feel an instant jump (although this can happen) into or out of this state, but once in the midst of it, the individual always feels no connection to the previous moment(s) or the coming moment(s).

Another occasion where someone may feel a moment to be singular and not flowing is when, all of a sudden, all seven bits of conscious attention are diverted elsewhere (whether that be to a single mind object or not). So, in our roller example, if we imagined a block and its rollers completely disappearing and reappearing somewhere else then this jump has taken place and the preceding moment is experienced as discrete and separate from the moment afterwards. On Planet X we would see this as every sprite abandoning its object(s) of attention and finding another object(s) elsewhere. All is that is required is that seven new objects of attention are suddenly focused upon by the sprites. It does not matter whether the Sprites focus on the same object or seven separate objects (or any combination in between). In reality, such a sudden jump would be most likely caused by a very novel stimulus or emergency.

The 'startle response', in reaction to a loud bang, would be a perfect example of when this kind of process would happen. A similar one would be to find one's self suddenly falling into ice cold water; all of the seven sprites (the seven bits of our conscious attention) would suddenly rush to Uptime-kinesthetic as we become instantly aware of the cold on our skin. The depressed or anxious, the paranoid or discontented individual would lose their 'dysfunction' during this moment of immediate redirection of attention. This is exactly what happened to the depressed man

229

when he dropped a brick on his foot.

So to be clear, we should approach some formal definitions of the terms 'moment' and 'time vista'.

<u>Moment</u>: any length of time where the contents of consciousness remain unchanged. In practice, the subjective feeling of discrete moments is rare as the contents of consciousness will change on a rolling basis, as expressed in the 'rolling moment' model.

<u>Time vista</u>: the 'width' of our time perception at any given moment. If the seven bits of conscious awareness spread widely into the past and future, we will experience the moment as being large or wide, but if the entire contents are located entirely at one point in time we will experience a 'timeless moment'. The time vista operates as a type of buffer that plays a part in the creation of meaning by creating causation and continuity, even during all (but the most absolute) Uptime. This time vista is reflected in how 'wide' or how long we perceive the rolling moment to be, even as we live it.

TOTES and Moments

A third condition, where we might like to model moments as being discrete and jumping from one to the next, would be when someone is running very strong TOTEs. Although in this instance the actual individual is less likely to actually feel the jumps from one moment to the next.

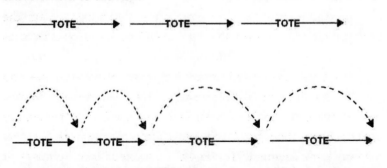

The jump form one TOTE to the next separates moments as we

are largely 'unaware' during the running of a TOTE, so it's the gaps in between that act as moments for our conscious awareness. A learner driver, for example, with very small TOTEs for the actions needed to drive, would experience far more moments (and so a different subjective speed of passing time) than would the experienced driver. So, we can see that the breaking of established TOTEs, or the acquisition of new TOTEs whilst one is learning a new behavior, are situations whereby one's Huxley valve is operating somewhat more widely. This means that there are two ways to widen the Huxley valve: 1. Engage in new and novel experiences; this is good but it's hardly a long term strategy because the experiences will begin to become familiar and very ordinary. You will build up larger TOTEs and create ordinary moment out of experiences which were once novel. Like Toad of Toad Hall, you'll have to forever keep jumping from one interest to the next.

2. Break larger existing TOTEs into more numerous smaller TOTEs; we've already covered how to do that in the chapter on TOTEs.

In the discussion of TOTEs, so far, we have only discussed behavioral-TOTEs; the expression of TOTEs in external bodily behavior. If we take thoughts to be 'internal behavior', an unbroken chain of thought is a 'thought-TOTE'. If left unchecked and unbroken, these TOTEs will grow larger and more 'unwieldy***' as one goes over the same old ground; the same old thoughts. Our adult on the train station platform enters the 'identify the train as a single object' TOTE, whereas the child does not.

Even if they originate in other forms, we often formalize and express our thoughts (to ourselves as well as others) in words. Just as we can become entrenched through longer behavioral TOTEs, these 'thought-TOTEs' show the same patterns. We may take on large linguistic TOTEs in the form of stock phrases or words that seem to make up a large amount of our external (and internal) speech: "Basically dude, at the end of the day, it's like 'yeah whatever', you know what I mean, yeah?" Conversely, some authors and speakers like to break up phrases or sentences in order to draw our attention to the sometimes unquestioned meanings behind words; two perennial favourites are 'dis-ease' and 'his-story'. This word-fracture effectively invites us to break the thought-TOTEs of our words.

Moments and Events

Event: the subjective projection of a boundary (or 'outline') onto a given length of time that makes it into a discrete mind-object.

Our discussion of moments has, so far, been about micro-time units; the experience of time at-that-time. Strictly speaking, of course, all time perception is retrospective; that is to say, we can only judge time when looking back at it. Yet there are times when an experience can seem to last for a long time, but in retrospect, it seemed to have whizzed by. To explain this we have macro-time units or 'Events'. Whilst *moments* mostly roll and only rarely jump, *events* are discrete in our mind and jump. Often huge gaps between pertinent events have been edited out – these gaps will be full of 'everyday mundane' activities that have little pertinence or novelty (according to one's arbitrary and subjective constellation of frames) and so are, therefore, not really remembered in any meaningful way because there is nothing to make these experiences stand out. This is especially true of repetitive activities.

On a longer-term basis we chunk our lived time, not into moments or clock time but as 'events'. For example, a night in one bar may be one event, but a bar crawl might be seen by us to be several events. And these events seem to group together to make larger events the further in the past it was. So the day after a wedding we might remember the breakfast, the church, the disco, the meal etc. all as separate events. A year after the wedding, the events have all been clumped together in our mind into the one event – 'the wedding'. As we clump more numerous smaller events into less numerous larger events, the time we look back on seems to shrink. We psychologically measure perceived 'living-in time' as moments, not clock time, and we measure longer-term lived time in events, not clock time. So as we look back at a few years ago, the resolution of those memories becomes lower (on average). Yet if we compare the known and constant measure of clock time against this ever increasing compression of perceived lived time, we may think to ourselves – "My god! Was the wedding really three years ago? Time has flown by," and this can give us the impression that time is flying by so fast that we are speeding to the grave. The further we look back, as a general rule, the more we have clumped many smaller events into fewer larger events and, as we look back at fewer events, so the time seems compressed.

This will only happen when are stuck in Downtime looking backwards though, and the enlightened individual, who is in the present place and moment, will not have this experience. Similar drifts of time can occur when we drop into Downtime to imagine the future and, accordingly, we ration out our own future in 'events' which, according to certain biases in thinking, can appear too long away from, or too near to, the present moment.

Continuity

Further distortions of moments and events can occur with regard to the continuity of moments and events. If a moment or event naturally leads from one to the next (like a story that makes sense) they can be easily arranged, but during extreme, abstract or nonsensical experiences (where one struggles to encode and make meaning of events) the continuity is difficult to maintain. To illustrate, imagine you were, as an experiment, sitting in a room and listening to numbers being counted out (there are no clocks in the room) and then asked later to judge how long you had been there. There are three conditions:

In the first condition you just hear:
1,1,1,1,1,1,1,1,1,1,1,1,1,1,1,1,1,1,1,... And so on.
In the second condition you just hear:
1,2,3,4,5,6,7,8,9,10,11, 12, 13, 14, 15... And so on.

In the third condition you just hear:
1,67,63,178,12,15,7,88,910,10,23, 444, 987, 4, 50, 23... And so on
(these are just random numbers).

You can imagine how your perception of time passing would be dictated by the continuity and novelty of the numbers. Your perception of time passing at-the-time and after the event will be affected by different variables.

The Narrative of the Self

The speed of time is relative to how strong and separate our ego is.
Steve Taylor

The Myth of the Self requires an adequate narrative that extends both forward and backwards in time; for these reasons, the Myth of the Self often compels us to send our awareness forward or backward, to other scenarios, or to simulations of other minds to gather verification of its existence. This is analogous to the constant assurance-seeking behavior manifested as the demands for certainly we see in people; this requires a position of 'it's not-OK to be not-OK' to persist.

In cases where people have retrograde amnesia, having no past story of who they are, they have less of a narrative from which to draw upon in knowing what to think and how to react to situations. With less information to draw upon to tell them 'who to be', we would see a corresponding drop in the strength of the personality. This produces anxiety and installs a great desire to find out who they are, or to quickly create a sense of identity; one that can inform them how to act, what to like, what to hate and so on. Of course, the older you are, generally speaking, the more time you've had to build up this narrative and the more entrenched this is likely to be. This correlates with the expected increasing of chunk size and reduction of time resolution and the subsequent speeding up of subjective time.

Despite the tendency to shrink time as we get older, we know that old people are still able to expand time during emergencies or times of novelty. We can infer from this that the physical apparatus in the brain is still capable of expanding time and so we conclude that the tendency to shrink time, as we get older, is a cognitive habit (the Huxley valve has a tendency towards being narrow), not an organically-driven state of an aging brain. The upshot of this is the recognition that the time-shrinkage we experience as we age is a trend, not a necessity.

The strength (or 'size') of the Myth of the Self has a direct relationship with our time-resolution. An expansion of time (a decrease in moment size) often comes along with a reduction in the narrative of the self. Certain drug experiences, fevers, emergency situations and metal illnesses can also affect this. This is something the Myth of the Self will fight against in the long term as it relies upon this narrative for its existence. The Myth of the Self requires, and to some degree drives, larger moment and event sizes in order to strengthen itself, yet to assume that the Myth of the Self alone governs time perception would be a mistake. In order to live in a shared and sophisticated world and to service certain survival needs, it is necessary to extend our time perception (that is to say reduce our time resolution) and to do this we require a sense of self, a story and a narrative. So much like the proverbial chicken and egg, we find the 'magnitude' of our time perception and our Myth of the Self to be locked into a self-reciprocating relationship whereby each enhances, requires and drives the other.

This reciprocal enhancement of each other gradually grows

Myth of the self

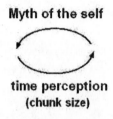

time perception
(chunk size)

over time, whereby the Myth of the Self drives a need for greater time perception (lower resolution), which drives the need for a larger Myth of the Self and so on. Is it any wonder then that, as a trend and a cliché, we find that, as we get older, time speeds up and as well as that, we also get more 'stuck in our ways'? It's no surprise because the two are connected. And so greater time spent in the social institutions of civilisation and within familiar environments appears to drift towards a deeper and deeper decent into inautheticity. Above, we saw how the time vista created moment sizes and as we know, the magnitude of the Myth of the Self is linked to the perception of time. The time vista is not only a *time*-vista then, but it is a vista of both time and *sense of self* – the two being inextricably linked. We will call this the 'time/Myth of Self-vista'.

As we get older (or more habituated in any circumstance), on average we descend downwards on the diagram below; the magnitude of both processes grow as they feed off each other. (Yes, that's right; I said both *processes*. Remember even though we talk about and model the Myth of the Self, the Huxley valve and many other concepts as psychic structures, they are in fact just processes.)

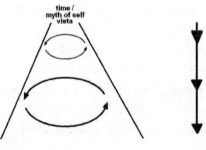

Despite the tendency of socialization and civilization pushing us towards inauthenticity, this is a trend that can be reversed. All of the exercises and the models in this book point towards one goal – the breaking down of the magnitude of the time/Myth of Self vista.

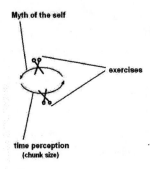

Just as, toward the beginning of the book, we surmised that the average default direction of awareness is Downtime (with Uptime being the option); I believe that 'everyday perception' is dominated by having the Huxley valve very much in place and operating strongly (narrowly) within us. So, for the less 'enlightened', the perceptive filters are working very 'tightly' to constrain their awareness and direct it largely towards social and survival-based cognition. The 'tightness' of a filter describes its tendency to show us less of what things are *in-themselves* and more of what things are *for-us*. This increases our disconnection from the World at Large as our experiences, things, people, situations and feelings shift from being an *end* in themselves and more of a *means* to some other deferred end or value. As we systemize our relationship to things (as our value hierarchies begin to habituate), we create 'roles' for ourselves which eventually come between our awareness and the World at Large. It is important not to strive or force results in all of this; to do so would be to open up the back door once again to the old ways. For example, if I decide that the next time I meet you, instead of relating to you through our roles, I will make an active attempt to relate to you more directly, then I have still turned you into a means to end. You have become the object which I can use in creating, for myself, the role of 'person who relates directly to others'. This is why, to progress in our venture, we have encountered many exercises to condition our experience to become effortlessly more authentic, and more direct. <u>You cannot simply think, or will, your way out of the old ways – this is why people generally find lasting personal change so difficult</u>. To involve effort, to strive, is to set an arbitrary goal, and if we do this, it is the goal (and not things-as-they-are) which determines our relationship (our responses) to everything, at which point every end becomes another means once it is achieved and this drags us back onto the merry-go-round of the constant deferment of value.

I don't want the money per se – I want the computer.

I don't want the computer per se – I want to send and e-mail.

I don't want to send an e-mail per se – I want to communicate with someone.

I don't want to communicate with someone per se – I want to make a sale.

I don't want to make the sale per se – I want the money.

I don't want the money per se – I want the car.

I don't want the car per se – I want the status.

I don't want the status per se – I want ....

Just as our venture requires a reversal of the default, with respect to Uptime and Downtime, so also, the whole venture begins to indirectly reverse our default with respect to this Huxley valve. So, we can expand our definition of the practical enlightenment venture, as one where we are essentially seeking to hack into the length of these processes to reduce (we can never eliminate) the degree to which our perceptual filters prevent us from being what we already are and living where and when we already live. That is to say, we disrupt the notions of becoming something else, somewhere else at some other time. And then, quite automatically, we find ourselves 'Being in the Here and Now'.

* In fact, as social animals - social information would be considered as a subset of survival information. The social group primarily reflects a survival strategy.

** We know that our eyes take approximately twenty-five pictures a second, not as one long continuous moving picture; this can be easily demonstrated in the strobe effect – an example of which would be when we 'see' a cartwheel slowing down, stopping or running backwards. It is assumed that our other senses are digitized in a similar fashion.

*** 'Unwieldy' with respect to direct perception. More wieldy with respect to social and survival concerns.

Chapter19

Relevant Philosophies: Who has been Here before you?

To teach how to live without certainty and yet without being paralysed by hesitation is perhaps the chief thing that philosophy, in our age, can do for those who study it.
Bertrand Russell

The greatest discovery of my generation is that man can alter his life simply by altering his attitude of mind.
William James

There is some philosophy in this section; it's here to increase understanding, not to tell you exactly what the currently fashionable interpretation is amongst scholars today.

You may be wondering where the ideas expressed in this book have come from. My intention was to design a system that distilled all the essential elements of a range of disparate ideas to their most basic form and to take these ideas and display them in an easy to follow, no-nonsense format for the everyday person.

Here you will learn how the 'it's OK to be not-OK' maxim fits in with other great thinkers and philosophies. The wisdom contained within 'it's OK to be not-OK' is universal and has been expressed in a myriad of ways before, I've merely reduced it to its algorithmic state so that you have the formula now to continue to learn to apply this everywhere.

Within ancient Greek philosophy there was a movement called Stoicism.

Stoicism

The philosophically-minded reader might have already noticed a Stoic line running through the ideas of the book. A great degree of the Stoic philosophy can be summed up by this most famous Stoic quote.

Man is not disturbed by events in the world by the meaning he attaches to those events.
Epictetus

Albert Ellis, in the 1950s, takes this as his starting point and gives us the discipline of Rational Emotive Behavior Therapy. The REBT ideas of compound emotions, belief disputing, reality testing, frustration tolerance and the inference of facts before beliefs, all inform many aspects of Practical Enlightenment. Those with a psychological background may also recognize the debt owed to Cognitive Behavioral theory, Neuro Linguistic Programming, Semantics and contemporary Hypnotherapeutic theory.

Albert Ellis' Rational Emotive Behavior Therapy was a major influence when I was designing the Practical Enlightenment Venture. Although he credits Stoicism in his development of REBT, I think he has really gone some way to reconciling the popular and central views of both Stoicism and Epicureanism.

That is to say that we can hold preferences about how we would like things to be yet not let these preferences become demands in our minds. A complete immersion in what we want (and a belief that we can only affect our state of well being through external circumstances) is bound to demise into unbridled hedonism and, therefore, a sense of always striving, always having some incompleteness. On the other hand, a complete denial of the body and its needs/desires can descend into out and out asceticism which, at the extreme, could be characterized by a hermit who has given away all connections, all possessions and all comforts. This extreme asceticism comes from a certain denial of our fragile and imperfect human bodies and the needs of those bodies and an over-idolisation of the mind. Ironically, this can appeal to the Myth of the Self, and possibly the reinforcer of 'status'. Although we will see later that higher motives may be at the core of extreme asceticism, it still represents a life-denying position.

Serenity

For those who like a little sugar with their medicine, someone has penned this catchy little ditty below, called 'the Serenity Prayer', that I believe is very popular amongst addiction re-habilitation interest groups.

God grant me the serenity
to accept the things I cannot change;
courage to change the things I can;
and wisdom to know the difference.
Living one day at a time;
Enjoying one moment at a time;
Accepting hardships as the pathway to peace;
Taking, as He did, this sinful world
as it is, not as I would have it;
Trusting that He will make all things right
if I surrender to His Will;

That I may be reasonably happy in this life
and supremely happy with Him
Forever in the next.
Amen.

There seems to be some controversy regarding who wrote this poem; one version has it that it was a Stoic poet who made the original. The Stoic original probably had a stronger accent on personal responsibility rather than magical intervention. Two quotes from one Stoic thinker are certainly consistent with the ideas expressed:

Make the best use of what is in your power, and take the rest as it happens.

There is only one way to happiness and that is to cease worrying about things which are beyond the power of our will.
Epictetus

One who has been credited most often as the author of the Serenity Prayer (particularly in the form it takes above) is Reinhold Niebuhr who also said *"The final wisdom of life requires not the annulment of incongruity but the achievement of serenity within and above it."* He is inviting us to another level. It seems implicit in his quote that he finds incongruity is not-OK, yet one can find another level above this where things are OK. So to be serene about incongruence is one example where *it is OK to be not-OK.*

The Serenity prayer has most likely been adapted by Reinhold to suit Christian sentiment, and as it is more useful to perceive control of one's interpretations and actions as emanating inside the self (the true self, not the Myth thereof) instead of outside, one could possibly reason thusly:

I'm not directly conscious of God.
God operates unconsciously for me.
God is the unconscious.
I substitute the word 'God' in the poem with the term 'unconscious mind'.

(Unconscious mind) grant me the serenity
to accept the things I cannot change;
courage to change the things I can;
and wisdom to know the difference.

We have now rested back control and response-ability of our thoughts, feelings and actions. Perhaps a desire to 'commune with the unknowable' (to be one with God) is actually just the expression, through a religious paradigm, of the desire for an integration of all our 'parts' i.e. an end to internal conflict? See if you can, bearing in mind that we are equating our unconscious processes with our experience of God, reverse the paradigm of the story below from the religious to the psychological:

A man is stuck on a peninsula. The tide is rising rapidly and soon the man will be drowned, so he prays to God for savior. Then along comes a dolphin and asks (yes dolphins can talk in this story) if the man would like a lift back to shore. He tells the dolphin, "*No thanks, I have faith that God will save me.*" He answers identically to the helicopter and boat that pass him who also offer assistance. The man drowns. In heaven, the man asks God "*why didn't you save me?*" God answers the man, "*I tired. I sent a dolphin, a boat and a helicopter. I guess you missed them.*"

The angle of this parable is similar to those who posit that heaven and hell are states on earth. Imagine if, when you die, it's just 'lights out' – that's it, nothing. Now for some reason you come back to awareness for just a moment and you ask "well, I'm dead, where is heaven?" and God answers, "*I tried. I sent an entire planet, an entire universe for you, I guess you missed it.*" So what God would be telling us, in this instance, is that it was really up to you to choose to interpret your situation as you wished.

The mind is its own place, and in itself Can make a heaven of hell, a hell of heaven.
John Milton

When Sartre talks of freedom, he states that if we choose to strive for freedom, it should be 'Authentic freedom within conditions, not freedom of conditions'. That is the freedom to choose to retain our ability to define the meaning of the events that happen in the World at Large, even if we are not free to control those events themselves. There is no singular 'grand narrative'; meaning is created, not discovered. He's not saying that it is desirable not to act upon the World at Large (the World at Large is known as 'Facticity' in Sartre's parlance), but we should know that if changing our circumstances is not within our control at anytime, we have recourse to the meaning we give to those circumstances. To act in such a manner is to have 'good faith' – that is to say acting authentically. Go back and have a look at how this ties in with the first four lines of the serenity prayer.

Sartre also distinguishes between reflexive and un-reflexive consciousness. Reflexive consciousness is the term he uses to describe an awareness of our own consciousness and ourselves; we can literally reflect consciousness back at itself. Un-reflexive consciousness is simply an awareness of only the contents of awareness. In reflexive consciousness, we can watch our own thoughts by splitting the actor and observer, and becoming aware of our ability to determine both the direction of our awareness, and the flavor of our unconscious beliefs and meanings. Once we have become aware of our value hierarchy chains, and altered them accordingly, it is time to leave reflexive consciousness behind and find that, in un-reflexive consciousness, we can be without the need for meaning and so enjoy living in the moment.

Below you can see reflexive consciousness at some level depicted in the planet X model.

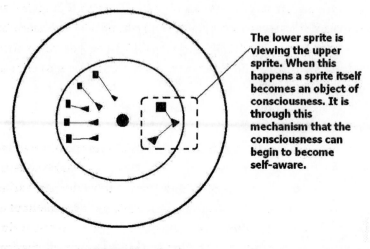

The lower sprite is viewing the upper sprite. When this happens a sprite itself becomes an object of consciousness. It is through this mechanism that the consciousness can begin to become self-aware.

Planet X

Given that we know what we want and why we want it, that is to say we are fully aware of our value hierarchies. For everyday life, the following formula seems to suffice.

1.   ASK THE WORLD – this is not a wish that things will just change without any action from you. Experiment to see what you can change; there are bound to be things for which you hold yourself accountable that are actually outside your remit, and yet other issues that you have believed you could not influence, when, in fact, you can.

2.   ASK YOURSELF – have an honest and incisive look at the beliefs you would need to hold to continue to feel a particular way about a given situation. Assess how usefully that belief is operating for you as it governs your relationship with your lived world.

You see here that this is the serenity prayer in a different order. It is necessary to 'ask the world (to change)' i.e. to try to change the things you can in order to discover "the knowledge to know the difference" (between what we can change and what we cannot). Only finally do we need recourse to "the serenity to accept the things I cannot change." This should follow a detailed assessment of what we want and why we want it; although it may be necessary to reassess our wants in light of what we learn by having 'asked the world (to change)'. By 'asking the world' first, we find out what *is* and what *is not* within our power to dictate; this is known as *reality testing*.

Kierkegaard

One of Sartre's forerunners, and one who is largely considered the father of existentialism, is Kierkegaard. He states that he believes our very personality to be made up of our values. In earlier chapters we've seen how the Myth of the Self can be thought of as the (anthropomorphized) collective coagulation of our value hierarchies. Kierkegaard also agrees that as much as changes occur in our values (our values expressed through our actions – not our overt assertions) this represents a change in 'who we are'. Kierkegaard also posits that facts (in the World at Large) will never be a motivation for action and that a fact will only affect us (become a pretext for action) in the light of the context of our values. He tells us here that in the World at Large there are no problems, only situations, and that our minds must actively intervene by coloring our interpretations of facts in order to create problems. He also sees existence as a-conceptual, that is to say; to create an idea of 'existence' in our minds is to create a concept of something which cannot be conceptualized. Various philosophies, such as Zen, and to some degree quantum physics, suggest that existence requires awareness. Existence is awareness. Kierkegaard tells us that 'existence will always require some risk and some anxiety', and this falls into line with Sartre's assertion that any life involving freedom (all authentic life at least) will cause some anxiety. There are two responses to anxiety:

1. Denial (it's not-OK to be not-OK) leading to avoidance, but at

the price of our freedom.
2. Acceptance (it's OK to be not-OK) leading to an embrace of the human condition and its freedom.

Coming back to the value-hierarchies, we will remember that all values ultimately lead to the primary reinforcers (hunger, shelter, sex, thirst), and that above them, the single 'grand reinforcer' is *existence* then we could suppose that the ascetics (those who deny worldly, bodily pleasures and even needs) sought to not only bypass all the sublimated and fetish-ized convolutions of the primary reinforcers, but also sought to jump the primary reinforcers themselves and so come face to face with existence. How obvious is it that for biologically-constrained creatures, such a venture is doomed to failure?

Sisyphus

Camus, in his essay, 'The myth of Sisyphus', demonstrates a mythological understanding of the principles of controlling what you can and managing what you cannot. Sisyphus is condemned for eternity to push a rock up a mountain, yet when nearing the top of the mountain, the rock always tumbles down to the bottom and the task starts again. Camus explains that, in becoming aware of the futility of the meaningless struggle and his lack of control over the situation, Sisyphus becomes free to create his own meaning, even if that meaning is absolute absurdity. Sisyphus cannot control his burden, yet he controls the meaning he assigns to it. Sisyphus is the ultimate 'absurd hero'. Although an involvement with the gods, eternity and a scenic backdrop give Sisyphus a certain glamorous élan, one must imagine him taking the same attitude to any repetitive task devoid of any intrinsic meaning. Working on an assembly line, wrestling with the in-tray, cleaning, perhaps even carrying water or chopping wood and a million other tasks all represent a never ending and essentially meaningless struggle against decay (Entropy).

Objects in life move toward a position of uniform chaos – a position of ultimate decay. No pile of rust ever makes itself into a bike, no floor gets cleaner and no lunch is free. It seems that, in our relentless battle against decay, we too are doomed to encounter this repetitive struggle that will eventually lead to naught; after all – even the sun will die eventually. How will you rise to the challenge of creating your own meaning, your own dignity, and perhaps even a little nobility, in the face of this dread inevitability?

Sisyphus is able to take one step at a time and guard himself from the terror of eternity; by being mindful of his task and living in the moment, he creates a reality for himself that is both useful and OK. To implement this state of consciousness, the Uptime-anchor would have come in particularly useful for him. *"The struggle itself is enough to fill a man's heart. One must imagine Sisyphus happy."*

Oriental wisdom

Ancient oriental philosophy (my limited understanding thereof) also lays a claim to being some inspiration during the conception of Accelerated Practical Enlightenment. Some time ago I read that a path to finding peace is to know it is possible to become peaceful even about those things which are un-peaceful. If you can't find the higher peace then simply don't worry, i.e. become peaceful about your inability to find peace about things which are un-peaceful. This idea speaks of one of the core strategies used in changing your interpretation of the world. If you find you are feeling two conflicting things, your only decision is in which level to dwell upon. If I'm comfortable about my discomfort I have only to make the simple choice to focus on the comfort, not the discomfort. Most of the time, our unconscious processes will take care of this after we have created the two options. Where those options do not exist we must create them.

What we are really being told here, about peace, is that <u>it's OK</u>

to be not-OK, and if you can't find your way to doing that, let yourself know that is OK.

Samurai warriors, Shoalin monks and other martial artists found it useful not to color their experience with internal dialogue, emotion or meaning when fighting, as this simply soaks up some of the conscious attention and reduces the mind's computing power to make good decisions*. Trusting the unconscious processes to make the decisions and to direct attention outward – this is Uptime. Once in Uptime, the warrior can choose which TOTEs to string together, finding a certain level of drilled-spontaneity within the gaps between TOTEs.

The Oriental tradition seems to value rational decision making, in the heat of battle, over a more Western bent towards increasing power-through-fury. Anger, when it is felt, is only a motivator to overcome frustration. Whilst the power-through-fury strategy (observable in any good town center at closing time) must have its time and place; it seems to me that it would be in a mainly physical setting, whereas, in today's society, we most often find that frustration is not of the simple, "this rock is too heavy to lift" variety. Today's frustrations come as ideas, meanings, pervasive long term situations where the Eastern philosophy is much more useful.

The Samurai had a kind of Uptime-generating practice you may wish to try. The practice is simple: just stare at a spot somewhere out in front of you and become intensely aware of that point and, whilst keeping your eyes where they are, let yourself become aware of everything just to the sides and to the top and bottom of that point. And so you are increasing the size of the spot you are becoming aware of. Just allow the increase in the direction of your attention to continue, either in steps or smoothly – as you wish.

When you get to the edges of your peripheral vision, don't let this stop you; allow this awareness to keep growing. This is not as absurd as it seems; you often have an awareness of where people or objects are around you and behind you; maybe by tapping into sounds or feelings. As a variant, you could go further, beyond the limits of your senses, and so you could start tapping into pure awareness itself; just be careful that this doesn't descend into simply imagining (in Downtime) what is 'out there' beyond your senses. Once it has been generated, anchor the state if you feel it to be beneficial so that you may access it again more easily and strongly as you wish.

Dogs Chase their Tails, Humans Chase their Tales

The tools of the mind become burdens when the environment which made them necessary no longer exists.
Henri Bergson

In literature, or even films or on TV, characters all have some sort of back-story that tells us 'who they are', and this helps us to make sense of their actions. Another literary device seems to be to have a group of friends or colleagues who all define each other, or bring a particular quality to the group. This is particularly visible in children's TV programs. So there will be the leader, the strong one, the crazy one, the master of disguise, the technical one, etc. And in a similar fashion in everyday life, we use both our own back-story and comparisons to define who we are.

As we come to define our own 'characters' (Myth of the Self) we have recourse to the meaning we assign to the past and comparisons with our peers, giving us a subjective, relative identity. Without this identity, we feel we would be overwhelmed and paralyzed by our anxiety in the face of our absolute freedom to do anything; we feel we would act entirely spontaneously, even randomly, and this too causes anxiety. The Myth of the Self perpetuates itself by constantly masking this existential angst from us. If we do act outside our idea of ourselves then fear grips us and that fear is actually the death-cry of the Myth of the Self.

As it dies a little it desperately tries to pull us 'back into line'. At this point, immediate repair is needed to keep the self consistent. If our actions continue to transgress our sense of self, then the Myth of the Self must change. If the Myth of the Self, and all the things which reinforce it, is strong enough then strategies will be implemented to strictly regulate future behavior. Past behavior that does not fit into our personality can be reconciled with the Myth of the Self by recourse to the idea that we were being controlled by outside agency. This position could be characterized by the temporary assertion that "I am the product of my environment," yet it ignores and denies our active choice of how we interpret our environments and the ever attendant freedom and responsibility this entails. Alternatively, faulty logic is often used to reconcile past actions with the Myth of the Self, as is the case with 'trance logic'. This faulty logic can be seen in the processes know as *cognitive dissonance*, whereby the logic under-pinning our beliefs and assertions will shift around according to the situations. This happens in order to bring differing values into the foreground to assuage the Myth of the Self. In less formal terms, we change what we think we value in order to make us feel better in the face of the circumstances. When we consider that *cognitive dissonance* entails some denial and dissociation, it becomes apparent this is one of the ways that the requirements of the Myth of the Self can sequester a massive amount of our psychic energies and promote within us an alienation from ourselves (from our true values).

The Building Blocks of the Myth of the Self
As we have seen so far, our basic drives can be met by many separate means. We have a huge mass of value hierarchies, all interacting with each other and reinforcing or conflicting with each other, and these are the variables in the equation that defines the shape of our Myth of the Self at any one time. The 'self' here is just a *descriptive* model that explains actions after the fact. As

long as the choices we make through our actions and thoughts are at least seen to be consistent then we can infer a sense of self. This idea of 'who we are' can then be extended into the future and so the model moves from description to *prediction* in an attempt to preempt actions before the fact. This gives us the illusion of an assurance of certainty within our future. This demand for certainty is both expressed by, and a necessitating factor of, the Myth of the Self.

As our preferred ways of meeting our most basic needs change, this can be interpreted as a change of the Myth of the Self. As much as we relate differently to our tales about whom we are, then this constitutes a change in the Myth of the Self. In as much as we have tendencies towards habitually using certain value hierarchies, the cluster of value deferments we operate at any moment is synonymous with our sense of self (our 'personality'). Naturally, as external situations change, then our priorities will change and this represents a very real shift in our 'personality' at that time, although this shift will normally only last as long as the external changes that caused it. Having said this though, our tendencies towards certain value hierarchies will govern the subjective meaning we make of external situations (objective events in the World at Large) initially and so we tend to gravitate towards a fixed way of relating to the world. This perpetuates unless a large destabilizing event happens in the World at Large that forces a lasting shift in our value-hierarchy tendencies, or we go out of our way to use appropriate techniques to make the change by volition. The first mechanism is inferior in as much as it acts in a random and undirected way.

Our personality (our convolution of value hierarchies) both governs and is governed by the preferred methods that our Myth of Self uses to 'keep us in line'. The punishments and rewards that the Myth of the Self uses in order to direct us into identifying with it (and so acting, thinking and feeling certain ways) only exist in the four Downtime dissociations of Past, Future,

Elsewhere and Other-mind(s). No present situation, in and of itself, can ever coerce us in this way. For different people, or for the same person in different situations, the Myth of the Self will choose a dissociation that is most effective; although, in practice, these can operate in any combination. In a moment we will take a look at what happens within each separate dissociation, but before we do we will have a look at something quite interesting. If we intersect the four dissociations of the Downtime diagram as seen below, then the three levels seem to correspond with the three psychic structures of psychodynamics* (on the left) and Transactional Analysis (on the right).

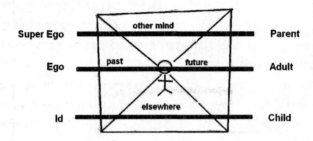

When the Myth of the Self coerces us by dragging our attention into Other-mind(s), then we respond to values based upon ideas of right and wrong, upon ethics and rules and upon concepts. In practice then, we might feel we are being looked down upon and judged by others and because this is happening only within our own mind, those 'others' could be anyone or anything. Any internalized other will do; a parent, the world population, the state, Big Brother, the Panopticon, a deity, or even some outside idea of ourselves. Likely expressions of this would include; self-downing, perfectionism, piety, guilt, shame, pride and righteousness.

When the Myth of the Self coerces us by dragging our attention into Past and Future then we are concerned with time and achievement and the attempt at creating and projecting an objective sense of self. Likely expressions of this would include micromanaging, time obsession, boredom, 'becoming', anxiety, despair, overwhelm, anticipation, waiting, self-denial and creating ordinary moments.

When the Myth of the Self coerces us by dragging our attention into Elsewhere then we are concerned mainly with instant gratification. In so far as this style of coercion is best suited to values nearer to the animalistic primary reinforcers (sex, shelter, thirst, hunger), we could argue that this is the most authentic. Likely expressions of this would include; discontent, distraction, mania, hyper-activity, superficiality, multi-tasking, job-hopping, hobby-hopping, constant redecoration of the house, constant upgrading of material possessions/social connections/status indicators, feeling that the grass is greener somewhere else (i.e. feeling you want to be doing something else) and indulging in discomfort distractions, such as over-eating, drinking or drug use etc.

It's interesting to note that traditional establishment, societal and religious values see the higher level as the location of virtue (i.e. dogma). Would it be cynical to suggest that this may be because things become more convoluted and more coercive the higher you go up from elsewhere; up to time, up to other-minds?

Psychodynamics, Terminology and Authenticity

Various other initiatives involved with mindfulness/enlightenment/present moment awareness/spirituality and so on, often speak of 'undoing the ego'. Within Accelerated Practical Enlightenment we talk, instead, of 'decommissioning the Myth of the Self' – at least to the degree that we can better control the Myth of the Self and relegate it to the background. The term 'Myth of the Self' is partially synonymous with the Ego, talked about in many other meditative and 'undoing' practices, but within Accelerated Practical Enlightenment, we do not use the term 'Ego' due to its psychodynamic connotations that could confuse matters. If we must relate all this to psychodynamics at all, we can say that the Myth of the Self differs in that it is a bunch of processes, not a structure, and also that it encapsulates all of the processes that all three of the psychodynamic structures seek to explain. Any defense mechanisms that the Myth of the Self uses also operate through all three levels of Space, Time and Mind (not just the 'Ego' level of time), as we can see in the diagram below. There are two other levels; the level of the World at Large and the level of Awareness (or 'spirituality'). Authenticity is achieved through the connection (with as little obscuration as possible) of Awareness and the World at Large. In Downtime, as we can see in the diagram below, there are three quite 'opaque', separating factors that impede that connection; these are the factors of Time, Space and Mind.

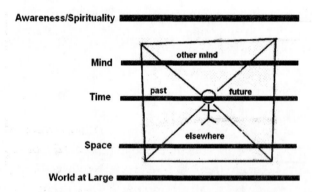

In Uptime (see diagram below), the unlabelled sense perceptions allow us, as much as is possible, a much more 'translucent' medium through which the Awareness can connect to the World at Large. Still the connection between Awareness and the World at Large will never be completely pure for two reasons:

1. The conduit, that is our senses, is very limited in its bandwidth and its range, whereas the World at Large and Awareness approach infinity.
2. The Fifth position will always project some notions of Time, Space and Mind onto the raw sensory data. Think of it here like a lens that will distort a little yet not obscure. We try to flatten

this lens as much as possible, but it will always exert a small effect.

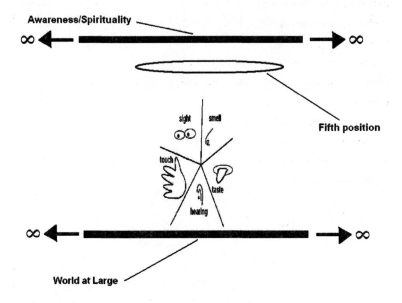

The qualitative difference is that, in Downtime, Time, Space and Mind create sensations themselves and massively obscure the connection between Awareness and the World at Large, if not impeding it altogether. But in Uptime, layers of Time, Space and Mind are projected onto present sensations and only color them. Even though there is some Deletion, Distortion and Generalization, the connection between Awareness and the World at Large is direct. We could phrase it like this; although Space, Time and Mind always project themselves onto the World at Large, to a lesser or larger degree:

- In Downtime, Space, Time and Mind exist *for us* (that is to say they exist for the Myth of the Self) as a means to an end.
- In Uptime, Space, Time and Mind exist *in and of themselves* and as an end in themselves.

In Downtime, Time exists within which to conceive goals, and create a sense of self, Space exists within which to gratify goals, and Mind exists within which to create high concepts that drive goals. In Uptime, Space, Time and Mind are just 'there'.

Death and Re-birth of the Self

Our 'true' values (our true value hierarchies) can be inferred only *after* our actions. We assume that the values we tell ourselves that we hold (the very building blocks of the Myth of the Self) drive our actions. So the Myth of the Self would like to think that our values *drive* our actions yet those values are actually *driven* by our actions.

As actions that are inconsistent with our Myth of the Self mount up, the Myth of the Self will try to absorb and reconcile these actions into some form of consistency. Sooner or later, at some sort of tipping-point, the Myth of the Self can no longer absorb the inconsistencies (assimilation) and must modify itself (accommodation). This will often come at some sort of crisis point. These crises can be either small and often, or infrequent, large and dramatic.

Incidentally, for anyone looking to set them self up as a guru of any kind, I strongly urge you to make much use of re-telling the story of your transformation crises; it will lend you a mystical aura. The more dramatic and complete the crises the better. A drastic death and re-birth of the self is the ultimate epiphany. Sadly, the creation of Accelerated Practical Enlightenment has no such metamorphosis tale to tell that is any more drastic than the slow accumulation of theory consistently applied and tested to petty everyday life – and the odd flash of insight.

The Myth of the Self will resist any change as this will result in its death, and accordingly, most of the time, we are very predictable to others and to ourselves. From time to time, if drastic events happen to us then we feel this to be uncomfortable or even painful, and it is a mistake to equate the discomfort with the situation itself. The discomfort is the Myth of the Self protesting at, and resisting, how the situation is forcing a change within itself. There are a few times in life though where the self must be transformed, and ancient rituals and rites of passage have regulated these times since the dawn of civilization. Within shamanism and ancient culture, the death-rebirth archetype can be seen again and again even in cultures entirely isolated from each other. This is often depicted as a real and complete death, yet it only stands for the death and rebirth of the Myth of the Self. The 'real' self always remains unchanged – after all, it has no definite qualities other than awareness.

The function of the culturally instigated death-rebirth ceremony (the rites of passage) is to make this change in an individual before this transformation becomes overdue and the outdated sense of self causes turmoil. Likewise, on most car engines, the cam belt is replaced at regular intervals to preempt any failure of the component. Should the belt fail, a more drastic and prolonged crisis takes place, often resulting in massive engine damage.

The self cannot choose another self to be without recourse to its own existing values. New values, and so a new Myth of the Self, need to be installed in a timely fashion and this will ideally happen day to day through action, appropriate to any given situation, as and when it happens. So each time we act directly in response to the present moment (and only the present moment) we instigate our own small, but accumulative, rites of passage.

Dualism

I contradict myself. I am large. I contain multitudes.
Walt Whitman

Apparently, very young children have no sense of self and other; they are just blissfully at one with the universe. During childhood, an important milestone for the child's social development is the rejection of their singular perspective through the formation of the conception of self and the recognition of 'the other'. This separation is, no doubt, useful for a shared civilized world, but perhaps the unquestioned assumption, that we have to take one perspective or the other, in short that 'we should be consistent', is at fault. Perhaps there is some way we can have both or either perspective as and when needed as they both fulfill useful functions. One perspective helps us to live and one helps us to be alive.

Just as *hot* is defined partially by the concept of *cold* so any sense of 'self' needs a 'not-self' with which to compare itself. When we divide the world into self and not-self then this is Dualism. A Non-Dualistic perspective is to see the universe as singular and no longer split into self and not-self.

A non-dualistic perspective seems to be desirable per se, with its benefits of the destruction of the Myth of the Self and its tendency to move one away from discontent and conflict. Contentment must come with the dissolution of the split between self and non-self and the according dissolution of the split between existence and possibility. But non-duality contains some questionable elements in its internal logic and may be a position born of a category error (bias rather than error really) and also, it is an unpractical stance in many day-to-day practical matters. As we are concerned with *Practical* Enlightenment, reconciliation is most desirable. Two options come to mind here in designing a perceptual perspective incorporating the benefits of both dualism and non-dualism:

1. To intellectually recognize both perspectives as viable but to really feel, at the gut level, that non-dualism is the most valid. As regards dualism, you might regard it as a conceptual tool necessary for navigating the social world.

2. To set non-dualism as a default (just as we would set Uptime

to the default) perspective, only entertaining dualism for practical matters then returning to non-dualism once practical matters have been addressed. This position differs from the first in that, as I entertain each perspective, I actually feel its reality to be most valid at the gut level.

One of these two options could be installed in your experience using techniques similar to the Uptime exercises. Indeed, extreme and permanent perception of the non-dualistic perspective may represent a more *absolute* enlightenment. As with all the absolute enlightenment options, though, it is not entirely practical or possible without major lifestyle changes and is probably only open to someone who has others to cater for many of their practical needs.

It could even be argued also that *absolute* enlightenment is quite a decadent venture and one that is necessarily not available to everyone. Perhaps society will support some shaman or diva or other spiritual type but it follows that it could not support the entire population in this pursuit. Everyone can attain practical enlightenment though. The first option (1) above seems the most desirable as it honors non-duality in both modes, and it's the most feasible as a shift between two perspectives at the academic cognitive level is much easier than a shift between two gut feelings of what is 'reality'. In the same way, it is easy for me to mathematically model my body as either moving or being stationary as the train next to me moves off from the station, but it is much harder to actually feel that it is I who is moving because my benchmark of what is stationary (the ground, everything apart from the other train) must move with me. 1. is tantamount to me playing monopoly, understanding and abiding by the rules yet knowing that none of it really matters. Position 2 is tantamount to me playing and really believing in the value of the money and the transactions going on within the game. It is OK for us to entertain a perspective even though we do not feel it to be reality at the gut level. In a debating exercise, one may be asked to defend a position they do not actually agree with; this is actually a very good exercise in objectivity between one's intellectual capacity and one's values and beliefs. The earlier exercise in the chapter *Freeing yourself from identification with the Myth of the Self*, is a good practice to create and install a gut belief in nonduality yet afterwards to hold this position and still interact, where necessary, from a dualistic perspective.

The way is perfect and complete like boundless space; nothing is lacking, nothing redundant, but, because the mind continues to make distinctions, its suchness is obscured.
Seng T'san

The term *interconnectedness* can nicely sum up the pragmatic perspective that allows the reconciliation of dualism and nondualism within the spirit of *practical* enlightenment. The boundaries are blurred again so as to find an enlightening, yet useable, balance. Interconnectedness allows us to see that we are all separate in ourselves, but also interconnected in the entirety of the whole universe. The default perspective of the pre-enlightened individual is, at the human level, focusing on human institutions, human concerns, their concerns and, generally, just perceiving the universe at a human level of definition. The boundaries are blurred, though; in reality, we impose this meaning on the World at Large: it is not 'out there'. Try this experiment; spit on a plate then try to put that spit back in your mouth. As soon as it has left the body it becomes 'not-I' (other), but at what point did this separation take place? Apparently, the cells of the body are renewed every seven years or so. Even the hands I type these words with right now are not made up of the same molecules they were a decade ago.

The self/other distinction is so pervasive that we humans often feel ourselves to be the population of the universe. In fact, we are part of it, as much as space, air, water, nuclear waste, the sun, time, oil, atoms and everything else is. Have a look at your body; it's irrevocably wired into the universe, particularly the earthly environment. There is always some air in your lungs, water in your body, pre-digested and post-digested matter passing through your body. If you think about it, your body is really one long tube with stuff going through all the time. All the apparatus surrounding that tube are secondary in that they all serve to keep negative entropy (complexity) running through this tube. The tube's job is to extract the complexity from the matter running through it in order to perpetuate itself and more tubes.

We are all parts of the universe with no clear division; we are not *in* the universe; we are *part of it*. Despite our social and, perhaps, survival-driven preoccupation with creating self and other, our very consciousness is actually part of the universe; we humans are just one of the ways that the universe has of becoming conscious of itself. In becoming conscious of itself, the universe is actually brought into existence as an object of consciousness – a *mind-object*. Choosing to play the game according to the dualistic rules, and recognizing them as arbitrary, does not prevent us from seeing and feeling (at the gut level) the interconnectedness of everything. Understanding this interconnectedness helps us to dis-identify with the myth, the cult, of just how central and important we are.

To any readers interested in non-dualism, and who may have spotted many dualist perspectives throughout the book so far, I must say that this has been no mistake. A synergy and reconciliation between dualist and non-dualist perspectives has been a concern throughout. I have chosen to write much that has been written so far from a dualist frame as there seemed no other way to explain many of the concepts. I see no barrier here to Accelerated Practical Enlightenment leading to 'a state of non-dualism' (for want of a better phrase) for those who strive for this, yet to write non-dualistically would be, no doubt, beyond my writing ability, and I dare say (if I wrote it) beyond any readers comprehension. Many writers on non-dualism openly admit the difficulty of explaining non-dualism, and I would agree with them, and I will follow the familiar caveat route of 'explaining' that all that comes before and after in this book could be considered to be 'pointers' towards a deeper and unexplainable understanding. Have I really said anything in saying this?

Non-dualism often teaches that nothing is to be done – that there are no problems; this is understandable from the absolutist perspective but we still have to live day to day and live in a shared world. Practical enlightenment incorporates the belief that the Myth of the Self cannot be totally 'undone'; it must be managed as we still need it for the day to day running of life in the world with all its structures of civilization and deferment of value. We need to make the Myth of the Self into a servant of our true awareness instead of becoming subservient to it. Non-dualistic perspectives often talk of the conditioned mind (our cognitive and behavioral faculties), the non-conditioned (true awareness) and the 'undoing' of the conditioned mind as if unraveling a ball of wool or a big knot. The conditioned mind cannot be undone; it cannot be dissolved and even if it could, this would totally undesirable. A look at a plethora of degenerative brain diseases that rob the afflicted of various higher faculties will show this be evident.

Short of messing with the physical substance of the brain itself, there is no *un*-conditioning, there is only *re*-conditioning; nature abhors a vacuum and so it is prudent for us to actively choose what will replace it instead of leaving that to chance. It is possible to re-condition the mind to become lighter in its touch, to be spacious and unobtrusive, to be in the background, to become transparent, but the very idea of 'undoing' or 'un-conditioning' is certainly a reification of a state each of us will never see again, we can not go back to the womb, we must move forward.

In short, practical enlightenment holds, implicit in its outlook, a natural suspicion of any idea that there is nothing to be done; no method; no need to clear away the obscuration caused by the

Myth of the Self and the cognitive processes it relies on hijacking in order to assert itself. If the realization of an epiphany-experience should happen to grace the odd guru-to-be with an immediate deep and lasting change in the conditioned mind, this path need not apply to all of us; surely it is the exception and not the rule. A denial of the mind and the ways in which its tendencies can be swayed would seem a little short-sighted as it is the mind which, for most people, constantly obscures the true awareness that is already present in all of us. Insight does not equal cure. It is not even a prerequisite for 'cure'. Practical enlightenment *conditions* the mind to act in a manner closest to that which we would expect from an *unconditioned* mind and in doing so we avoid the trap of denying our physical and secular aspects, which is the mistake of all ascetic practices. Through this denial, all ascetic practices lead one to judge him or her self against an impossible bench-mark based on the ideas of a non-corporal form leading to perfectionist tendencies, shame, guilt, inadequacy, self-hatred, hatred of the physical, dogmatism and ideology.

I will leave you with one more thought that convinced me to leave non-dualism, mostly, alone: it seems to me that to have 'non-dualism' as a concept, a dualism must exist with which to define, by contrast, the non-dualistic perspective. That is to say, the very name 'non-dualism' (as opposed to 'monism', which I believe is something slightly different) defines itself not by what it *is*, but by what it is *not*. So to have non-dualism, one must have dualism – and this appears to be a dualism in and of itself. Dualism (not in and of itself, as a concept, but as it is often taught) always lapses into dualistic language to give us 'pointers'. Don't get me wrong, I appreciate non-dualism and I like non-dualism; the practice of Practical Enlightenment prepares the ground for the non-dual experience to arrive spontaneously. The non-dualist suspicious of technique has fallen into the error of assuming that the technique makes the changes. In fact, technique is to change, what gardening is to growing plants; that is to say, the environment is prepared so as to invite, more readily, things that will or won't happen of their own accord. And at that point where, if there is nothing more to be done, nothing more to explain and nothing more to say, it seems appropriate to say no more about it.

* I am not suggesting that a more direct experience was sought after just because of its use within battle. Although, perhaps the Samurai extended their battle philosophies to life, I think it more likely the Shoalin extended their pre-existing philosophy to the battle field.

Chapter 20

The Memory System and Awareness: Where is the true self? Behind the workings of the mind

Using the planet X model helped us to define the differences between Uptime and Downtime and showed us that we had only a few finite points of conscious attention, i.e. the seven bits of information that our conscious channel can handle. A brief look at the memory system will help us to locate all we have learnt into an overall picture. Despite my taking a seemingly structural approach here, because it appeals to the way our minds work, it is just as well to remember that what we are actually looking at are a series of processes.

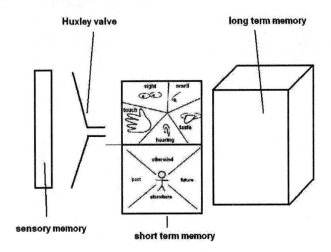

Take a look at the diagram above. Here we see a classic 'three store' memory model; this model is somewhat simpler than some expanded models, yet will serve adequately for our purposes here. Running from left to right, we have the sensory memory 'store'; it has around 150 bits capacity and can hold onto raw (unprocessed) sensations for only a few seconds. It may be that, when someone speaks to us and we aren't really paying attention, we may immediately ask them "what did you say?" only to find that we have just accessed this store and been able to replay what they said before they have a chance to repeat what they said. This is just one example of how this buffer store works for us.

The next 'store' we come to is the short-term memory; this has a capacity of seven 'bits'.* (sound familiar?) The short-term memory store is regarded as the 'seat of consciousness'. The classic three store model does not divide this into Uptime and Downtime perception, yet I have found it useful to do so in order to define enlightenment in terms of information processing theory – so there it is in the diagram. You will already be largely familiar now with the workings of the short-term memory store from the 'Planet X' model.

The classic three store model simply states that only a fraction of the information in the sensory memory will make it to the short-term memory. The three store model is structural and so makes no real provision of this process but, for our purposes, I have inserted the Huxley valve between the sensory and the short-term stores. Again, this system actually performs three processes (deletion, distortion and generalization of the incoming information), to vastly reduce the information making it's way from the sensory-store to the short-term store. We will consider how the Huxley valve makes choices about what to delete, distort and generalize later in the chapter. Finally, we have the long-term memory store; this is, to all extents, limitless. It contains our memories and habits and, to some degree, has some connection with our primitive brain which is that part which looks after our base biological functions. The Myth of the Self 'lives' here; bear in mind once again, and I feel I can't overstate this, that everything is actually process; the Myth of the Self is, in fact, just a personification (an anthropomorphism, a reification, a specter, a halluci-nation) of a bunch of 'lifeless' and sometimes conflicting or disconnected processes (lines of programming code, heuristics). Nevertheless, for now, let's just say that the Myth of the Self 'resides' in the long-term memory store.

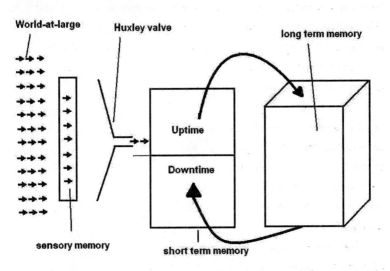

Now let's look at the above model again, from the point of view of a piece of information entering the system. Plenty of information, for our purpose a limitless amount, is just floating around 'out there' in the World at Large. This information can be loosely targeted by our actions; so, for example, if I decide to look out of the window, it's really not too likely that any visual infor-mation from inside the room will get to my sense receptors for that modality (i.e. my eyes). Apart from this level of directional control, the information just drifts in and a lot of the information will be unsolicited, from a sudden and unexpected wasp sting, to the mild and slow fluctuations of temperature in the room. The sensory memory performs a sort of scanning function; cycling over and over like the refresh of the picture on a television screen. The Huxley valve will only allow, according to its agenda, very few pieces of information to pass. Notice that the information doesn't make its way just into the short-term store, but only into the Uptime portion of the short-term store. If a piece of information is very unique or hangs around in the short-term store long enough, it's granted access to the long-term store. Information in the long-term store can then make its way back out to the short-term memory (the seat of consciousness) but only into the Downtime area.

So in the 'nightclub of the memory system', we have many bits walking past in the <u>World at Large</u>; only a few will join the long <u>sensory-store</u> queue of bits waiting to get in, then only a few of them will be allowed access into the club by Mr. '<u>Huxley Valve</u>', the door-man. If they dazzle with uniqueness (or can just hang around long enough) on the dance floor of <u>Uptime</u>, they will be granted lifetime membership to the vast VIP <u>long-term store</u> lounge. From here, the only dancing they will doing from now on is if they are called to the podium to dance; the club policy is only seven dancers at any time, whether they all be on the <u>Downtime</u> podium, all on the <u>Uptime</u> dance floor, or a mixture of each. Some long-term residents of the VIP lounge will dance on the <u>Downtime</u> podium a lot and repeatedly maybe, and some will never dance again and just languish in the lounge forever. For us to become more direct in our perceptions, we want to adjust our doorman's (Mr. Huxley Valve) entry policy and, as a general house rule, try to keep the dance floor full and the podium empty. In doing so, we move away from the detached, the closed and the circular, and towards the relevant, the open-ended and the linear. But who is it that sets the club policy? Who is the manger?

Have a look at the diagram opposite. Do you recognize 'who' is at the top there? Yes, it's our old friend, the 'Unseen Watcher', from Planet X. Remember, we are not really dealing with entities here but bundles of processes; the Unseen Watcher represents all processes that guide the flow of information and in doing so, dictates the contents of our consciousness system, but for now, we will see how the Unseen Watcher is (within the pre-enlightened

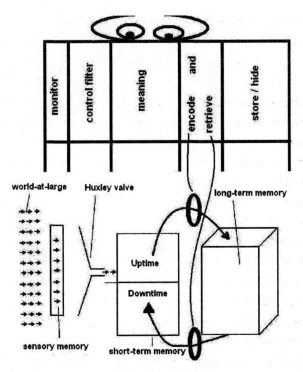

individual) very much under the direction of the Myth of the Self. This doesn't have to be the case; through Practical Enlightenment, we can help to liberate the Unseen Watcher from the grip of the Myth of the Self. The classic three store model contains a 'structure' called the 'central executive'. This name, at least, fits very well with the role that the Unseen Watcher plays in directing consciousness; it fulfills an executive function and exhibits, what looks like, a goal-orientated attitude. This 'central executive' role puts a 'head' (an operator) on the top of a lot of other drone (or 'slave') processes, like a general ordering around, blindly obedient, units of troops.

The same kind of qualities can also be said of the Myth of the Self when it has strongly hijacked the Unseen Watcher. When it does so, it also hijacks some of its powers and so can seem to act in a planned-out manner, with volition and with intelligence towards a long term goal. Yet, in actual fact, the Myth of the Self is only a bunch of processes and those processes can only really take place when the agency of the Unseen Watcher has been hijacked. I don't want to mix too many metaphors and models but this relationship seems to me very reminiscent an extremist, of some sort, who has been 'possessed' by the 'thought viruses of dogmatic ideology'. As a parasite, ideology needs a host and if it is denied access to a host then it dies or, at least, remains inert.

Continuing, we will look now at what the functions of the Unseen Watcher are, as it makes its way through our perceptual and memory process, exerting influence on the stream of information.

In the diagram above, you will see all the functions that the Unseen Watcher commands in order to build our lived experience. First of all, we can consciously move our sensory apparatus towards certain areas of the World at Large, but we can do this only so much as we have information within the seat of consciousness (the Uptime part of the short-term memory store) upon which to make the decisions as to where to point our senses. The Unseen Watcher can also exert influence on directing this sensory apparatus around and does so most of the time.

The next process is the monitoring of the contents of the sensory-store; some sort of knowledge of all this information is needed to make a 'decision' as to what is let through the Huxley Valve. At the Huxley valve itself, the Unseen Watcher must make that 'decision' as to what to let through the valve, and the Unseen Watcher sets the agenda as to what kind of information does get through and what doesn't. It is this agenda (that is to say, the tendency towards allowing in certain types of information) that we influence indirectly through some of the exercises in the book. It is not within our ability to perceive the Unseen Watcher, it's part of our 'Unconscious Mind' (our unconscious processes); it stands to reason that the monitoring and filtering, which take place in the sensory-store and the Huxley valve, must take place unconsciously because they are 'preconscious' – they are deciding what should be let into the consciousness. At the risk of repeating myself – do the exercises. It is only through conditioning and the addressing of confounding factors that we can exert control over the unconscious processes. We can never exert control through the will directly. This model should show that we can never directly/consciously control the very factors which feed and define the contents of our consciousness. We can't consciously choose what to be conscious of.

The next process after that is to create a 'meaning' to the information held in the short-term store; the Unseen Watcher has access to the long-term store and can use tendencies, we have expressed before, to streamline this process, and so our perceptions of given information can become very habituated. This meaning-making process happens at the 'fifth position', and we are already familiar with what happens there. Depending on the saliency and relevance to existing frames we hold (existing tendencies to make meaning of given information), the Unseen Watcher may 'encode' the information, and its interpreted meaning, into a form where it will be accepted into the long-term store. Depending on the contents of the short-term store, the Unseen Watcher can also retrieve information from the long-term store and allow it back into the Downtime part of the short-term store. This information will likely bring back, not only, itself but also 'tagged to it' will be the underlying interpretations (the meaning) that it was given when it initially made its way into the long-term store. When this old information makes its way back out like this, only a copy of the information comes out; the 'original' master copy is still there in the long-term store. Whilst this 'copy' is on the Downtime part of the short-term store, one of two things may happen. Most likely, when the information's presence is no longer required in the short-term store, it will make it's way back into long-term store and overwrite the 'original' in the long-term store; this represents a status quo, as it overwrites with the identical information and its attendant tagged meaning. The second and more interesting option is that, when it's out in the Downtime part of the short-term, the Unseen watcher may change the meaning attached to the information. Now, when it makes its way back into the long-term store, it overwrites the original with something different; the actual information stays largely the same but its meaning is changed. Not only does it change the original, but any similar information lurking in the long-term store may also undergo a change of its attached interpretations without ever having to make its way out into the short-term store. It is largely this process, the changing of the meaning of 'facts', that a lot of therapy seeks to manipulate.

These changes in this type of information can begin to influence, not only the actual interpretation of meaning of new information as it comes in through the Uptime route, but also the selection of information at the Huxley valve and even at the point where decisions are made as to where to point the sensory apparatus in the first place. This shows that it is largely the attendant and attached interpretations (meanings) that are given to the information, we have lurking in the long-term store, that determine our habits, our preferences, our tendencies, in other words – 'who we are'. This is no surprise because we know that the Myth of the Self resides in the long-term store; in fact, the Myth of the Self is actually built out of this information and, more importantly, the meaning that attaches to this information. As the meaning attached to both the incoming information and information in the long-term store becomes 'looser', this weakens the Myth of the Self, who then has less and less power to hijack the Unseen Watcher, and the effect becomes accumulative and begins to snowball you towards Practical Enlightenment.

So, as we do the exercises and instigate Practical Enlightenment, we will see a 'quickening' of the throughput of information through the system; this can lead to a slower perception of lived time, as we have already seen. This quickening will happen as smaller chunks are allowed through the Huxley

valve, and less depth of meaning will be attached to this information; as a result of this, a more direct and authentically-lived
perception occurs. This will also have the upshot of less information making its way out of the long-term store and into the
Downtime part of the short-term store. Meaningless information
does not make its way into the long-term store and so, in peak
experiences of direct perception, you may have no real memories
of what happened. This process happens on a sliding scale; so, in
everyday life, you may find that you are laying down less
memories; common sense tell us that this will be problematic, but
as you're living in the Here and Now and trusting that you are
responding more directly and authentically to all the situations
you find yourself in, this will not be a problem. Remember that
the old ways will still be available to you for everyday concerns,
but now that is the option and no longer the default.

This is how we eject a large proportion of our 'baggage'. The
idea of laying down less long-term memories may seem scary to
some people; this scariness, this anxiety is, as you've probably
guessed, the Myth of the Self expressing its fear of death through
one of its defense mechanisms. It is often the case that any holes
in one's memory are scary; you may have experienced this
through drugs, or alcohol, or even a knock on the head and
experienced the anxiety of trying to find out what happened
during those lost hours. In essence; this is a miniature version of
the overwhelming urge to find out 'who I am' that is felt by the
sufferer of full blown retrograde amnesia – where there is a
complete personality loss. If a person has a trust that they were
who they were at those moments in the past, and they were acting
and reacting authentically, then this urge to recover lost
memories, or even a lost personality, would not operate.
Interestingly, we all suffer this small identity loss, to some degree,
every time we wake from a deep sleep; it actually takes different
amounts of time for all our systems to 'come online' and the
downloading of the essentially inert information about who we

are (information and its attendant tagged meanings) can take longer to make its way to the Unseen Watcher (where the information becomes 'active') than it does for the Unseen Watcher itself to 'boot up'.

This delay can be seen most clearly, because it is so dramatic, in the case of someone who is grieving or depressed, as they wake up there are a few seconds before their sadness/depression/anxiety is 'downloaded'. For these moments, they feel directly in contact with the world and peaceful. Then, as that information downloads and that person's affect changes accordingly, they experience a very real shift as a nasty wave of doom and gloom descends and begins to color the interpretation of everything. This wave (that is to say, this veil of interpretation that descends), needn't be just unpleasant though, it may just as easily descend over someone who is in love and so skew the interpretation of the world to just as large a degree, only more pleasantly. In fact, I dare say, although I have never made any observation, that the glassy eyes and daydreaming traits, so indicative of being in Downtime, are equally present in the person who is in love as they are in the depressed individual.

Awareness

Finally, we venture now into territory that gets a little metaphysical as we consider exactly for whom, or for what, this interpretational veil exists.

Kant used the analogy of the spyglass; a piece of filtered glass that colors what we see of the world through it, just like rose-tinted spectacles do. So I shall now shift my analogy from the 'veil' I have talked about earlier to a 'lens', and despite my use of the visual metaphor in the rest of the chapter, keep in mind that, in actual fact, we are talking about all the senses and even beyond any particular sense modality at all, to the domain of pure awareness in and of itself. One distinction that I have not made overtly, until now, is the distinction between *awareness* and the *contents of consciousness.* It is tempting to think, but would be a mistake to assume, that the short-term store actually is consciousness itself. The short-term store, which is comprised of Uptime and Downtime, is a slave-process – just a screen upon which the contents of consciousness are projected and held.

The short-term store is the 'seat of consciousness', not *consciousness (awareness)* itself. In some existential/phenomeno- logical philosophy, awareness is seen as 'intentional' and, in this case, 'intentional' means that it must be directed *at* something. This is certainly true of our experience most of the time. To be *aware* at all we must be aware *of* something. This is not the only form of awareness available though – we can simply be *aware*. And this means just *aware* – and nothing else. This is awareness- *of*-awareness but it cannot show itself as an object upon the screen of the short-term store. Awareness can never become the contents of consciousness. It is simply awareness – nothing more, nothing less. This raw awareness is quite apart from whom we are, or any interpretation of meaning and so, the thinking mind can never hope to capture or perceive it and will try to deny it. Yet, when the systems of the mind are dormant, this awareness is in the fore.

To make the mind dormant, through direct will, would involve some effort on the part of the mind, so will always lead to failure. Furthermore, the mind will seek to represent *awareness* by converting it into a mind-object within the short-term store and this can never happen. To attempt to know awareness like this is like trying to shine a torch (seven torches if you will) at the sun in order to get a better look at it. Any conception of *awareness* that our mind can devise is simply a model and can never reflect true awareness. Awareness can never be an object within the contents- of-consciousness (within the short-term store), just as much as I could never psychically climb inside myself.

Yet, for the most part, the contents-of-consciousness is what we are aware of. It seems a little weird perhaps but the mind is a madcap bundle of responses and programs and does not contain our awareness itself. Let me repeat – <u>awareness is not of the mind</u>.

Now, I've stated that awareness can never be modeled, so the irony is not lost upon me as we move on to model awareness. We know the model is doomed to be deficient from the outset and it is not so much the awareness itself I seek to model. I think we can still usefully glimpse some small 'pointer' as to the relationship of Awareness to the contents of consciousness.

If you look at the diagram above, you'll see I have isolated the

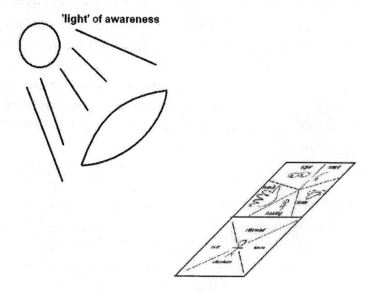

'light' of awareness

short-term store with its Uptime at the top and its Downtime at the bottom; think of it a bit like a towel on the beach. For our intents here, all the other processes of the mind are ancillary and simply exist to regulate what is projected upon this screen. It is true that, for Accelerated Practical Enlightenment, we need to be aware of all the other components of the mind but only so we can learn to influence them. And, in doing so, we influence the contents of the short-term store; that is to say, we can influence the contents-of-consciousness. At the top of the diagram is the light of awareness (a bit like a sun), and between the light of awareness and the short-term store is the lens (the fifth position – the meaning-making process of the Unseen Watcher) that skews the light of awareness. The stronger this lens is – the more distortion happens. We can never remove this lens but we can certainly make it flatter, maybe even approaching complete flatness, so that the light is not bent at all as it passes through. When we identify with the mind, we are receiving the 'sunlight' of awareness. Yet, when we identify with awareness itself, then we become the sun – the very source of light itself. Now for one final leap, and this is just an idea! What if there was not an individual, personal, 'light of awareness' for each us but only one large light for all of us?

One thing is for sure though; there is only one time and one place where we can take our 'place in the sun' – Here and Now.

Whilst out on the lake the other day, a further metaphor struck

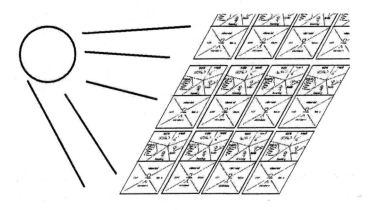

me as nice depiction of the relationship between our awareness and our cognition, so bear with me if you will. I was out windsurfing on a cold day when one of the staff at the sports centre had remarked "you must be mad" and naturally, I assumed that he was referring to the cold. But then he added (not so much to me as to his friend) "if it hasn't got an engine, I'm not interested." He was referring to the jet skiers out on the water. I later pondered his distaste of the wind-powered sport; maybe the windsurfing was just too slow for him, maybe too much work? But another possibility came across my mind; maybe he only liked the idea of the independence of the motor powered craft.

If you were to watch this stretch of water on the day, you'd have seen that there were two types of craft out – windsurfers and jet skiers. Each jet ski has its own internal source of power, un-reliant on anything else for its movement. The jet ski will power its way across the waves and currents of the water, almost regardless of the water and wind conditions. If we take the power source to be analogous to 'awareness', the jet ski is now repre-senting the traditional model of consciousness as emanating from within us. Each jet ski can travel across the water (the prevailing and uncontrollable conditions in the World at Large) through an act of independent, self-contained, will. With the windsurf, however, one would be hard pressed, if examining the equipment, to find the power source on the craft itself.

I remember first seeing sailing boats as a young child and seeing them as quite 'magical' in the way they moved around with no visible means of locomotion, probably because I had grown up around cars that had their own internal power, just like the Jet Ski. Contrast this with a man of the fifteenth century, say, for whom the sailing boat would seem more natural and the car would seem fantastical. I think a lot of the modern day conception of awareness is very much like this assumption that 'internal power' is the default way of things, and this keeps a lot of us from recog-nizing consciousness as an all-pervasive field or 'wind'.

If we look at the windsurf, then we can see it has no power of its own, it is merely an apparatus that is designed to harness (to 'tune into') an all-present 'field' of power. And so, in this metaphor, the windsurf stands for our brain. It's merely the correct 'shape' to harness the all-pervasive field of awareness. Of course, any bystander will be able to see that all the windsurfing boards on the water are in some sense separate, yet they are all 'tuned' into the same power source – the same will. The windsurf is a means of converting this power into desired movement across the water. The water and its tides and waves represent the goings-on of the World at Large, and sometimes the movements help us in our desired direction and sometimes they hinder us.

A further extension of this metaphor led me to look at my own progress as I learnt to windsurf; at first, I was always more concerned with the arrangement of the board and sail itself. I never took any formal tuition, but people passing on other windsurfers would sometimes shout, things like "look where you are going, not at your feet," or "watch out for that gust coming," (if you look upwind you can see the effect of the wind as a gust moving across the water). As I became more adept, I found my attention was not so much on the board and sail but on the wind and the water conditions. I think all good sailors probably direct the majority of their attention on the wind and water and less on the boat (or board).

Whilst still a beginner, if I was being pounded by waves, my mind would (irrationally, I know) shout out internally "can't these waves just give me a break – can we not just turn them off for second, I'm having trouble here." I soon came to accept the prevailing conditions as the unchangeable 'is-ness' of things outside my control that had to be managed. You could say that I was beginning to accept 'what is' with respect to the watery World at Large.

Like any beginner sailor, we first may struggle to become accustomed to manipulating the sails and the craft, but as we get the hang of things, then it leaves us free to turn our attention towards the will of the wind and the 'is-ness' of the water.

* Actually, the accepted number of bits our short term memory can handle is 7 +/- 2 (seven plus or minus two). There is no way to really change this amount. Whilst it is possible that at different times we all display different amounts of awareness

between five and nine, the plus or minus factor is actually more likely to be influenced by experimental factors involved in obtaining these numbers and the plus or minus two factor is more likely to be largely a result of the measurement process than of any major fluctuation. The actual bandwidth of conscious awareness is not too important; you don't really experience it as a number of bits anyway. Just know that your bandwidth is ridiculously small compared to the amount of stimuli you could choose to direct your attention towards and this bandwidth is, alas, fixed. The short-term memory can handle 120 bits of information per second, so this dictates the speed at which the sprites may move around upon Planet X; their movement is not instantaneous, but it is very fast.

Chapter 21

Conclusion

The time is right now to reiterate here that the Accelerated Practical Enlightenment protocol is not intended as an entirely definitive, all-inclusive, or ultimate system with which to attain enlightenment. In fact, some may consider the operationalization of enlightenment I have used as somewhat wanting, but it has been designed to be practical and achievable and inclusive of all the ideas about enlightenment that I could find and systemize.

It's a pretty good bet that you are interested in living in the Here and Now because you have this book in front of you – and you've got this far. One should always be careful, of course, to understand what one wants and why one wants it, so we really need to know what Practical Enlightenment looks like to assess why we would want it.

Just to recap here; we know now that Practical Enlightenment is all about living in the Here and Now as a default choice, with as few labels upon our sense perceptions as possible, we call this 'Uptime'. We have further made the distinction of 'usefulness'; we would always prefer the most useful state of mind, whether this be Uptime or Downtime, as the situation demands.

Usefulness and Uptime, like so many things, are not to be prized for themselves but because they answer deeper (or should that be higher?) values. I think the Practical Enlightenment protocol addresses and reconciles our desires for comfort and acceptance with the equally important quest to realize our authenticity and freedom of thought and action, i.e. to become that which we already are. What this reconciliation does for us, exactly, is anyone's guess; it is something that is always talked about axiomatically; perhaps self realization, through a better quality relationship with ourselves, the universe and existence itself, needs no further justification? One thing we have learned is that spending time in Unuseful-Downtime can lead us to various problematic processes; anxiety, depression, paranoia and discontent.

We have encountered the various levels at which we judge the world and our situation and found them to be completely arbitrary and contingent. And we know now that any given situation in the World at Large holds no definite or necessary response.

Furthermore, whether or not we can affect changes in situations in the World at Large, we can always choose how we *feel about* those situations. This comes into play most notably when we choose to recognize our freedom to say that, we can feel comfortable about discomfort, or more generally and importantly, that <u>it's OK to be not-OK.</u>

Even the processes which we use to judge 'OK-ness' and 'not-OK-ness at any level are up for grabs; none of the boundaries we so easily take for granted are absolute. The boundaries of objects (mind-objects) are projected by ourselves so we always play a part in creating (not just discovering) our lived world. Even our wants and values are deferred; every want and value reflects the convoluted paths we choose to address our primary reinforcers – the very base drives that our mortal forms demand; sex, thirst, hunger and shelter. These choices of deferments of value, in so far as these choices remain consistent, can even be conceived to be the very building blocks of our 'personality'. Further thoughts on the self lead us to consider the notion of the *Myth of the Self* (a story, a fiction) that guards us from the anxiety of our spontaneity, yet demands the high price of our ultimate freedom for its services. We make this bargain an unnecessary evil by finding some way of resolving this anxiety. We do this first by simply tolerating the anxiety by saying 'it's OK to be not-OK' until we realize, on the deepest level, that the anxiety just isn't really called for at all.

Our Myth of the Self aside, we are only conscious in the

moment, but we are built for survival and this demands that we carve the world into object and subject (self and other, you and me) but this too is a projection. As with any game, we can play by the rules, even though we know them to be contingent. The game of existence, the game of the human condition, the game of life, the game of society is no different. We can know at the gut level, the whole universe to be interconnected with no absolute boundaries, whilst at the same time, understanding intellectually (and operating within) the consensual hallucination of dualism.

Practicality demands that we recognize our preferences and wants as long as we exercise authenticity, and to do so it is imperative that we know how our wants operate. Wants are something we desire (another want) to destroy; in fact, they are created solely to be destroyed – they are the crash-test dummies of the mind. The satisfaction of wants can take place at the supply or the demand end. We can strive to satisfy our wants temporarily and indirectly within the world or we can dissolve them directly by denying them at the source. A third synergistic option is to become aware of our values hierarchies and find the higher (deeper) values that any want seeks to ultimately address and address this higher value more directly; perhaps through action in the mind, perhaps through action in the world. Confusion of wants can lead to all sorts of conflicting and self defeating behavior.

All this requires that we really take responsibility – a kind of existential responsibility – by recognizing our own role in creating our experienced world. Nowhere is this more relevant than in the area of our beliefs and our freedom to change those beliefs; again the recognition of what is inside and outside of our control is crucial. So often we confuse what is and is not within our power, leading to confusion, frustration and conflict.

Much of our adventure through the human condition has been an attempt to head off the obstructions to Living in the Here and Now that our culture and our survival-based make up creates. It is for this reason that all of the exercises and models within the book should be seen as aides to the removal of obstacles obscuring 'where' we already are and will always be, and not as a means to getting 'somewhere' else.

Remember that practicality, achievability and pragmatism are a prime concern when exploring How to Live in the Here and Now. Never should we lose sight of the primary motivations driving our quest. Success will come in degrees and as apparent setbacks occur (and they will, you can rely on it!), it is preferable to recognize and seize the very opportunity that those errors represent.

To hold yourself to overly strict aspirations is the most insidious trap of an *absolute enlightenment* venture, and the very epitome of the *second error!* To see Practical Enlightenment as something you will 'get to' or 'perfect' in your future is an error; indeed it is, necessarily, practiced only ever within the ever-present moment you are actually in. Your first and last step will be the appreciation and wholehearted embrace of the present moment. The understandings and exercises in this book will bring this to a default, more automatic, habit; yet, ultimately they all bring you to Awareness and the present moment. Or should that actually be; 'they all bring Awareness to the present moment?' Sometimes we can't change *the* world, but we can always change *our* world.

So just tune into your senses, relax and realize, right Here and right Now, that it's OK to be not-OK.

Further Reading

Some of the authors below have written more than one book relevant to the venture of Accelerated Practical Enlightenment, where this is so, I have included the book I think the most accessible. I have included in **bold** and in [square brackets] the issues relating to Accelerated Practical Enlightenment that each book addresses to some extent. The books denoted "mindfulness" are the most directly related titles.

Bandler, Richard & Grinder, John. *Frogs into Princes: Neuro Linguistic Programming* **[uptime]**

Bodenhamer, Bob. & Hall, L. Micheal. *The User's Manual for the Brain* **[uptime and anchoring]**

Brantley, Jeffrey. *Calming Your Anxious Mind: How Mindfulness and Compassion Can Free You from Anxiety, Fear, and Panic* **[mindfulness]**

Byron, Katie. *Loving What Is* **[seeing yourself in others and mindfulness]**

Camus, Albert. *The myth of Sisyphus* **[accepting meaninglessness]**

de Botton, Alain. *Status Anxiety* **[Myth of the Self, confusion of wants]**

Dilts, Robert. & Hallbom & Suzi Smith. *Beliefs: Pathways to Health and Wellbeing* **[belief change]**

Dryden, Windy. *Overcoming Anxiety* **[it's OK to be not-OK]**

Duncan, Shannon. *Present Moment Awareness: A Simple step by step guide to living in the Now* **[mindfulness]**

Ellis, Albert. & Lange, Arthur. *How To Keep People From Pushing Your Buttons* **[beliefs and it's OK to be not-OK]**

Erving, Goffman. *The Presentation of Self in Everyday Life* **[Myth of the Self]**

Freud, S. *Civilisation and its discontents* **[Myth of the Self, confusion of wants]**

Gray, John. *Straw Dogs: Thoughts on Humans and Other Animals*

287

[Myth of the Self]

Huxley, Aldous. *The Doors of Perception* and *Heaven and hell* [creation of meaning]

Jung, Carl. *The Undiscovered Self* [Myth of the Self]

Kelly, George, A. *Theory of personality: The Psychology of Personal Constructs* [Myth of the Self and creation of meaning]

Neenan, Michael & Dryden, Windy. *Essential Rational Emotive Behavior Therapy* [it's Ok to be not-OK]

Nietzsche, Friedrich. *Beyond Good and Evil* [creation of meaning]

Lem, Stanislaw. *The Futurological Congress* [creation of meaning]

Levy, David A. *Tools of Critical Thinking: Metathoughts for Psychology* [creation of meaning]

Palmer, Donald. *Sartre for Beginners* [creation of meaning and Myth of the Self]

Russel, Bertrand. *The Problems of Philosophy* [category error]

Sartre, Jean Paul. *Being and Nothingness* [creation of meaning and Myth of the Self]

Schwartz, Barry. *The paradox of choice: Why more is less* [confusion of wants]

Sheehy, Gail. *Passages: Predictable Crises of Adult Life.* [Myth of the Self]

Skinner, B.F. *Beyond Freedom and Dignity* [Myth of the Self and anchoring]

Spinelli, Ernesto. *The Interpreted World: An Introduction to Phenomenological Psychology* [creation of meaning and Myth of the Self]

Taylor, Steve. *Making time: Why time seems to pass at different speeds and how to control it* [mindfulness, time vista and myth of self]

Tolle, Eckhart. *The Power of Now* [mindfulness]

Williams J. Mark G. & Teasdale, John D. & Segal, Zindel V. & Kabat-Zinn, Jon. *The Mindful Way through Depression: Freeing Yourself from Chronic Unhappiness* [mindfulness]

Glossary

Any terms that appear in **bold** in the definitions within the glossary appear, themselves, as terms elsewhere in the glossary (except where a term appears in its own definition).

The glossary has been prepared with a view to aiding knowledge and ease of comprehension when reading the book, but many of the concepts will aid the reader further, simply by expanding their conceptual vocabulary regarding the subject of Accelerated Practical Enlightenment. Scholars of dualism, psychology or existentialism may have just cause to take pedantic issue with my interpretation of a few of the existing terms I have adopted. I have endeavored to keep the logic of the terminology consistent, at least within this book.

Absolute enlightenment: a flavor of enlightenment that is strictly true to the concepts of hard-line **non-dualism** (monism) and an entirely unlabelled perception of the World at Large aside from any values or agenda at all. This position is destined to remain a metaphysical concept as it can never be realized by us in our mortal (our only) form. An attempt to achieve absolute enlightenment is a guarantee of disappointment.

Access stimulus: when a particular **TOTE** is set in motion there must be a particular **stimulus** that first sets it off; this is the access stimulus; it invites access for a **TOTE** to begin. **Anchoring** is the intentional use of an access stimulus. **Anchoring** can be used to make the access stimulus for one **TOTE** become the identical **stimulus** for another, more useful, different **TOTE**, which allows a choice to be exploited as one single cue is inviting two different TOTEs.

Anchor: an **arbitrary** [behavioral] **association** that enables one to recreate a state of mind and body at will, whenever needed.

Anxiety: findings one's **direction of awareness** unusefully in future-**Downtime.**

Arbitrary association: an arrangement whereby meaning is connected to something else that has no necessary connection.

Aureola: the depiction of interconnectedness; the most notable and prominent example is the halo.

Authenticity [AKA 'Good faith']: often talked about as a state, but more accurately it is a process. Strictly speaking, one does not *have* authenticity, one is *not* authentic; one *acts* (in thought or deed) authenti*cally*. To act authentically is to have self-honesty and self-awareness of one's **value hierarchies** about one's freedom in thought and action. Authenticity is not to be confused with conventional honesty or morality which relies on a singular inter-pretation of the world; authenticity is the act of **response**-ability in one's choice among arbitrary and contingent values.

Awareness: see **consciousness**.

Behavioral belief: a belief that is held outside of the conscious awareness, on such a level as to be unquestioned (sometimes because it is 'so obvious' to the human condition, e.g. "I would rather keep my blood in my veins and arteries" – yet even this belief rests upon certain arbitrary values). Behavioral beliefs show up as implicit in one's actions.

Boredom: socially speaking, boredom is a lack of a role and a lack of identity through an activity – and so a lack of meaning. Cognitively speaking, boredom is an inability to see any novelty in a given **stimulus** due the deletion of the complexity of one's incoming **sensory information** through over-generalized labeling which, in turn, creates **ordinary moments**.

Bracketing: the attempt, never fully possible in practical terms, to separate **sensory information** from its attendant meaning, created through interpretation.

Category error [error of categories]: the confusion of multiple logical levels, often leading to paradox and/or conflict of values as those values operate upon themselves.

Confusion of wants: a confusion of wants can take two forms; a confusion of *what* one really wants, or a confusion of *why* one really wants what they appear, prima face, to want. This is a direct result of an unexamined or unclear **value hierarchy**.

Consciousness: a term I have chosen to sue interchangeably with **'awareness',** not to be confused with the **'consciousness – contents of'** (i.e. contents of awareness); consciousness itself is the 'light of awareness'.

Consciousness (contents of -): the collection of **mind-objects** or raw sensations that are held, at anytime, within the short-term memory store, i.e. the contents of both **Uptime** and **Downtime.**

Cognitive dissonance: a tendency of the mind to interpret one's situation in such a way as to serve the **Myth of the Self,** mainly by strengthening it (e.g. being selective in the criteria one chooses to use when comparing oneself to others). This mechanism also operates, quite notably, in response to one's own behavior that does not fit in with one's **Myth of the Self.**

Default: the situation that persists in the absence of any active decision or choice otherwise.

Defense mechanism: the use of any unpleasant feelings, but

largely anxiety, used by the **Myth of the Self** in order to promote behavior and thoughts that create and perpetuate the existence of the **Myth of the Self.**

Direction of (conscious) awareness: the conscious awareness may be directed towards external or internal **mind-objects,** and this is what is meant by the direction of conscious awareness.

Discomfort distraction: an activity that seeks to distract one from discomfort; it is the result of holding the position of it's not-OK to be not-OK. Engaging in discomfort distractions do not preclude a practical **authenticity** as long as there is awareness of *what* and *why* one has chosen.

Discontent: findings one's **direction of awareness** unusefully in elsewhere-**Downtime.**

Depression: findings one's **direction of awareness** unusefully in past-**Downtime.**

Downtime: having one's **direction of awareness** focused on internal **sensory information.**

Dualism: a projection onto the **World at Large** of a split between the self and the other i.e. a dichotomy creating both object and subject.

Epiphany: an experience that is sufficient, but not necessary, to reveal that the **direction of awareness** and/or meaning is entirely arbitrary and mind-created. Not to be confused with **enlightenment** itself.

Error of categories: see *category error.*

Event: the subjective **projection** of a boundary (or 'outline') onto a given length of time that makes it into a discrete **mind-object**.

Explicit belief: a belief that one is aware of as explicit idea. Contrast this with **behavioral belief**.

Grand narrative: ('the big, and only, story') the idea that there exists some objective truth or interpretation 'out there' in the **World at Large**. An idea that requires, and is perpetuated by the belief in, some monotheistic deity or 'prime mover' from which all true values axiomatically spring forth.

Huxley valve: a mechanism that restricts the in-flow of information. It represents the processes of distorting, deleting and generalizing information as it comes in to the consciousness. The valve is thought to help us focus only on information that is relevant to survival. It makes the choice as to what this is through the use of **meta-filters**.

Inauthenticity: to be acting inauthentic*ally* through self-deception and a denial of one's freedom of thought and action.

Inner voice: the voice we 'hear' in our heads that is actually a device of the **Myth of the Self**. Often the words 'chattering', 'incessant' and 'intrusive' are used to describe this voice. Actually, the inner voice could, theoretically, take on any modality, not just a voice. It would be possible for one to experience the 'voice' as pictures, or symbols, such as writing.

Interconnectedness: a reconciliation between **dualism** and hard **non-dualism** (monism) whereby one can feel **non-dualism** to represent a valid position, yet can still operate intellectually through the **dualism** that is necessary for practical social and survival matters.

Just-world hypothesis: a belief (often a **behavioral belief** and/or unconscious belief) that the universe will somehow deliver justice. Many religions incorporate this idea, most notably 'Karma' and 'Judgment'. The belief, in fact, is an example of **cognitive dissonance.**

Map/territory distinction: (AKA the menu/meal distinction.) A discrepancy between facts or tendencies in the **World at Large** and one's interpretations of the world. Map/territory confusion can lead to one making demands of the world that, when unmet, will lead to disappointment. During Map/territory confusion, assertions that there is something wrong with the world are not uncommon.
More **authentic** map/territory distinctions play a large part in differentiating what is within one's power and what is not.

Meta filters: a **Neuro linguistic Programming (NLP)** model of the filters that frame incoming information according to certain categories.

Mind object: the mental conception of an object as a whole (the creation of a 'gestalt'), whose boundaries are arbitrarily created by the mind.

Modality: in this book, the term refers to our senses. So, Visual, Auditory, Olfactory, Gustatory and Kinesthetic are the five 'modalities'. Although, in actual fact, the Kinesthetic modality is a collection of around six separate senses.

Moment: any length of time where the **contents of consciousness** remain unchanged. In practice, the subjective feeling of discrete moments is rare as the contents of consciousness will change on a rolling basis, as expressed in the 'rolling moment' model.

Myth of the Self: a convolution of **value hierarchies,** set up in a particular way that causes the host individual to act consistently and so infer a self, a personality, out of this consistency. The term 'Myth of the Self' is often used structurally, as if it was an object or entity – it is not. The Myth of the Self is shorthand for us to understand the processes of the mind as it attempts to exercise its ability to create meaning and to address the anxiety attendant, with one's freedom of thought and action, within an essentially meaningless **World at Large.**

Negative identity: this is not a position where one's identify is 'not good', as the name might suggest. The term actually describes a situation whereby an individual or group derives some identity not primarily from what they are, but by what they are not.

Neuro linguistic Programming (NLP): a certain way of looking at the mind and behavior that generates many techniques. No small definition will really suffice, but it has been called 'the study of excellence'.

Non-Dualism: in its hard sense (monism), a belief that there is only one substance. In its soft form (**interconnectedness**), a belief that everything is connected in as far as all boundaries are projected onto the **World at Large** by the mind.

Ordinary moment: the unenlightened position of becoming jaded with one's incoming **sensory information** and so perceiving none of the complexity in one's lived experience. This position is driven by a tendency to infer the *similarities* between situations instead of *differences*. The over-generalization of incoming **sensory infor-mation,** effectively, deletes the incoming raw **sensory infor-mation** from one's experience and leads to the illusion that there is nothing worthy of one's attention in the outside world at that given moment.

Paranoia: findings one's **direction of awareness** unusefully in Other-mind(s) **Downtime.**

Practical enlightenment: a flavor of enlightenment that accepts our lot as mortals with basic bodily needs (**primary reinforcers**) and higher drives derived from them through **value hierarchies.** Practical enlightenment sets achievable limits that reconcile the everyday human condition with the purity of the concept of absolute enlightenment. Practical enlightenment is a form of enlightenment designed to be achievable and workable. Its main tenets are practical-authenticity and the setting of the **direction of awareness** to **Uptime** as a **default** tendency.

Primary reinforcer: a basic, animalistic drive that requires no deferment of value to another level or value, but is valued on and of itself. I.e. Sex, Hunger, Thirst and Comfort

Preference: an expression of what an individual would like to have happen in the **World at Large.** Many of our preferences are held at an out-of-consciousness level, as **behavioral beliefs,** yet they can be set through various behavioral means. The enlightened individual can express a preference whilst, at the same time, not allowing any outcome in the **World at Large,** either way, to operate upon them.

Problem: a situation that has been arbitrarily allowed to operate problematically according to arbitrary values.

Project: (verb) referring to the action of sending meaning out into **the World at Large,** like a cinema projector. The word 'project' is only used in its verb sense within the book. At anytime, where I was tempted to use 'project' in its sense as a noun, such as the 'existential project', I have substituted the word 'venture'.

Reality testing: the experimentation of what effects are produced under certain **stimuli**. This is particularly relevant with respect to ascertaining the level of one's control over **the World at Large** and also to assess one's own response to a given stimuli in **the World at Large**.

Reinforcer: a term from the 'behaviorism' branch of psychology; they can be thought of as motivators and rewards. As humans, we show strong tendencies to convolute the four basic **primary reinforcers** in a way which all other animals do not.

Response: a behavior that happens as a result of a **stimulus**.

Second[ary] (2nd) error: an error of categories, whereby one will make a more fundamental 'error' in **response** to an earlier 'error', leading to a logical double bind. This encourages one's **direction of awareness** *towards* unuseful **Downtime** and so *away from* **Uptime**.

Sensory information: the raw building blocks of awareness; Sight, Sound, Smell, Taste and Touch.

Sensory acuity: the acuteness (sensitivity) of one's mind to become aware of the contents of their own experience that is made up of sensory information.

Solution focused: a focus on solutions instead of on causes; a paradigm that encourages a moving *toward* what is desired, as opposed to *away from* what is undesired.

Sprite: part of the Planet X model that represents a 'bit' of the finite bandwidth of the mind's **direction of awareness**.

Stimulus [plural – 'stimuli']: a **mind object** that operates as an invitation, or coercion to act (**respond**).

Stress: a motivation strategy that is generated internally, and within one's control, whereby uncomfortable feelings motivate one's self away from a situation that is undesirable. If the undesirable situation is constructed according to tight enough criteria, the only 'escape route' will be the direction of what is actively desired.

Three-store model: a memory model that consists of three basic stores; the sensory, short-term and long-term store. There are many variant models that expand upon the three stores.

Timeline: an imaginary line that is the means by which a mind represents time, and the movement of time, to itself.

Time vista: the 'width' of our time perception at any given **moment**. If the seven bits of the **contents of our consciousness** (i.e. the contents of the short-term memory store) spread widely into the past and future, we will experience the **moment** as being large or wide, but if the entire contents are located entirely at one point in time we will experience a 'timeless **moment**'. The time vista operates as a type of buffer that plays a part in the creation of meaning by creating causation and continuity, even during all (but the most absolute) Uptime. This time vista is reflected in how 'wide' or how long we perceive the rolling **moment** to be, even as we live it.

TOTE: **Test®Operate®Test®Exit**. The smallest 'indivisible' piece of behavior that operates outside of conscious awareness. The TOTE can be divided using the right techniques.

Unseen watcher: part of the Planet X model that represents

functions that the mind carries out, normally out of conscious awareness. For the purposes of the Planet X model, this part controls one's **direction of awareness** both between **Uptime** and **Downtime** and between the different directions of **Sensory information**.

Uptime: having one's **direction of awareness** focused on external **sensory information**.

Value hierarchy: the chain of deferment from one value to another. Each Value hierarchy theoretically leads to a **Primary reinforcer** at the ultimate level. The inability, or disinclination, to examine a **Value hierarchy(s)** can lead to a **confusion of wants**.

Venture: a task or an undertaking. I have used the word 'Venture' in place of '**project**' in its sense of use as a noun – to prevent confusion – due to my liberal use of '**project**' in its sense as a verb. Existentialists used to write about the *existential project*, not the *existential venture*.

World at Large (the) [AKA facticity/phenomena]: the physical 'mad dance of atoms'; the physical 'facts' of the outside world that exist without any meaning at all. This is the *territory* we can only ever know through the *map* we make of it in our own heads.

Zone (the): a state of body and mind particularly associated with sports performances, where one performs particularly well. The operationalization of this state defines this state as a complete absorption in externally generated **sensory information**.

Appendix/Addendum

In creating the Accelerated Practical Enlightenment protocol, it was my primary intention to simply extol the tools and models necessary, not to write an academic book.

Many of the ideas and techniques in this book have been directly inspired through various psychological technologies and approaches and deserve recognition, most notably Nuero Linguistic Programming. Regrettably, in retrospect due recognition would ideally have been included in the text.

I have always asserted that my contribution has been 90% innovation and 10% invention.

What follows is a late and informal list perhaps not of the primary sources, but of major works and theorists who I am aware influenced me personally – so I consider them to be some of *my* most primary sources. Whilst there is overlap, I have cited where I myself first came to the ideas.

Sub modalities strategies (own the world) / TOTEs / Anchoring / VAKG model: Bandler, R. & Grinder, J. *The Hypnotic Techniques of Milton Erickson Vol. ii .& Frogs into Princes &* Heller, S. *Monsters and Magical sticks*

Parts conflict / Timelines / Uptime & Downtime / Meta-frame notation: Bodenhamer, B. & Hall, L.M.. *The User's Manual for the Brain Vols. i & ii*

3 store model: Atkinson & Schiffer

Toward & away from frames / The NLP presuppositions: Hall, L.M. *The sourcebook of magic*

Deconstruction of emotion: Philips, P. & Watts, T. *Rapid Cognitive therapy*

'Ourselves in others' matrix: Byron Katie, *Loving what is*

'Freeing identification' exercise: Assagioli, R. *Psychosynthesis*

Fractionation for insomnia: Progressive muscular relaxation - Jacobson, E. and the Elman induction – Elman, D.

Belief ABC model and disputing / Preferences vs. Demands: Nenan, M. and Dryden, W. *Essential rational emotive behaviour therapy*

7 +/- 2 & VAKG: Miller, G. *The magical number seven, plus or minus two: Some limits on our capacity for processing information*

BOOKS

O is a symbol of the world, of oneness and unity. In different cultures it also means the "eye", symbolizing knowledge and insight. We aim to publish books that are accessible, constructive and that challenge accepted opinion, both that of academia and the "moral majority".

Our books are available in all good English language bookstores worldwide. If you don't see the book on the shelves ask the bookstore to order it for you, quoting the ISBN number and title. Alternatively you can order online (all major online retail sites carry our titles) or contact the distributor in the relevant country, listed on the copyright page.

See our website **www.o-books.net** for a full list of over 400 titles, growing by 100 a year.

And tune in to myspiritradio.com for our book review radio show, hosted by June-Elleni Laine, where you can listen to the authors discussing their books.

mySpiritRadio